BUS HANDBOOK 10
SCOTLAND

Iain MacGregor

Capital Transport

ISBN 185414 141 4

Published by Capital Transport Publishing
38 Long Elmes, Harrow Weald, Middlesex

Printed by The KPC Group, Ashford, Kent

© Capital Transport Publishing 1992

Front cover upper **A 1985 Alexander-bodied Leyland Olympian of Grampian Transport in the impressive setting of Aberdeen's Union Street.** Gavin Booth

Front cover lower **Midland have very quickly adopted a Grampian 'family' livery in two shades of blue on a base of cream. No.298 is seen freshly painted in the beautiful Trossachs area between Gartmore and Aberfoyle on route for Stirling in the summer of 1991.** Donald MacRae

Back cover upper **The A1 Co-operative still present one of the most varied fleets in the country, generally turned out to the highest standard. Amongst the more recent secondhand acquisitions are seven former Tayside Volvo Ailsas of which NSP338R is seen in sunny conditions at Irvine Cross in August 1991.** Donald MacRae

Back cover lower **Kelvin Central's Leyland National 2s were previously with Kelvin Scottish, but originated with a variety of Scottish Bus Group companies. No.1138 was new to Central SMT and is seen in KCB's current livery in Osborne Street, Glasgow.** Max H. Fowler

Title page **The long and the short — one of Lothian's 81-seater Alexander RH bodied Olympians is contrasted with Royal Mail Post Bus 6770007, a Land Rover, photographed at Kyle of Lochalsh prior to setting out for Arnisdale three hours and 20 minutes away.** Murdoch Currie

Acknowledgements
We are grateful to Ernest Barnett, David Donati, Mark Jameson, Colin Lloyd, Sandy MacDonald, Geoff Mills, the PSV Circle and the operating companies for their assistance in the compilation of this book.

Contents correct to March 1992

Series Editor: Bill Potter
Third edition (formerly Scottish Bus Handbook)

CONTENTS

A1 SERVICE

Ayrshire Bus Owners (A1 Service) Ltd, Parkhouse Road, Ardrossan, KA22 8AA

The limited company celebrated its sixtieth birthday in 1991, but in fact the A1 association dates back to 1926. Whereas there were 22 owners in 1931, there are now only 10, but the basic principles of operation and commitment to service remain, as does the interesting variety of vehicles.

A1 has neither sought to expand its operation on deregulation nor has it been subjected to undue pressure from other operators who are no doubt aware of the fierce loyalty of A1's passengers. There has been some experimentation using four minibuses which unusually, to spread the risk, are owned by the company rather than individual shareholders as is normal.

Recent acquisitions have tended to be good secondhand vehicles from South Yorkshire, Tayside or West Midlands. The livery is blue and white, with maroon on some vehicles. Each owner has his own depot as shown in the fleet list.

Former Tayside 134 leaves Irvine Cross for Ardrossan. NSP334R is one of seven former Tayside Ailsas now with the A1 operation and one now working for Docherty. Sandy MacDonald

Alexander-bodied Volvo Citybus TSD285, inherited the registration of a Leyland PD3 when it was new to Docherty in 1985. It was the first of Alexander's RV style for the group and was photographed in Irvine in September 1991. Sandy MacDonald

Operating a local service in Irvine is HGD213T, a Leyland Atlantean with Alexander AL bodywork that was formerly with Graham's of Paisley. Sandy MacDonald

The Alexander AL body style fitted to Daimler Fleetline or Leyland Atlantean and Fleetline chassis was once almost the A1 standard bus. NCS16P is a Fleetline example operated by Meney and was photographed at Saltcoats. David Little

There are three Roe-bodied Atlanteans in the A1 fleet. DSD55V passes through Dreghorn and is operated by Steele, who continues to favour the maroon waistband no longer incorporated into the livery by many A1 members. Sandy MacDonald

Former West Midlands Fleetlines have recently been a popular acquisition. An MCW-bodied example, originally with Leyland engine, passes through Stevenston still showing the Hartshill allocation disc. Sandy MacDonald

The newest double deckers for the group are Leyland Olympians dating from 1989, most fitted with the Leyland body built at Workington. F149XCS is seen in Irvine. Sandy MacDonald

Because of the experimental nature of their operation, the two Iveco Daily 49s are owned by the A1 company rather than individual members. G575YTR was photographed in Saltcoats. David Little

A1 SERVICE Fleet List

Note: Owner codes used in this list:-

A1	Ayrshire Bus Owners (A1 Service) Ltd		
B	Brown, Dreghorn	MK	McKinnon, Kilmarnock
D	Docherty, Irvine	MM	McKenemy, Ardrossan
DF	Duff, Ardrossan	RS	Steele, Stevenston
HD	Hunter, Dreghorn	SM	Stevenston Motor Co (Hill)
ME	Meney, Saltcoats	SS	Stewart, Stevenston

D	JHK500N		Leyland Atlantean AN68/1R		Eastern Coach Works		H43/31F	1975	Ex Colchester, 1989
SS	LKP381P		Ailsa B55-10		Alexander AV		H44/35F	1975	Ex Maidstone & District, 1983
SM	LKP384P		Ailsa B55-10		Alexander AV		H44/35F	1975	Ex Maidstone & District, 1984

			Leyland Fleetline FE30AGR		Alexander AL		H43/31F	1976	
ME	NCS11P	ME	NCS17P	DF	NCS18P	DF	NCS19P	B	NCS21P
SM	NCS16P								

SS	NCS13P		Leyland Atlantean AN68A/1R		Alexander AL		H43/31F	1976	
ME	NCS15P		Leyland Atlantean AN68A/1R		Alexander AL		H43/31F	1976	
D	NCS25P		Ailsa B55-10		Alexander AV		H44/35F	1976	
D	NCS26P		Leyland Leopard PSU3C/4R		Duple Dominant E		DP51F	1976	
MK	KON336P		Leyland Fleetline FE30ALR		MCW		H43/33F	1976	Ex West Midlands Travel, 1991
MM	MTV753P		Leyland Leopard PSU3C/4R		Duple Dominant E		DP53F	1976	Ex Nottingham, 1983

			Ailsa B55-10		Alexander AV		H44/31D	1976	Ex Tayside, 1990
D	NSP331R	D	NSP333R	D	NSP335R	ME	NSP336R	ME	NSP338R
D	NSP332R	D	NSP334R						

MK	OCS114R		Daimler Fleetline CRG6LXB		Alexander AD		H44/31F	1976	
MK	NOC380R		Leyland Fleetline FE30ALR		MCW		H43/33F	1976	Ex West Midlands Travel, 1991
MM	NOC407R		Leyland Fleetline FE30ALR		MCW		H43/33F	1976	Ex West Midlands Travel, 1991

B	OJD161R	Leyland Fleetline FE30AGR	Park Royal	H45/32F	1977	Ex London Transport, 1984
B	OJD162R	Leyland Fleetline FE30AGR	Park Royal	H45/32F	1977	Ex London Transport, 1984
MK	OJD214R	Leyland Fleetline FE30AGR	MCW	H45/32F	1977	Ex Graham, Paisley, 1985
SS	TSD163S	Leyland Atlantean AN68A/1R	Roe	H43/33F	1977	

		Leyland Fleetline FE30AGR	MCW	H43/33F	1977-78	Ex West Midlands, 1990-91

MK NOC450R   MK NOC458R   B SDA563S   B TVP900S   MK WDA914T

B	SDA655S	Leyland Fleetline FE30AGR	Park Royal	H43/33F	1978	Ex West Midlands Travel, 1991
RS	UCS186S	Ailsa B55-10	Alexander AV	H44/31D	1978	
D	UCS896S	Ailsa B55-10	Alexander AV	H44/35F	1978	

		Leyland Fleetline FE30AGR	Alexander AL	H45/33F	1979	

ME ASD25T   DF ASD26T   DF ASD27T   SM ASD28T   MK ASD29T

RS	HGD213T	Leyland Atlantean AN68A/1R	Alexander AL	H45/33F	1979	Ex Graham, Paisley, 1990
D	KMA399T	Leyland National 11351A/1R		B49F	1979	Ex Blackpool, 1990
B	WDA664T	Leyland Fleetline FE30AGR	Park Royal	H43/33F	1979	Ex West Midlands Travel, 1990
D	AYR332T	Leyland National 10351A/2R		B36D	1979	Ex London Buses, 1991
ME	ASD30T	Leyland Atlantean AN68A/1R	Alexander AL	H45/31F	1979	
SS	ASD31T	Leyland Atlantean AN68A/1R	Alexander AL	H45/31F	1979	
SM	ASD32T	Ailsa B55-10 MkII	Alexander AV	H44/35F	1979	
RS	DSD55V	Leyland Atlantean AN68A/1R	Roe	H43/34F	1979	
D	ECS56V	Ailsa B55-10 MkII	Alexander AV	H44/35F	1979	
SS	ECS57V	Ailsa B55-10 MkII	Alexander AV	H44/35F	1979	
MM	GTO798V	Leyland Leopard PSU3F/4R	Duple Dominant E	DP53F	1980	Ex Nottingham, 1991
B	JPE235V	Leyland Atlantean AN68B/1R	Roe	H43/30F	1980	Ex Luton & District, 1991
B	HSJ61V	Leyland Atlantean AN68B/1R	Roe	H43/32F	1980	
MM	KSD62W	Leyland Atlantean AN68B/1R	Alexander AL	H45/33F	1980	
MK	DWH700W	Leyland Fleetline FE30AGR	Northern Counties	H43/32F	1980	Ex GM Buses, 1991
SS	KSD2W	Leyland Leopard PSU3F/4R	Duple Dominant II Express	C53F	1981	
SS	JKW310W	Leyland Atlantean AN68B/1R	Marshall	H45/29D	1981	Ex South Yorkshire, 1991
SS	JKW316W	Leyland Atlantean AN68B/1R	Marshall	H45/29D	1981	Ex South Yorkshire, 1991
SS	JKW322W	Leyland Atlantean AN68B/1R	Marshall	H45/29D	1981	Ex South Yorkshire, 1991
SS	JKW335W	Leyland Atlantean AN68B/1R	Marshall	H45/29D	1981	Ex South Yorkshire, 1991
B	OSJ1X	Leyland Tiger TRCTL11/2R	Duple Dominant Express	C53F	1981	
MK	OSJ35X	Leyland Tiger TRBTL11/2R	Wadham Stringer Vanguard	DP49F	1982	
MK	OSJ36X	Leyland Tiger TRBTL11/2R	Wadham Stringer Vanguard	DP49F	1982	
RS	GHS215X	Fiat 60F10	Caetano Beja	C18F	1982	Ex Southern, Barrhead, 1986

		Leyland Olympian ONLXB/1R	Roe	H47/29F	1982-83	Ex West Yorkshire PTE, 1986-87

DF CUB50Y   HD CUB73Y   HD EWY74Y   ME EWY75Y   ME EWY76Y
HD CUB72Y

D	A308RSU	Volvo B10M-50	East Lancashire	H47/36F	1983	Ex Volvo demonstrator, 1985
MM	A93PKJ	Volvo B10M-61	Duple Caribbean	C51F	1984	Ex Truman, Pontypool, 1991
D	TSD285	Volvo B10M-50	Alexander RV	H47/37F	1985	
ME	B24CGA	Volvo B10M-50	Alexander RV	H47/37F	1985	
RS	B312UNB	Volvo B10M-61	Van Hool Alizée	C53F	1985	Ex Shearings, 1991
B	C100HSJ	Scania N112DRB	East Lancashire	H47/33F	1986	
SM	C800HCS	Leyland Olympian ONLXB/1R	Eastern Coach Works	H45/32F	1986	
SM	OAG765	Volvo B10M-61	Plaxton Paramount 3500	C53F	1987	Ex Doig, Glasgow, 1991
A1	E402TBS	Renault S56	Alexander AM	B25F	1987	Ex Highland Scottish, 1992
A1	E403TBS	Renault S56	Alexander AM	B25F	1987	Ex Highland Scottish, 1992
ME	E660UWU	Volvo B10M-61	Van Hool Alizée	C49FT	1988	Ex Black Prince, Morley, 1991
MM	F881VSJ	Volvo B10M-61	Ikarus Blue Danube	C49FT	1988	
DF	F149XCS	Leyland Olympian ONCL10/1RZ	Leyland	H47/31F	1988	
SM	F524WSJ	Leyland Olympian ONCL10/1RZ	Leyland	H47/31F	1989	
HD	F41XCS	Leyland Olympian ONCL10/1RZ	Leyland	H47/31F	1989	
MM	F747XCS	Leyland Olympian ONCL10/1RZ	Alexander RL	H47/32F	1989	
RS	F680LGG	Toyota HB31R	Caetano Optimo	C21F	1989	Ex Southern, Barrhead, 1991
ME	G164ECS	Volvo B10M-60	Van Hool Alizée	C51FT	1990	
ME	G165ECS	Volvo B10M-60	Van Hool Alizée	C51FT	1990	
DF	G569ESD	Volvo B10M-55	Plaxton Derwent	B55F	1990	
A1	G575YTR	Iveco Daily 49.10	Phoenix	B25F	1990	
A1	G576YTR	Iveco Daily 49.10	Phoenix	B25F	1990	

Previous Registrations:
OAG765   D812SGB

AA BUSES

AA Motor Services Ltd, Boswell Park, Ayr, KA7 1NR
Dodds (Coaches Ltd), 72 Portland Street, Troon, KA10 6QY

AA, born as a breakaway from the A1 co-operative with seven members, now has only two members remaining, Dodds of Troon and Young of Ayr.

AA has had to contend with competition from a number of operators and has had to seek new opportunities such as those offered by the opening of the new South Ayrshire hospital outside Ayr.

While Young has had an all single deck fleet for some years, Dodds has now moved towards the elimination of double deckers from the fleet. Dodds has taken two new Scania saloons, but secondhand Nationals in the standard livery of green and cream are very much the order of the day.

On the 1st April 1992 the Youngs fleet was due to pass to Dodds ownership. To accommodate the additional fleet Dodds premises in Troon are being expanded by redevelopment of the adjacent area. Young's garage and filling station are to be sold.

EHJ29X features the unusual combination of Marshall bodywork on the Scania BR112DH. This example has had the windscreen modified since its period of operation with CIE in Ireland. Murdoch Currie

AA was the first operator in Scotland to buy a Leyland National. Its first, purchased in 1972, is still going strong. It has been joined by other, mostly secondhand examples including EUM889T, one of three acquired in 1991 and originating from the West Riding fleet. Sandy MacDonald

A feature of the operation has been the choice of engines. Young, whose fleet merged with Dodds on April 1st 1992, took the Leyland engine option for the Leyland Lynx while Dodds chose Gardner. D330LSD is the first example for the Dodds fleet. Sandy MacDonald

Dodds operation uses several vehicles of Scania manufacture. E77RCS (above) is one of the N112CRB city bus chassis fitted with East Lancashire coachwork. In contrast is H455WGG, the later Scania K113 model, here fitted with Alexander's PS bodywork. Both are seen passing through Irvine. David Little

AA BUSES Fleet List

Note: Owner codes used in this list:-

D - Dodds, Troon   Y - Formerly Young's fleet   C - Dodds Coaches

D	OKM317	AEC Regent III	Saunders	H30/26R	1951	Ex Saunders demonstrator, 1952
Y	XSD789L	Leyland National 1151/1R/2001		B52F	1972	
Y	RCS518M	Leyland National 1151/1R		B52F	1974	
Y	MOD816P	Leyland National 11351/1R		B52F	1976	Ex Annis, Felling, 1989
Y	MOD817P	Leyland National 11351/1R		B52F	1976	Ex Annis, Felling, 1989

D	MGR535P	Leyland National 11351A/1R		B49F	1976	Ex Go-Ahead Northern, 1988
D	MGR536P	Leyland National 11351A/1R		B49F	1976	Ex Go-Ahead Northern, 1988
Y	SGR106R	Leyland National 11351A/1R		B52F	1976	Ex United, 1990
Y	MFN113R	Leyland National 11351A/1R		B49F	1976	Ex East Kent, 1991
D	NSJ380R	Leyland Fleetline FE30ALR	Alexander AL	H43/31F	1976	Gardner engine fitted
D	NSJ381R	Leyland Fleetline FE30ALR	Alexander AL	H43/31F	1976	Gardner engine fitted
D	OOX824R	Leyland National 11351A/1R		DP45F	1977	Ex West Midlands Travel, 1990
D	OOX829R	Leyland National 11351A/1R		DP45F	1977	Ex West Midlands Travel, 1990
D	OOX828R	Leyland National 11351A/1R		DP45F	1977	Ex West Midlands Travel, 1991
Y	PSD561R	Leyland National 11351A/1R		B52F	1977	
C	RCS712R	Seddon Pennine 7	Alexander AT	C49F	1977	Ex Western Scottish, 1988
C	RCS713R	Seddon Pennine 7	Alexander AT	C49F	1977	Ex Western Scottish, 1988
D	TVP859S	Leyland National 11351A/1R		DP45F	1977	Ex West Midlands Travel, 1991
D	YYE283T	Leyland National 10351A/2R		B36D	1979	Ex London Buses, 1987
D	YYE296T	Leyland National 10351A/2R		B36D	1979	Ex London Buses, 1987
D	EUM889T	Leyland National 11351A/1R		B49F	1979	Ex West Riding, 1991
D	EUM895T	Leyland National 11351A/1R		B49F	1979	Ex West Riding, 1991
D	EUM897T	Leyland National 11351A/1R		B49F	1979	Ex West Riding, 1991
Y	YSJ14T	Leyland National 11351A/1R		B52F	1979	
Y	CSD199T	Leyland National 11351A/1R		B52F	1979	
C	ASD44T	AEC Reliance 6U3ZR	Plaxton Supreme IV	C51F	1979	
D	ASJ206T	Leyland Fleetline FE30AGR	Alexander AL	H45/33F	1979	
Y	FSD687V	Leyland National 2 NL116L11/1R		B52F	1980	
Y	JSD595W	Leyland National 2 NL116L11/1R		B52F	1980	
Y	LSD732W	Leyland National 2 NL116AL11/1R		B52F	1981	
D	LSJ871W	Leyland National 2 NL116AL11/1R		B52F	1981	
D	LSJ872W	Leyland National 2 NL116AL11/1R		B52F	1981	
D	EHJ29X	Scania BR112DH	Marshall	H45/33F	1981	Ex CIE, Dublin, 1984
Y	NSJ550X	Leyland National 2 NL116AL11/1R		B52F	1981	
C	PSJ101X	Volvo B10M-61	Plaxton Supreme V	C51F	1982	
C	7076LJ	Volvo B10M-61	Plaxton Paramount 3200	C57F	1983	
C	8028LJ	Volvo B10M-61	Plaxton Paramount 3500	C49FT	1983	
C	MDM371	Volvo B10M-61	Van Hool Alizée	C46FT	1983	Ex Watson, Dundee, 1988
C	OJE533	Volvo B10M-61	Van Hool Alizée	C46FT	1983	Ex Watson, Dundee, 1988
Y	USJ491Y	Leyland National 2 NL116TL11/1R		B52F	1983	
C	WSV540	Volvo B10M-61	Van Hool Alizée	C53F	1984	Ex Park, Hamilton, 1986
C	WSV541	Volvo B10M-61	Van Hool Alizée	C53F	1984	Ex Park, Hamilton, 1986
D	A522YSD	Leyland National 2 NL116HLXCT/1R		B52F	1984	
D	A523YSD	Leyland National 2 NL116HLXCT/1R		B52F	1984	
Y	A306YSJ	Leyland National 2 NL116TL11/1R		B52F	1984	
Y	C112GSJ	Leyland National 2 NL116TL11/1R		B52F	1985	
C	B122ECS	Mercedes-Benz L608D	PMT Bursley	C19F	1985	
Y	D573LSJ	Leyland Lynx LX112TL11FR1	Leyland	B51F	1986	
D	D330LSD	Leyland Lynx LX5636LXCTFR1	Leyland	B51F	1986	
D	D340LSD	Leyland Lynx LX5636LXCTFR1	Leyland	B51F	1986	
D	E76RCS	Scania N112CRB	East Lancashire	B51F	1987	
D	E77RCS	Scania N112CRB	East Lancashire	B51F	1987	
C	E755TCS	Scania K112CRB	Van Hool Alizée	C49FT	1988	
C	E760TCS	Scania K112CRB	Van Hool Alizée	C49FT	1988	
C	E312OPR	Volvo B10M-61	Van Hool Alizée	C46FT	1988	Ex Excelsior, Bournemouth, 1989
C	E314OPR	Volvo B10M-61	Van Hool Alizée	C53F	1988	Ex Excelsior, Bournemouth, 1989
C	E315OPR	Volvo B10M-61	Van Hool Alizée	C53F	1988	Ex Excelsior, Bournemouth, 1989
C	E318OPR	Volvo B10M-61	Van Hool Alizée	C46FT	1988	Ex Excelsior, Bournemouth, 1989
C	E878SSJ	Toyota HB31R	Caetano Optimo	C18F	1988	
D	E499TSJ	Mercedes-Benz 609D	Devon Conversions	C23F	1988	
C	F350WCS	Mercedes-Benz 609D	Scott	C24F	1988	
D	F262WSD	Leyland Lynx LX112LXCTZR1S	Leyland	B51F	1989	
Y	F85XCS	Leyland Lynx LX112L10ZR1R	Leyland	B51F	1989	
D	H455WGG	Scania N113CRB	Alexander PS	B51F	1990	
D	H466WGG	Scania N113CRB	Alexander PS	B51F	1990	

Previous Registrations:

EHJ29X	450UZO	WSV540	A650UGD	WSV541	A641UGD

Special Liveries:
Scottish Citylink: WSV540, WSV541, E760TCS, E312OPR, E318OPR.

BLUEBIRD NORTHERN

Bluebird Northern Ltd, Guild Street, Aberdeen, AB9 2DR

Bluebird was formed in 1961 as W.Alexander & Sons (Northern) Ltd responsible for the northern area of the old Alexander company. It became Northern Scottish Omnibuses Ltd in 1985 shortly before the Tayside area was restructured to form Strathtay Scottish.

The ambitions of Stagecoach to obtain a share of the privatisation of the Scottish Bus Group companies were first realised when Northern Scottish was acquired in March 1991.

The company has depots throughout the Grampian Region with services reaching Dundee in the south and beyond Inverness to the west. It was operating in competition with Grampian Transport on city services in Aberdeen, though most of the city services ceased in mid-1991 as, coincidentally, Grampian withdrew from country services which duplicated Northern routes.

Stagecoach already had a base in Inverness in Inverness Traction and this increased in importance in autumn 1991 through competition with Highland's new owners. Consequently, an additional base was established at Tain. Responsibility for Inverness and Tain has passed to Bluebird, but the Inverness Traction trading name continues to be used for services and on vehicles in that area. The company was renamed Bluebird Northern Ltd in March 1992.

A feature of Stagecoach operation is the regular movement of vehicles between group companies. Bluebird has provided more modern Olympians to Stagecoach in Perth, Cumberland and United Counties, while there have been acquisitions from the south of Bristol VRTs and Leyland Leopards.

Depots are situated in Aberdeen, Alford, Ballater, Braemar, Buckie, Elgin, Ellon, Forres, Fyvie, Inverness, Inverurie, Macduff, Mintlaw, Peterhead, Stonehaven and Tain. The livery is white with orange, red and blue bands, though some vehicles retain the former yellow and cream with blue scheme.

Bluebird Northern's dual door Leyland Olympians were obtained to compete with Grampian in Aberdeen. Now that most of these services have been withdrawn, many of the type are being rebuilt to single door while some others have gone south to other Stagecoach companies. One of those that remain is 069, still to be found in its original layout at Aberdeen. Murdoch Currie

The requirement for additional vehicles in Inverness caused several of the 1991 Stagecoach order for Leyland Olympians to be reallocated. Three of the early examples destined for Cumberland never arrived, being replaced by three later deliveries. New to this fleet, and now 092, this latest delivery features a modified windscreen layout aimed at reducing driver glare. Murdoch Currie

Leyland National 587 is one that was new to the Northern fleet but went with the Tayside operations into the Strathtay fleet, from where it returned in 1987. It is seen in Stagecoach livery on an Aberdeen city service just before these were curtailed. Graeme Yuill

The Inverness developments of 1991 required the drafting in of many Stagecoach group vehicles that were part of the reserve fleet. From Cumberland came some Bristol VRTs that had been replaced by new Olympians. One of the early examples is 118, seen in Inverness in December 1991, complete with Inverness Traction motif. Murdoch Currie

Probably the first open-top service in the Inverness area commenced in 1991 when Inverness Traction introduced 'The Inverness & Culloden Tour' using two former Southdown Bristol VRTs fitted with convertible Eastern Coach Works coachwork to their standard design. Stewart Brown

The unique front-engined Volvo B57 bus fitted with Alexander Y-type bodywork was one of the first vehicles of the Bluebird Northern fleet to receive Stagecoach colours. Now numbered 401, it is seen in Aberdeen. Stewart Brown

All of the Leyland Tiger type TRBLXB/2RH production was for the Scottish market. Typical of the type is Bluebird 428 which was photographed while on the Fraserburgh Town Service. The angular, P-type front, may be contrasted with the Singapore inspired PS front seen on the AA Scania. Stewart Brown

Bluebird has two of the shorter Leyland Tigers fitted with Duple 320 bodies that were once in the Central fleet. Now numbered 455 and 456, the former was photographed in Inverness in September 1991. Alistair Douglas

The provision by the Government of bus grant brought modifications to several coach designs. Duple produced an Express version of the Dominant with a wide doorway. Still going strong some fifteen years later is such an example. Bluebird 133, is one of the original batch of Duple-bodied Leopards. Murdoch Currie

The first of five short Leyland Tigers with Alexander TC-type delivered in 1985 is seen parked at Aberdeen bus station. This example is now numbered 442. Murdoch Currie

The English Stagecoach companies supplied several vehicles to Inverness Traction during 1991. Formerly with Cumberland is 209, a Leyland Tiger fitted with the Eastern Coach Works body produced for National Bus. It is seen in Inverness on local service.
Murdoch Currie

A number of Mercedes-Benz minibuses were gathered from various sources in recent times, all being second-hand purchases. The only example with Reeve Burgess Beaver bodywork is 234, one that came to Bluebird from Carr and Robinson.
Murdoch Currie

A former Hastings & District Mercedes-Benz van conversion is 240, seen in Peterhead. The conversion of this example was undertaken by Alexander and was part of the National Bus Company order when minibus purchase was in its infancy.
Stewart Brown

002-007

Leyland Olympian ONLXB/1R — Alexander RL — H45/32F — 1981

002	SSA2X	004	SSA4X	005	SSA5X	006	SSA6X	007	SSA7X
003	SSA3X								

017	TSO17X	Leyland Olympian ONLXB/1R	Eastern Coach Works	H45/32F	1982
023	TSO23X	Leyland Olympian ONLXB/1R	Eastern Coach Works	H45/32F	1982
029	TSO29X	Leyland Olympian ONLXB/1R	Eastern Coach Works	H45/32F	1982
031	TSO31X	Leyland Olympian ONLXB/1R	Eastern Coach Works	H45/32F	1982

033-060

Leyland Olympian ONLXB/1R — Alexander RL — H45/32F* — 1983-85

033	YSO33Y	039	YSO39Y	045	A45FRS	051	B351LSO	056	B356LSO
034	YSO34Y	040	YSO40Y	046	A46FRS	052	B352LSO	057	B357LSO
035	YSO35Y	041	YSO41Y	047	A47FRS	053	B353LSO	058	B358LSO
036	YSO36Y	042	YSO42Y	048	B348LSO	054	B354LSO	059	B359LSO
037	YSO37Y	043	YSO43Y	049	B349LSO	055	B355LSO	060	B360LSO
038	YSO38Y	044	A44FRS	050	B350LSO				

061-066

Leyland Olympian ONLXB/1RV — Alexander RL — DPH43/27F — 1986

061	C461SSO	063	C463SSO	064	MHS4P	065	MHS5P	066	C466SSO
062	C462SSO								

067-072

Leyland Olympian ONLXB/1RV — Alexander RL — H47/26D* — 1986-87 *071/2 are H47/30F

067	C467SSO	069	C469SSO	070	C470SSO	071	GSO1V	072	GSO2V
068	C468SSO								

082	OCY910R	Bristol VRT/SL3/501	Eastern Coach Works	H43/31F	1976	Ex East Midland, 1992
083	PRU917R	Bristol VRT/SL3/6LXB	Eastern Coach Works	H43/31F	1976	Ex Hampshire Bus, 1992

085-089

Leyland Olympian ONLXB/1RV — Alexander RL — DPH43/27F — 1987

085	D385XRS	086	D386XRS	087	D387XRS	088	D388XRS	089	D389XRS

090-099

Leyland Olympian ON2R56G13Z4 — Alexander RL — DPH47/27F* — 1991 *093-5 are H51/33F

090	J120XHH	092	J122XHH	094	J621GCR	096	J196YSS	098	J198YSS
091	J121XHH	093	J620GCR	095	J622GCR	097	J197YSS	099	J199YSS

106	UWV608S	Bristol VRT/SL3/6LXB	Eastern Coach Works	CO43/31F	1977	Ex Stagecoach, 1991
108	UWV609S	Bristol VRT/SL3/6LXB	Eastern Coach Works	CO43/31F	1977	Ex Stagecoach, 1991

110-115

Bristol VRT/SL3/6LXB — Eastern Coach Works — H43/31F — 1977 — Ex Stagecoach, 1991

110	URB160S	112	URB162S	113	URB164S	114	URB165S	115	URB166S
111	URB161S								

117-126

Bristol VRT/SL3/501 — Eastern Coach Works — H43/31F — 1976-78 Ex Cumberland, 1991

117	PHH407R	119	PHH409R	121	SAO411R	123	SAO413R	125	WHH415S
118	PHH408R	120	SAO410R	122	SAO412R	124	WHH414S	126	WHH416S

130-138

Leyland Leopard PSU3E/4R — Duple Dominant Express — C49F — 1977

130	RRS44R	132	RRS47R	134	RRS49R	136	RRS51R	138	RRS53R
131	RRS46R	133	RRS48R	135	RRS50R	137	RRS52R		

139-144

Leyland Leopard PSU3E/4R — Alexander AT — C49F — 1979

139	CRS60T	141	CRS62T	142	CRS63T	143	CRS68T	144	CRS69T
140	CRS61T								

145	CRS70T	Leyland Leopard PSU3E/3R	Duple Dominant I	C49F	1979
146	CRS71T	Leyland Leopard PSU3E/3R	Duple Dominant I	C49F	1979
147	CRS73T	Leyland Leopard PSU3E/3R	Duple Dominant I	C49F	1979
148	CRS74T	Leyland Leopard PSU3E/3R	Duple Dominant I	C49F	1979

149-158 — Leyland Leopard PSU3E/4R — Alexander AYS — DP49F* — 1980 — *155/7 are B53F

149	GSO82V	151	GSO84V	153	GSO90V	155	GSO92V	157	GSO94V
150	GSO83V	152	GSO89V	154	GSO91V	156	GSO93V	158	GSO95V

No.	Reg	Chassis	Body	Seating	Year	Notes
159	KRS529V	Leyland Leopard PSU3E/4R	Duple Dominant II Express	C49F	1980	
160	KRS531V	Leyland Leopard PSU3E/4R	Duple Dominant II Express	C49F	1980	
161	KRS532V	Leyland Leopard PSU3E/4R	Duple Dominant II Express	C49F	1980	
162	KRS533V	Leyland Leopard PSU3E/4R	Duple Dominant II Express	C49F	1980	
163	JSA101V	Leyland Leopard PSU3F/4R	Alexander AT	C49F	1980	
164	JSA102V	Leyland Leopard PSU3F/4R	Alexander AT	C49F	1980	
165	JSA103V	Leyland Leopard PSU3F/4R	Alexander AT	C49F	1980	
166	JSA104V	Leyland Leopard PSU3F/4R	Alexander AT	C49F	1980	

167-171 — Leyland Leopard PSU3G/4R — Duple Dominant II Express — C49F — 1981

167	PSO27W	168	PSO28W	169	PSO29W	170	PSO31W	171	PSO32W

No.	Reg	Chassis	Body	Seating	Year	Notes
201	OLS536P	Leyland Leopard PSU3C/3R	Alexander AYS	DP49F	1975	Ex Midland Scottish, 1987
202	OSJ629R	Leyland Leopard PSU3C/3R	Alexander AY	DP49F	1977	Ex Western Scottish, 1988

203-212 — Leyland Leopard PSU3G/4RT — Eastern Coach Works — C49F — 1982 — Ex Cumberland, 1991

203	RRM633X	205	RRM635X	207	RRM637X	209	VAO639Y	211	VAO641Y
204	RRM634X	206	RRM636X	208	VAO638Y	210	VAO640Y	212	VAO642Y

No.	Reg	Chassis	Body	Seating	Year	Notes
213	HNE252V	Leyland Leopard PSU5C/4R	Duple Dominant II Express	C53F	1980	Ex Ribble, 1991
214	HNE254V	Leyland Leopard PSU5C/4R	Duple Dominant II Express	C53F	1980	Ex Ribble, 1991
215	JND260V	Leyland Leopard PSU5C/4R	Duple Dominant II Express	C53F	1980	Ex Ribble, 1991
230	D435RYS	Mercedes-Benz 609D	Scott	C24F	1987	Ex Airpark, Linwood, 1990
231	D436RYS	Mercedes-Benz 609D	Scott	C24F	1987	Ex Airpark, Linwood, 1990
233	E364YGB	Mercedes-Benz 609D	Scott	C24F	1988	Ex Airpark, Linwood, 1990
234	E842KAS	Mercedes-Benz 609D	Reeve Burgess	C25F	1988	Ex Carr & Robbins, Tomintoul, 1990
235	E947BHS	Mercedes-Benz 609D	Scott	C24F	1988	Ex Whitelaw, Stonehouse, 1990
236	F77HAU	Mercedes-Benz 609D	Scott	C24F	1988	Ex Skill, Sheffield, 1990
237	F164XCS	Mercedes-Benz 609D	Scott	C24F	1989	Ex Clyde Coast, Ardrossan, 1990
238	F862FWB	Mercedes-Benz 609D	Whittaker	C24F	1989	Ex Metcalfe, Ferryhill, 1990
249	B875GSG	Mercedes-Benz L608D	Northern Scottish	C24F	1984	Ex Edinburgh Spastics, 1988
250	A121XWB	Mercedes-Benz L608D	Whittaker	C23F	1983	Ex Stagecoach, 1991

258-314 — Mercedes-Benz 709D — Alexander AM — B23F* — 1990 — Ex Stagecoach, 1991-92
*258-74 are B25F, 304-14 are DP25F

258	G258TSL	272	G272TSL	280	G280TSL	287	G287TSL	304	G193PAO
259	G259TSL	273	G273TSL	281	G281TSL	288	G288TSL	305	G194PAO
260	G260TSL	274	G274TSL	282	G282TSL	289	G289TSL	304	G195PAO
261	G261TSL	276	G276TSL	283	G283TSL	290	G290TSL	305	G196PAO
262	G262TSL	277	G277TSL	284	G284TSL	291	G291TSL	313	G202PAO
270	G270TSL	278	G278TSL	285	G285TSL	292	G292TSL	314	G203PAO
271	G271TSL	279	G279TSL	286	G286TSL				

No.	Reg	Chassis	Body	Seating	Year	Notes
361	FBV271W	Bristol LHS6L	Eastern Coach Works	B35F	1980	Ex Stagecoach, 1991
362	FBV272W	Bristol LHS6L	Eastern Coach Works	B35F	1980	Ex Stagecoach, 1991

363-367 — Bristol LH6L — Eastern Coach Works — DP37F — 1977-78 — Ex Stagecoach, 1991
*363 is B43F

363	SNU851R	364	SNU853R	365	WVO854S	366	WVO855S	367	WVO856S

No.	Reg	Chassis	Body	Seating	Year	Notes
401	XSA5Y	Volvo B57	Alexander AYS	B51F	1983	
421	A116ESA	Leyland Tiger TRBTL11/2R	Alexander P	B52F	1983	
422	A117ESA	Leyland Tiger TRBTL11/2R	Alexander P	B52F	1983	
423	A118ESA	Leyland Tiger TRBTL11/2R	Alexander P	B52F	1983	

424-430 — Leyland Tiger TRBLXB/2RH — Alexander P — B52F — 1984

424	A121GSA	426	A123GSA	428	A125GSA	429	A126GSA	430	A127GSA
425	A122GSA	427	A124GSA						

431	1412NE	Leyland Tiger TRCTL11/3R	Duple Dominant IV	C47FT	1982	
432	CSU920	Leyland Tiger TRCTL11/3R	Duple Dominant IV	C44FT	1981	Ex Kelvin Scottish, 1989
433	VSS3X	Leyland Tiger TRCTL11/3R	Duple Goldliner IV	C46FT	1982	
434	CSU921	Leyland Tiger TRCTL11/3R	Duple Dominant IV	C44FT	1981	Ex Kelvin Scottish, 1989
435	CSU922	Leyland Tiger TRCTL11/3R	Duple Dominant IV	C51F	1981	Ex Central Scottish, 1989
436	CSU923	Leyland Tiger TRCTL11/3R	Duple Goldliner IV	C46FT	1982	Ex Eastern Scottish, 1987

437-441

| | | Leyland Tiger TRCTL11/2R | Duple Dominant II Express | C47F* | 1983 | 438/9 are C49F |

| 437 | TSV777 | 438 | TSV778 | 439 | TSV779 | 440 | TSV780 | 441 | TSV781 |

442-446

| | | Leyland Tiger TRCTL11/2RP | Alexander TC | C47F | 1985 |

| 442 | TSV718 | 443 | TSV719 | 444 | TSV720 | 445 | TSV721 | 446 | TSV722 |

447	126ASV	Leyland Tiger TRBTL11/2R	Alexander TE	C46F	1983	Ex Kelvin Scottish, 1986
448	127ASV	Leyland Tiger TRBTL11/2R	Alexander TE	C46F	1983	Ex Kelvin Scottish, 1986
449	128ASV	Leyland Tiger TRBTL11/2R	Alexander TE	C46F	1983	Ex Kelvin Scottish, 1986

450-454

| | | Leyland Tiger TRCTL11/3RH | Alexander TC | C57F | 1987 |

| 450 | D436XRS | 451 | D437XRS | 452 | D438XRS | 453 | D439XRS | 454 | E640BRS |

455	C110JCS	Leyland Tiger TRCLXC/2RH	Duple 320	C47FT	1986	Ex Central Scottish, 1989
456	C111JCS	Leyland Tiger TRCLXC/2RH	Duple 320	C47FT	1986	Ex Central Scottish, 1989
457	A165TGE	Leyland Tiger TRCTL11/3RZ	Duple Caribbean	C48FT	1984	Ex Western Scottish, 1989
458	A166TGE	Leyland Tiger TRCTL11/3RZ	Duple Caribbean	C48FT	1984	Ex Western Scottish, 1989
459	A40XHE	Leyland Tiger TRCTL11/2R	Alexander TE	C49F	1983	Ex East Midland, 1991

501-512

| | | Dennis Dart 9.8SDL3017 | Alexander Dash | B41F | 1992 |

501	J501FPS	504	J504FPS	507	J507FPS	509	J509FPS	511	J511FPS
502	J502FPS	505	J505FPS	508	J508FPS	510	J510FPS	512	J512FPS
503	J503FPS	506	J506FPS						

548-553

| | | Volvo B10M-61 | Van Hool Alizée | C53F | 1987 | Ex Shearings, 1991 |

| 548 | D548MVR | 549 | D549MVR | 551 | D551MVR | 552 | D552MVR | 553 | D553MVR |

581-590

| | | Leyland National 2 NL106L11/1R | | B44F* | 1980 | 585-7/9 ex Strathtay, 1987 |
| | | | | | | *587 is B41F |

| 581 | KRS534V | 583 | KRS539V | 585 | KRS541V | 587 | MSO9W | 589 | MSO11W |
| 582 | KRS538V | 584 | KRS540V | 586 | KRS542V | 588 | MSO10W | 590 | MSO12W |

Previous Registrations:

126ASV	BMS511Y	KRS542V	GSO8V
127ASV	BMS513Y	MHS4P	C464SSO
128ASV	BMS515Y	MHS5P	C465SSO
1412NE	KSL41X	PSO27W	ORS106W, TSV718
CSU920	BSG549W, 630DYE, WGB175W	PSO28W	ORS107W, TSV719
CSU921	BSG547W, WLT741, WGB176W	PSO29W	ORS108W, TSV720
CSU922	BSG545W	PSO31W	ORS109W, TSV721
CSU923	MSC556X	PSO32W	ORS110W, TSV722
GSO1V	C471SSO	TSC718	B328LSA
GSO2V	C472SSO	TSV719	B329LSA
KRS529V	HSA96V, CSU920	TSV720	B330LSA
KRS531V	HSA97V, CSU921	TSV721	B331LSA
KRS532V	HSA98V, CSU922	TSV722	B332LSA
KRS533V	HSA99V, CSU923	TSV777	ASA7Y
KRS534V	GSO1V	TSV778	ASA8Y
KRS538V	GSO4V	TSV779	ASA9Y
KRS539V	GSO5V	TSV780	ASA10Y
KRS540V	GSO6V	TSV781	ASA11Y
KRS541V	GSO7V		

Special Liveries:
Overall Advertisements: 037/48/54, 423.
Scottish Citylink: 432/4/57/8.

CLYDESIDE 2000

Clydeside 2000 plc, 4 Gordon Street, Paisley, PA1 1XE

This employee-owned company commenced trading as recently as October 1991, having purchased the Glasgow, Renfrewshire and Largs operations of Western Scottish immediately on the privatisation of the latter company. It covers an area similar to that of Clydeside Scottish Omnibuses Ltd which operated from 1985 until 1989, the main difference being that Rothesay has remained with Western Scottish.

The new company has chosen to revive the former Clydeside colours of red and yellow, but applied in a different style. Many of the fleet retain former Clydeside livery, including some in the silver and white Quicksilver coach scheme.

There have been considerable incursions into the Clydeside area by small operators, often using minibuses, and Strathclyde Buses has a significant presence in Paisley. The company plans to recover some of the business lost and to assist in this task it has added a number of former Merseyside Dodge minibuses to the fleet.

Depots are located in Greenock, Inchinnan, Johnstone, Largs, Paisley and Thornliebank.

Western acquired Kelvin Central's stock of Leyland Fleetlines in 1989 and most are used in the Clydeside area. ULS668T, now Clydeside 818, lacks destination information when seen as it loads in Johnstone on the town service. Graeme Yuill

Ailsa 912, one of two from the batch to be fitted with coach seats for longer distance work, was photographed while on a local service at Paisley Cross.
Stewart Brown

Alexander-bodied Leyland Fleetline 878 is seen at Govan bus station having arrived on a route from Erskine. These were among the last AD-type bodies delivered to the group. Max Fowler

Western Scottish have frequently taken deliveries from Northern Counties over the years. Northern Counties-bodied Leyland Fleetline 827, now with the Clydeside fleet, was photographed in Bath Street, Glasgow on one-time Routemaster service 11. Max Fowler

Seen crossing the Clyde by Glasgow Bridge, is the fourth prototype Leyland Olympian which was known at that time as the B45. It was exhibited at the motor show and used as a demonstrator, in Midland Scottish livery, before joining the Northern Scottish fleet. It came south in 1989 and was one of the last vehicles to receive Clydeside livery in Western days. Max Fowler

Passing through Glasgow city centre, 926 is one of four Rolls-Royce engined Dennis Dominators that began life with Central Scottish fleet. Murdoch Currie

Two of the rare Leyland Lions are to be found in Citylink livery for work that their engineering design makes them eminently suitable. The remainder of the Lions are in Quicksilver colours. One of the latter, 162 is seen leaving the soon-to-be-closed Anderston bus station in Glasgow on the Linwood Clipper service. Max Fowler

All but two of Clydeside's Routemasters were withdrawn under Western control. One of the survivors is this front entrance example which had been extensively refurbished with coach seating. Now numbered 100, it is normally found on driver shuttle duties. Stewart Brown

Just prior to the formation of Clydeside 2000, No.662 was painted from an overall advertisement into the previous Clydeside livery. The new company then added its early style of a new fleetname. It is seen in Paisley in November 1991. Murdoch Currie

Several vehicles in the Clydeside fleet are in one of Western's liveries. Leyland Leopard 703, seen on the former Graham's Linwood-Hawkhead service, sports the black, white, grey and red style. Stewart Brown

Alexander-bodied Renault 355 is one of two from the batch to have coach seats. It received Western's dual-purpose livery in 1990 and is seen in Paisley with a Strathclyde MetroRider behind. Stewart Brown

Alexander-bodied Renault-Dodge minibuses form the majority of the minibus fleet and were originally marketed as Skippers. No.319 awaits the green traffic light at Paisley Cross.
Murdoch Currie

The new management of Clydeside 2000 acquired 13 Northern Counties-bodied Dodges from the Merseybus fleet. Many of these originated with Greater Manchester Buses. One new to Merseybus is 290, photographed on a Paisley town service.
Alistair Douglas

CLYDESIDE 2000 Fleet List

All vehicles were formerly Western Scottish in 1991, unless stated.

99	WLT900	AEC Routemaster 5RM	Park Royal	H40/32R	1962
100	KGJ614D	AEC Routemaster R2RH2	Park Royal	DPH31/24F	1966
112	C112JCS	Leyland Tiger TRCTXC/2RH	Duple 320	C49FT	1986
113	C113JCS	Leyland Tiger TRCTXC/2RH	Duple 320	C49FT	1986
121	WGB589W	Volvo B10M-61	Duple Caribbean	C47FT	1981
122	WGB588W	Volvo B10M-61	Duple Dominant IV	C51F	1981

131-139   Dennis Dorchester   Plaxton Paramount 3500   C55F*   1985   *134-6 are C46FT

| 131 | WLT471 | 133 | WLT364 | 135 | 705DYE | 137 | 407CLT | 139 | VLT204 |
| 132 | 32CLT | 134 | FSU661 | 136 | VLT166 | 138 | WLT878 | | |

155-159   Dennis Dominator DD908   Alexander RL   DPH41/34F 1985

| 155 | C155FDS | 156 | C156FDS | 157 | C157FDS | 158 | C158FDS | 159 | C159FDS |

160-165

Leyland Lion LDTL11/1R Alexander RH DPH49/37F* 1987 *160/1 are DPH49/31F

160	E160YGB	162	E162YGB	163	E163YGB	164	E164YGB
161	E161YGB					165	D852RDS

170-186

Leyland Tiger TRCLXC/2RH Plaxton Paramount 3200 Ex C49F 1984

170	A170UGB	174	TCS174	177	WLT974	179	54CLT	181	A181UGB
172	WLT924	175	WLT956	178	VLT28	180	VLT234	186	A186UGB
173	A173UGB	176	VCS376						

201-206

Talbot Freeway Talbot DP12FL 1990

201	G826VGA	203	H903YUS	204	H904YUS	205	H905YUS	206	H906YUS
202	G832VGA							

287-299

Dodge S56 Northern Counties B22F* 1986-87 Ex Merseybus, 1991 *295-9 are B20F

287	D706TWM	290	D711TWM	293	E716VEM	296	D887MDB	298	D895MDB
288	D708TWM	291	D713TWM	294	E717VEM	297	D893MDB	299	D902MDB
289	D709TWM	292	D714TWM	295	D851LND				

301-322

Dodge S56 Alexander AM B25F* 1987 *322 is DP25F

301	D261NCS	311	D311SDS	314	D314SDS	317	D317SDS	320	D320SDS
308	D308SDS	312	D312SDS	315	D315SDS	318	D318SDS	321	D321SDS
310	D310SDS	313	D313SDS	316	D316SDS	319	D319SDS	322	D300SDS

323-355

Renault S56 Alexander AM B25F* 1987-88 *354/5 are DP25F

323	E323WYS	330	E330WYS	337	E337WYS	344	E344WYS	350	E350WYS
324	E324WYS	331	E331WYS	338	E338WYS	345	E345WYS	351	E351WYS
325	E325WYS	332	E332WYS	339	E339WYS	346	E346WYS	352	E352WYS
326	E326WYS	333	E333WYS	340	E340WYS	347	E347WYS	353	E353WYS
327	E327WYS	334	E334WYS	341	E341WYS	348	E348WYS	354	E354WYS
328	E328WYS	335	E335WYS	342	E342WYS	349	E349WYS	355	E355WYS
329	E329WYS	336	E336WYS	343	E343WYS				

361	G421MWY	Renault S56	Reeve Burgess Beaver	B23F	1990	Ex Yorkshire Rider, 1992
362	G192NWY	Renault S56	Reeve Burgess Beaver	B23F	1989	Ex Yorkshire Rider, 1992
365	G195NWY	Renault S56	Reeve Burgess Beaver	B23F	1989	Ex Yorkshire Rider, 1992
366	G196NWY	Renault S56	Reeve Burgess Beaver	B23F	1989	Ex Yorkshire Rider, 1992

634-690

Leyland Leopard PSU3D/4R Alexander AY B53F 1977-78

634	VSJ216S	643	TSJ43S	652	TSJ52S	660	TSJ60S	674	TSJ74S
635	TSJ35S	644	TSJ44S	653	TSJ53S	661	TSJ61S	675	TSJ75S
636	TSJ36S	645	TSJ45S	654	TSJ54S	662	TSJ62S	681	TSJ81S
637	TSJ37S	646	TSJ46S	655	TSJ55S	663	TSJ63S	682	TSJ82S
638	TSJ38S	647	TSJ47S	656	TSJ56S	665	TSJ65S	684	TSJ84S
639	TSJ39S	648	TSJ48S	657	TSJ57S	666	TSJ66S	688	TSJ88S
640	TSJ40S	649	TSJ49S	658	TSJ58S	672	TSJ72S	689	TSJ89S
641	TSJ41S	650	TSJ50S	659	TSJ59S	673	TSJ73S	690	TSJ90S
642	TSJ42S	651	TSJ51S						

691-798

Leyland Leopard PSU3E/4R Alexander AY B53F 1978-80

691	BSJ891T	704	BSJ904T	719	BSJ919T	732	GCS32V	766	GCS66V
692	BSJ892T	705	BSJ905T	720	BSJ920T	734	GCS34V	767	GCS67V
693	BSJ893T	706	BSJ906T	721	BSJ921T	735	GCS35V	768	GCS68V
694	BSJ894T	707	BSJ907T	722	BSJ922T	739	GCS39V	788	YCS88T
695	BSJ890T	708	BSJ908T	723	BSJ923T	740	GCS40V	789	YCS89T
696	BSJ932T	709	BSJ909T	724	BSJ924T	742	GCS42V	790	YCS90T
697	BSJ897T	710	BSJ910T	725	BSJ925T	744	GCS44V	791	YCS91T
698	BSJ898T	712	BSJ912T	726	BSJ926T	750	GCS50V	793	YCS93T
699	BSJ899T	713	BSJ913T	727	BSJ927T	754	GCS54V	794	YCS94T
700	BSJ900T	714	BSJ914T	728	BSJ928T	755	GCS55V	795	YCS95T
701	BSJ901T	715	BSJ915T	729	BSJ929T	756	GCS56V	796	YCS96T
702	BSJ902T	716	BSJ916T	730	GCS30V	759	GCS59V	797	YCS97T
703	BSJ903T	718	BSJ918T	731	GCS31V	764	GCS64V	798	YCS98T

804-822

| | | | | | | Leyland Fleetline FE30AGR | Eastern Coach Works | H43/32F | 1978-79 |

804	GSC857T	807	ULS657T	815	ULS665T	818	ULS668T	821	OSG57V
805	GSC858T	811	ULS661T	816	ULS666T	820	ULS670T	822	OSG58V
806	ULS656T	813	ULS663T	817	ULS667T				

823-849

Leyland Fleetline FE30AGR — Northern Counties — H44/31F — 1979

823	XSJ663T	827	BCS867T	834	BCS874T	844	ECS884V	848	ECS888V
824	XSJ664T	828	BCS868T	835	BCS875T	846	ECS886V	849	ECS889V
826	BCS866T	832	BCS872T	841	ECS881V				

850-889

Leyland Fleetline FE30AGR — Alexander AD — H44/31F — 1980

850	LMS170W	862	LMS162W	872	HSD72V	878	HSD78V	884	HSD84V
853	LMS153W	863	LMS163W	873	HSD73V	879	HSD79V	885	HSD85V
854	LMS154W	867	LMS168W	874	HSD74V	880	HSD80V	886	HSD86V
857	LMS157W	869	LMS169W	875	HSD75V	881	HSD81V	887	HSD87V
858	LMS158W	870	HSD70V	876	HSD76V	882	HSD82V	888	HSD88V
859	LMS159W	871	HSD71V	877	HSD77V	883	HSD83V	889	HSD89V
861	LMS161W								

890-913

Ailsa B55-10 — Alexander AV — H44/35F* — 1980 — *910/2 are CH40/31F

890	KSD90W	895	KSD95W	901	KSD101W	906	KSD106W	910	KSD110W
891	KSD91W	897	KSD97W	902	KSD102W	907	KSD107W	911	KSD111W
892	KSD92W	898	KSD98W	903	KSD103W	908	KSD108W	912	KSD112W
893	KSD93W	899	KSD99W	904	KSD104W	909	KSD109W	913	KSD113W
894	KSD94W	900	KSD100W	905	KSD105W				

914	OMS910W	Leyland Olympian B45/6LXB/1R	Eastern Coach Works	H45/32F	1981
915	TSO15X	Leyland Olympian ONLXB/1R	Eastern Coach Works	H45/32F	1982
926	TYS256W	Dennis Dominator DDA135B	Alexander RL	H45/34F	1981
927	TYS257W	Dennis Dominator DDA135B	Alexander RL	H45/34F	1981
928	TYS258W	Dennis Dominator DDA135B	Alexander RL	H45/34F	1981
929	TYS259W	Dennis Dominator DDA135B	Alexander RL	H45/34F	1981

936-945

Dennis Dominator DDA161 — Alexander RL — H45/31F — 1983

936	GSB136Y	938	GSB138Y	940	GSB140Y	942	GSB142Y	944	GSB144Y
937	GSB137Y	939	GSB139Y	941	GSB141Y	943	GSB143Y	945	GSB145Y

946	GSB146Y	Dennis Dominator DDA163	Alexander RL	H45/31F	1983
947	GSB147Y	Dennis Dominator DDA163	Alexander RL	H45/31F	1983

948-954

Dennis Dominator DDA908 — Alexander RL — H45/34F — 1985

948	B148EGA	950	B150EGA	952	B152EGA	953	B153EGA	954	B154EGA
949	B149EGA	951	B151EGA						

Previous Registrations:

32CLT	B402OSB	VLT28	A178UGB	WLT878	B408OSB
407CLT	B407OSB	VLT166	B406OSB	WLT924	A172UGB
54CLT	A179UGB	VLT204	B409OSB	WLT956	A176UGB
705DYE	B405OSB	VLT234	A180UGB	WLT974	A177UGB
FSU661	B404OSB	WLT364	B403OSB	WGB588W	WLT471, NCS120W
TCS174	A174UGB	WLT471	B401OSB	WGB589W	FSU661, NCS116W
VCS376	A175UGB				

Special Liveries:

Airlink:	337
Overall Advertisements:	339, 713, 828/32/76/86/95, 927
Quicksilver:	100/38/9/56-9/62-5, 176-8/81
Scottish Citylink:	112/3/21/33-8/60/1/70/2-4/5/9/86.

FIFE SCOTTISH

Fife Scottish Omnibuses Ltd, Esplanade, Kirkcaldy, KY1 1SP

W. Alexander & Sons (Fife) Ltd (renamed Fife Scottish Omnibuses Ltd in 1985) was one of the new companies set up in 1961 when the vast Alexander empire was divided. Its principal operating area has always been the ancient Kingdom of Fife, the natural boundaries of which have until recently protected the company from the organisational changes experienced by others.

However, Fife hit the headlines during 1991 when there was a fierce negotiation between the Secretary of State and a management and employee buy-out team and the Stagecoach group for custody of the company. After a number of court actions, Stagecoach emerged as the preferred bidder, and thus Fife Scottish vehicles are now appearing in the Stagecoach corporate livery of white with orange, red and blue bands. Many vehicles still remain in Ayres red and cream.

The company has competition from Moffat and Williamson in Glenrothes and Kirkcaldy, but a challenge from Rennie in Dunfermline has waned. To deal with the former, a number of minibuses have been transferred in from Ribble's reserve after a period of loan to Southdown

The company has depots in Aberhill, Cowdenbeath, Dunfermline, Glenrothes, Kirkcaldy and St Andrews.

All of the Volvo Citybuses that were in Coastliner livery are now in the Stagecoach livery. The Fife Scottish logo had been devised prior to the company's acquisition by Stagecoach and is to be retained. Seen in Bathgate in August 1991 is 918. Murdoch Currie

All but one of
Highland's Ailsas
were new to Fife, and
most returned to Fife
in 1990. No.807
retains Highland's
red and grey livery
and is now allocated
to Dunfermline.
Murdoch Currie

Latest arrivals in the
Fife fleet are
Northern Counties-
bodied examples of
the Volvo Citybus
from Southdown.
Still waiting to be
programmed for the
electronic destination
board is 940,
photographed in
Buchanan bus
station, Glasgow.
Murdoch Currie

Below Leyland
Leopard 149 was in
Stagecoach
corporate livery
when photographed
as it arrived in
Dundee from St
Andrews. The
photograph shows
the narrow window
bays of the AYS-type
body.
Alistair Douglas

Above **Leyland National 388 began life with Midland Scottish in Perth, and then passed to Strathtay on that company's formation in 1985 before being moved to Northern two years later. It then came to Fife in 1989 and is seen leaving Kirkcaldy bus station.** M. Fowler

For a former SBG-company, Fife has relatively few Alexander T-types. One of the second batch, 293, is seen passing through Bridge of Earn. Max Fowler

An early recipient of Stagecoach livery was 412. The bodybuilder's name, moulded into the front panel, serves to remind that the bus was exhibited at the NEC Show in 1986. Murdoch Currie

Fife Scottish **33**

Fife took nine of Kelvin Central's Dodges in 1990. No.28 is seen on a Cowdenbeath local service. Graeme Yuill

Fife's MetroRiders are normally to be found on Kirkcaldy town services, but 70 was photographed while passing through Bridge of Earn on a long route from Perth to Kirkcaldy. Max Fowler

Leyland Tiger 563 began life with a Duple Goldliner III body for service on the London route. Like many of its contemporaries, it has since been extensively rebuilt and refurbished, losing much of the brightwork. It is also of interest in that it has recently been fitted with a Leyland-derived Polish-built Pezetel engine. Stewart Brown

FIFE SCOTTISH Fleet List

1-20 — Renault-Dodge S56, Alexander AM, B25F*, 1987-88 8, 19 are B23F; 14/5 DP25F

1	D891DSF	5	D895DSF	9	E809JSX	13u	E813JSX	17	E317NSX
2	D892DSF	6	D896DSF	10u	E810JSX	14	E814JSX	18	E318NSX
3	D893DSF	7	D897DSF	11u	E811JSX	15	E815JSX	19	E319NSX
4	D894DSF	8	D898DSF	12u	E812JSX	16	E316NSX	20	E320NSX

21	G21CSG	Renault S56	Reeve Burgess Beaver	B25F	1989	
22	G22CSG	Renault S56	Reeve Burgess Beaver	B25F	1989	
23	G23CSG	Renault S56	Reeve Burgess Beaver	B25F	1989	
24	G24CSG	Renault S56	Reeve Burgess Beaver	B25F	1989	

25-31 — Dodge S56, Alexander AM, B25F, 1987, Ex Kelvin Central, 1990

25	D825RYS	27u	D827RYS	29	D829RYS	30	D830RYS	31	D831RYS
26u	D826RYS	28	D828RYS				

32	E635DCK	Renault S46	Dormobile	B25F	1987	Ex Ribble, 1991
33	D823RYS	Dodge S56	Alexander AM	B25F	1987	Ex Kelvin Central, 1990
34	D824RYS	Dodge S56	Alexander AM	B25F	1987	Ex Kelvin Central, 1990

35-47 — Renault S46, Dormobile, B25F, 1987, Ex Ribble, 1991

35	E634DCK	38	E638DCK	41	E641DCK	44	E644DCK	46	E646DCK
36	E636DCK	39	E639DCK	42	E642DCK	45	E645DCK	47	E647DCK
37	E637DCK	40	E640DCK	43	E643DCK				

51-70 — MCW MetroRider MF150, MCW, B25F, 1988, 67-70 are DP25F

51	F51RFS	55	F55RFS	59	F59RFS	63	F63RFS	67	F67RFS
52	F52RFS	56	F56RFS	60	F60RFS	64	F64RFS	68	F68RFS
53	F53RFS	57	F57RFS	61	F61RFS	65	F65RFS	69	F69RFS
54	F54RFS	58	F58RFS	62	F62RFS	66	F66RFS	70	F70RFS

85-102 — Leyland Leopard PSU3D/4R*, Alexander AYS, B53F, 1977, *93,100/2 are PSU3E/4R

85	YFS85S	93	YFS93S	98	YFS98S	100	YFS100S	102	YFS102S
86	YFS86S	97	YFS97S	99	YFS99S				

104	TMS404Y	Leyland Leopard PSU3G/4R	Alexander AY	B53F	1982	Ex Ribble, 1992
122	XMS422Y	Leyland Leopard PSU3G/4R	Alexander AY	B53F	1982	Ex Ribble, 1992
123	XMS423Y	Leyland Leopard PSU3G/4R	Alexander AY	B53F	1982	Ex Ribble, 1992

135-160 — Leyland Leopard PSU3F/4R*, Alexander AYS, B53F, 1980-81 *159/60 are PSU3G/4R

135	WFS135W	138	WFS138W	141	WFS141W	148	WFS148W	158	CSF158W
136	WFS136W	139	WFS139W	142	WFS142W	149	WFS149W	159	CSF159W
137	WFS137W	140	WFS140W	147	WFS147W	150	WFS150W	160	CSF160W

180-189 — Leyland Leopard PSU3G/4R, Alexander AYS, B53F, 1982

180	PSX180Y	182	PSX182Y	184	PSX184Y	186	PSX186Y	188	PSX188Y
181	PSX181Y	183	PSX183Y	185	PSX185Y	187	PSX187Y	189	PSX189Y

200	XMS420Y	Leyland Leopard PSU3G/4R	Alexander AY	DP49F	1982	Ex Ribble, 1992
205	TMS405Y	Leyland Leopard PSU3G/4R	Alexander AY	DP49F	1982	Ex Ribble, 1992

206	TMS406Y	Leyland Leopard PSU3G/4R	Alexander AY	DP49F	1982	Ex Ribble, 1992
207	TMS407Y	Leyland Leopard PSU3G/4R	Alexander AY	DP49F	1982	Ex Ribble, 1992
210	CFS110S	Leyland Leopard PSU3E/4R	Duple Dominant I	C49F	1978	
215	CFS115S	Leyland Leopard PSU3E/4R	Duple Dominant I	C49F	1978	
216	CFS116S	Leyland Leopard PSU3E/4R	Duple Dominant I	C49F	1978	

219-227 — Leyland Leopard PSU3E/4R, Duple Dominant II Express, C49F, 1978

219	CFS119S	222	GSG122T	224	GSG124T	226	GSG126T	227	GSG127T
221	GSG121T	223	GSG123T						

229-234 Leyland Leopard PSU3E/4R Duple Dominant I C49F* 1978 *231 is C45F

229	GSG129T	231	GSG131T	232	NSU132	233	NSU133	234	NSU134
230	GSG130T								

261	CSF161W	Leyland Leopard PSU3G/4R	Alexander AYS	DP49F	1981
262	CSF162W	Leyland Leopard PSU3G/4R	Alexander AYS	DP47F	1981

263-269 Leyland Leopard PSU3F/4R Alexander AYS DP49F 1981

263	CSF163W	265	CSF165W	267	CSF167W	268	CSF168W	269	CSF169W
264	CSF164W	266	CSF166W						

270-294 Leyland Leopard PSU3G/4R Alexander AT C49F 1982

270	NFS170Y	273	NFS173Y	276	NFS176Y	279	NFS179Y	292	RSC192Y
271	NFS171Y	274	NFS174Y	277	NFS177Y	290	RSC190Y	293	RSC193Y
272	NFS172Y	275	NFS175Y	278	NFS178Y	291	RSC191Y	294	RSC194Y

304-313 Leyland National 11351A/1R B49F 1978 304 has a DAF engine

304	HSC104T	309	HSC109T	310	HSC110T	312	HSC112T	313	HSC113T
306	HSC106T								

314-325 Leyland National 2 NL116L11/1R B52F 1980 317 has a Gardner 6HLXB engine
319 has a Volvo THD100 engine

314	RSG814V	317	RSG817V	320	RSG820V	322	RSG822V	324	RSG824V
315	RSG815V	318	RSG818V	321	RSG821V	323	RSG823V	325	RSG825V
316	RSG816V	319	RSG819V						

326-335 Leyland National 2 NL106L11/1R B44F 1980-81

326	YSX926W	328	YSX928W	330	YSX930W	332	YSX932W	334	YSX934W
327	YSX927W	329	YSX929W	331	YSX931W	333	YSX933W	335	YSX935W

365	WAS765V	Leyland National 2 NL116L11/1R	B52F	1980	Ex Kelvin Scottish, 1987
367	WAS767V	Leyland National 2 NL116L11/1R	B52F	1980	Ex Kelvin Scottish, 1987
370	WAS770V	Leyland National 2 NL116L11/1R	B52F	1980	Ex Kelvin Scottish, 1987

380-388 Leyland National 2 NL116L11/1R B52F 1980 Ex Northern Scottish, 1989

380	DMS20V	382	DMS22V	384	MSO14W	386	NLS986W	388	NLS988W
381	DMS21V	383	MSO13W	385	MSO15W	387	NLS987W		

412-419 Leyland Tiger TRCTL11/3RH Alexander P B61F 1986-87

412	D512CSF	414	D614ASG	416	D516DSX	418	D518DSX	419	D519DSX
413	D713CSC	415	D615ASG	417	D517DSX				

420-424 Leyland Tiger TRBTL11/2RH Alexander P B57F 1987

420	D520DSX	421	D521DSX	422	D522DSX	423	D523DSX	424	D524DSX

466-470 Leyland Tiger TRBTL11/2R Alexander TE C49F 1983 Ex Kelvin Central, 1989
*470 is C47F

466	MNS6Y	467	MNS7Y	468	MNS8Y	469	MNS9Y	470	MNS10Y

477	D277FAS	Leyland Tiger TRCTL11/3RH	Alexander TE	C53F	1987	Ex Highland Scottish, 1987
478	D278FAS	Leyland Tiger TRCTL11/3RH	Alexander TE	C53F	1987	Ex Highland Scottish, 1987
479	D279FAS	Leyland Tiger TRCTL11/3RH	Alexander TE	C53F	1987	Ex Highland Scottish, 1987

507-511 Leyland Tiger TRBTL11/2RH Alexander TC C47F 1985

507	B207FFS	508	B208FFS	509	B209FFS	510	B210FFS	511	B211FFS

541	GSU341	Leyland Tiger TRCTL11/3R	Duple Laser	C55F	1983	Ex Leyland Bus, 1984
542	GSU342	Leyland Tiger TRCTL11/3R	Duple Laser	C51F	1984	Ex Highland Scottish, 1987
543	GSU343	Leyland Tiger TRCTL11/3R	Duple Laser	C51F	1984	Ex Highland Scottish, 1987
544	GSU344	Leyland Tiger TRCTL11/3R	Duple Laser	C51F	1984	Ex Highland Scottish, 1987
545	MSU445	Leyland Tiger TRCTL11/3R	Duple Goldliner IV	C51F	1983	

559	MSU499	Leyland Tiger TRCTL11/3RZ	Duple 340	C48FT	1987	Ex Kelvin Central, 1990
562	MSU462	Leyland Tiger TRCTL11/3RH	Duple 340	C55F	1987	Ex Kelvin Central, 1990
563	MSU463	Leyland Tiger TRCTL11/3R	Duple Goldliner IV	C51F	1983	
564	MSU464	Leyland Tiger TRCTL11/3RZ	Duple 340	C53FT	1987	Ex Kelvin Central, 1990

801-844

Ailsa B55-10 — Alexander AV — H44/35F — 1975/77 — 801-10/44 ex Highland Scottish, 1990

801	KSF1N	807	KSF7N	817	LSX17P	829	LSX29P	838	LSX38P
802	KSF2N	810	LSX10P	825	LSX25P	830	LSX30P	839	LSX39P
803	KSF3N	814	LSX14P	827	LSX27P	832	LSX32P	840	LSX40P
805	KSF5N	815	LSX15P	828	LSX28P	834	LSX34P	844	YMS714R
806	KSF6N	816	LSX16P						

847-866

Ailsa B55-10 MkII — Alexander AV — H44/35F — 1979

847	OSC47V	851	OSC51V	855	OSC55V	859	OSC59V	863	OSC63V
848	OSC48V	852	OSC52V	856	OSC56V	860	OSC60V	864	OSC64V
849	OSC49V	853	OSC53V	857	OSC57V	861	OSC61V	865	OSC65V
850	OSC50V	854	OSC54V	858	OSC58V	862	OSC62V	866	OSC66V

867-874

Volvo-Ailsa B55-10 MkIII — Alexander RV — H44/37F — 1984

| 867 | A967YSX | 869 | A969YSX | 871 | A971YSX | 873 | A973YSX | 874 | A974YSX |
| 868 | A968YSX | 870 | A970YSX | 872 | A972YSX | | | | |

875-884

Ailsa B55-10 — Alexander AV — H44/35F — 1977

| 875 | UFS875R | 877 | UFS877R | 878 | UFS878R | 879 | UFS879R | 884u | UFS874R |
| 876 | UFS876R | | | | | | | | |

901-920

Volvo Citybus B10M-50 — Alexander RV — DPH47/33F* — 1985-87 — 908 ex Volvo demonstrator, 1986
*909/10 are CH45/35F

901	C801USG	907	C807USG	910	E910KSG	915	C795USG	919	C799USG
905	C805USG	908	B108CCS	914	C794USG	918	C798USG	920	C800USG
906	C806USG	909	E909KSG						

940	F310MYJ	Volvo Citybus B10M-50	Northern Counties	DPH43/33F	1989	Ex Southdown, 1991
941	F311MYJ	Volvo Citybus B10M-50	Northern Counties	DPH43/33F	1989	Ex Southdown, 1991
942	F312MYJ	Volvo Citybus B10M-50	Northern Counties	DPH43/33F	1989	Ex Southdown, 1991

972-997

Volvo Citybus B10M-50 — Alexander RV — H47/37F — 1985-87

972	C802USG	979	B179FFS	984	B184FFS	988	C788USG	992	C792USG
973	C803USG	980	B180FFS	985	B185FFS	989	C789USG	993	C793USG
974	C804USG	981	B181FFS	986	B186FFS	990	C790USG	996	C796USG
977	B177FFS	982	B182FFS	987	C787USG	991	C791USG	997	C797USG
978	B178FFS	983	B183FFS						

Previous Registrations:

GSU341	VTY130Y		MSU463	SFS583Y, MSU445, PSP722Y
GSU342	A505PST		MSU464	D321RNS
GSU343	A506PST		MSU499	D319SGB
GSU344	A507PST		NSU132	GSG132T
MSU445	SFS582Y		NSU133	GSG133T
MSU462	D322RNS		NSU134	GSG134T

Special Liveries:
Overall Advertisements: 316, 855
Service 74: 334.

GRAMPIAN

Grampian Regional Transport Ltd, 395 King Street, Aberdeen, AB9 1SP

Grampian was the first Scottish council-owned bus company to be privatised when in January 1989 it was sold to its management and employees. The company is successor to the Corporation trams and later buses which served Aberdeen from the early years of the century.

Even before privatisation, Grampian had purchased two local firms, Mair of Aberdeen and Kirkpatrick of Banchory, and these continue to operate as separate and distinctive units. In September 1990, Grampian became the new owner of Midland Scottish Omnibuses based in the central belt, following the sale of that company by the government.

Faced with competition from Northern Scottish on city routes, Grampian ventured forth into the country and operated to places such as Ellon and Banchory. When Alexanders (North East) failed in November 1989, Grampian took over some vehicles and continued to operate from Aberdeen to Peterhead and Fraserburgh under the Alexanders name. Most of these country services ceased in mid-1991 at the same time as Northern Scottish, by then owned by Stagecoach, reduced its presence in the city.

While coaches have come and gone, there has been little movement within the bus fleet in recent years and the Atlantean remains in the majority.

The depot is in King Street, Aberdeen and the livery is cream, green and dark green.

The Leyland Atlantean is still very prominent in the Grampian fleet and 342 is seen at Marischal College. The ribbon through the fleetname displays 'Employee Owned — Caring for YOU' and was added to the fleet after its sale by the council. Murdoch Currie

The 1988 delivery of Leyland Olympians introduced the Lothian-style of destination display to this operator. Two of the batch of these longer Olympians have a single doorway while 128, one of the standard dual-doored bus versions, was photographed when operating in Guild Street, Aberdeen. Murdoch Currie

Six Reeve Burgess Beaver-bodied Mercedes-Benz, carrying appropriate logos, joined the Grampian fleet in 1991 mainly for use on service 6. Stewart Brown

Only two of the Gardner-engined Tigers remain in the parent fleet. No.52 is in the current multi-striped livery. Stewart Brown

A Scott-bodied Mercedes-Benz of Mair's is seen while on the forecourt of Aberdeen railway station. Alistair Douglas

Grampian supplies vehicles to both Citylink and Caledonian Express. Jonckheere-bodied Volvo 89, seen here in Caledonian Express livery, heads south from Montrose on service 372 to Middlesbrough. Stewart Brown

GRAMPIAN Fleet List

24	GRS114E	Leyland Atlantean PDR1/1	Alexander A	O43/34F	1967	
25	CRG325C	Daimler CVG6	Alexander	H37/29R	1965	
32	D32XSS	MCW MetroRider MF150/10	MCW	C23F	1987	
33	D33XSS	MCW MetroRider MF150/10	MCW	C23F	1987	

34-39							
		Mercedes-Benz 709D	Reeve Burgess Beaver	B23F	1991		
34	H34USO	**36**	H36USO	**37**	H37USO	**38**	H38USO	**39**	H39USO
35	H35USO						

40	ESK955	Volvo B58-56	Duple Dominant II	C45F	1979	Ex Kirkpatrick, Banchory, 1991
41	ESK956	Volvo B10M-61	Plaxton Paramount 3200 III	C53F	1988	Ex Alexander, Aberdeen, 1989
44	ESK957	Volvo B10M-61	Plaxton Paramount 3200 III	C57F	1988	Ex Alexander, Aberdeen, 1989
45	ESK958	Volvo B10M-61	Plaxton Paramount 3200 III	C49FT	1988	Ex Alexander, Aberdeen, 1989

48	WSU479	Leyland Tiger TRCTL11/3RH	Plaxton Paramount 3200 Ex	C49FT	1984	Ex Paramount Leisure, 1990
52	PSU623	Leyland Tiger TRCLXC/2RH	Plaxton Paramount 3200 Ex	C53F	1986	
53	PSU624	Leyland Tiger TRCLXC/2RH	Plaxton Paramount 3200 Ex	C53F	1986	
59	158ASV	Leyland National 11351A/1R		B52F	1978	Ex Midland Scottish, 1991
60	ORS60R	Leyland Leopard PSU4C/4R	Alexander AY	DP45F	1977	
65	KSO65P	Leyland National 10351/2R		B40D	1976	
82	WSU480	Leyland Leopard PSU5C/4R	Plaxton Supreme IV	C53F	1978	Ex Rennie, Dunfermline, 1990
87	TSU651	Volvo B10M-60	Jonckheere Deauville	C51FT	1989	
88	TRS333	Volvo B10M-61	Jonckheere Jubilee P50	C46FT	1987	Ex Hallmark, Luton, 1990
89	PSU968	Volvo B10M-61	Jonckheere Jubilee P599	C51FT	1987	Ex Tellings Golden Miller, 1990
90	542GRT	Volvo B10M-61	Plaxton Paramount 3500	C49FT	1986	Ex Tellings Golden Miller, 1990
91	TSU682	Volvo B10M-61	Jonckheere Deauville	C51FT	1989	Ex Hillingdon Travel, Uxbridge, 1991

101-110

Leyland Olympian ONLXB/1R   Alexander RH   H47/26D   1984

101	A101FSA	103	A103FSA	105	A105FSA	107	A107FSA	109	A109FSA
102	A102FSA	104	A104FSA	106	A106FSA	108	A108FSA	110	A110FSA

112-121

Leyland Olympian ONLXB/1RV   Alexander RH   H47/26D*   1985   *121 is H47/24D

112	B112MSO	114	B114MSO	116	B116MSO	118	B118MSO	120	B120MSO
113	B113MSO	115	B115MSO	117	B117MSO	119	B119MSO	121	B121MSO

122-131

Leyland Olympian ONCL10/2RZ   Alexander RH   H49/29D*   1988   *122/3 are CH47/33F

122	E122DRS	124	E124DRS	126	E126DRS	128	E128DRS	130	E130DRS
123	E123DRS	125	E125DRS	127	E127DRS	129	E129DRS	131	E131DRS

205-217

Leyland Atlantean AN68A/1R   Alexander AL   H45/29D   1977

205	ORS205R	209	ORS209R	211	ORS211R	213	ORS213R	216	ORS216R
206	ORS206R	210	ORS210R	212	ORS212R	215	ORS215R	217	ORS217R
207	ORS207R								

218-257

Leyland Atlantean AN68A/1R   Alexander AL   H45/29D   1977-78

218	XSA218S	226	XSA226S	235	YSO235T	243	DSA243T	250	DSA250T
219	XSA219S	227	XSA227S	236	YSO236T	244	DSA244T	251	DSA251T
220	XSA220S	228	YSO228T	237	YSO237T	245	DSA245T	252	DSA252T
221	XSA221S	230	YSO230T	238	DSA238T	246	DSA246T	253	DSA253T
222	XSA222S	231	YSO231T	239	DSA239T	247	DSA247T	254	DSA254T
223	XSA223S	232	YSO232T	240	DSA240T	248	DSA248T	256	DSA256T
224	XSA224S	233	YSO233T	241	DSA241T	249	DSA249T	257	DSA257T
225	XSA225S	234	YSO234T	242	DSA242T				

261-300

Leyland Atlantean AN68A/1R   Alexander AL   H45/29D   1979-80

261	HRS261V	269	HRS269V	277	HRS277V	285	HSO285V	293	LRS293W
262	HRS262V	270	HRS270V	278	HRS278V	286	HSO286V	294	LRS294W
263	HRS263V	271	HRS271V	279	HRS279V	287	HSO287V	295	LRS295W
264	HRS264V	272	HRS272V	280	HRS280V	288	HSO288V	296	LRS296W
265	HRS265V	273	HRS273V	281	HSO281V	289	HSO289V	297	LRS297W
266	HRS266V	274	HRS274V	282	HSO282V	290	HSO290V	298	LRS298W
267	HRS267V	275	HRS275V	283	HSO283V	291	LRS291W	299	LRS299W
268	HRS268V	276	HRS276V	284	HSO284V	292	LRS292W	300	LRS300W

301-330

Leyland Atlantean AN68C/1R   Alexander AL   H45/29D   1981-82

301	NRS301W	307	NRS307W	313	NRS313W	319	URS319X	325	URS325X
302	NRS302W	308	NRS308W	314	NRS314W	320	URS320X	326	URS326X
303	NRS303W	309	NRS309W	315	NRS315W	321	URS321X	327	URS327X
304	NRS304W	310	NRS310W	316	URS316X	322	URS322X	328	URS328X
305	NRS305W	311	NRS311W	317	URS317X	323	URS323X	329	URS329X
306	NRS306W	312	NRS312W	318	URS318X	324	URS324X	330	URS330X

331-345

		Leyland Atlantean AN68D/1R		Alexander AL			H45/29D	1983				
331	XSS331Y	**334**	XSS334Y	**337**	XSS337Y	**340**	XSS340Y	**343**	XSS343Y
332	XSS332Y	**335**	XSS335Y	**338**	XSS338Y	**341**	XSS341Y	**344**	XSS344Y
333	XSS333Y	**336**	XSS336Y	**339**	XSS339Y	**342**	XSS342Y	**345**	XSS345Y

Kirkpatrick fleet:

PRE205R	Bedford VAS5	Plaxton Supreme	C29F	1976	Ex Pilkington, Accrington, 1989
PSU626	Bedford VAS5	Plaxton Supreme	C29F	1977	Ex Bruce, Airdrie, 1983
PSU630	Leyland Leopard PSU5C/4R	Plaxton Supreme IV	C57F	1979	Ex Mair, Dyce, 1991
WSU447	Leyland Leopard PSU5C/4R	Plaxton Supreme IV	C57F	1979	Ex Lightfoot, Winsford, 1989
EVC371Y	Ford Transit 190	Dormobile	B12F	1983	
C200HGF	Mercedes-Benz L608D	Plaxton	C20F	1985	Ex Richmond, Epsom, 1990
781GRT	Leyland Tiger TRCLXC/2RH	Plaxton Paramount 3200 Ex C49F		1986	Ex Grampian fleet, 1991

Mair's fleet:

HSO61N	Leyland Leopard PSU4C/4R	Alexander AY	DP45F	1975	Ex Grampian fleet, 1988
KJD412P	Bristol LH6L	Eastern Coach Works	B39F	1976	Ex Grampian fleet, 1988
131ASV	Leyland Leopard PSU3E/4R	Duple Dominant Express	C49F	1977	Ex Midland Scottish, 1991
PSU609	Bedford VAS5	Duple Dominant	C29F	1979	Ex Jolly, Ulverston, 1981
WSU481	Leyland Leopard PSU3E/4RT	Plaxton Supreme III Exp	C48F	1980	Ex Grampian fleet, 1991
HSU955	Leyland Leopard PSU3F/4R	Plaxton Supreme IV Exp	C48F	1981	Ex Southdown, 1989
LSU717	Leyland Leopard PSU3F/4R	Plaxton Supreme IV Exp	C48F	1981	Ex Southdown, 1989
LSU917	Leyland Leopard PSU3F/4R	Plaxton Supreme IV Exp	C48F	1981	Ex Southdown, 1989
WSS904Y	Mercedes-Benz L508D	Devon Conversions	C19F	1982	
JSV426	Leyland Tiger TRCTL11/3R	Plaxton Paramount 3500	C55F	1983	Ex Armchair, Brentford, 1990
PSU629	Volvo B10M-61	Van Hool Alizée	C49FT	1984	
PSU631	Volvo B10M-61	Jonckheere Jubilee P50	C53F	1985	Ex Budden, Woodfalls, 1988
B490CGN	Mercedes-Benz L608D	Robin Hood	C19F	1985	Ex Driver, Rainham, 1989
D995ARE	Mercedes-Benz L608D	PMT	C24F	1986	Ex Collison, Stonehouse, 1989
XWL539	Volvo B10M-61	Jonckheere Jubilee P599	C51FT	1987	Ex West Kingsdown Coach, 1989
PSU628	Volvo B10M-61	Jonckheere Jubilee P599	C51FT	1987	Ex Budden, Woodfalls, 1990
737ABD	Volvo B10M-61	Jonckheere Jubilee P599	C51FT	1988	
E182DBB	Toyota HB31R	Caetano Optimo	C19F	1988	
F326WCS	Mercedes-Benz 609D	Scott	C24F	1988	
F327WCS	Mercedes-Benz 609D	Scott	C24F	1988	
F103HSO	Volvo B10M-61	Plaxton Paramount 3200 III	C57F	1988	Ex Grampian fleet, 1991
PSU627	Volvo B10M-61	Jonckheere Jubilee P599	C51FT	1989	Ex River Valley, Sutton Valence, 1990
F632JSA	MCW MetroRider MF154/26	MCW	C29F	1989	
F633JSO	Mercedes-Benz 609D	Made-to-Measure	C19F	1989	
F634JSO	Mercedes-Benz 609D	Made-to-Measure	C19F	1989	
G143SUS	Mercedes-Benz 609D	Scott	C22F	1990	
H386CFT	Toyota HB31R	Caetano Optimo	C18F	1990	
H193CVU	Mercedes-Benz 609D	Made-to-Measure	C24F	1990	

Previous Registrations:

131ASV	YMS262R	PSU626	WSC32R
158ASV	OLS805T	PSU627	F913YNV
542GRT	C109AFX	PSU628	D95BNV
737ABD	F950RNV	PSU629	B229LSO, 737ABD
781GRT	D55VSO	PSU630	FDF272T
ESK955	HSE696V	PSU631	B497CBD
ESK956	F101HSO	PSU968	D318VVV
ESK957	F104HSO	TRS333	D330VVV
ESK958	F105SSE	TSU651	F87CBD
HSU955	MAP346W	TSU682	F912YNV
JSV426	FNM863Y	WSU447	FDF275T
LSU717	MAP349W	WSU479	A75JFA
LSU917	MAP348W	WSU480	YYJ299T, 405DCD, FRX868T
PSU609	BFP131T	WSU481	GWV931V
PSU623	D52VSO	XWL539	D315VVV
PSU624	D53VSO		

Special Liveries:

Aberdeen Corporation Transport:	25
British Petroleum:	F633JSO, F634JSO, G143SUS
Caledonian Express:	89.
Overall Advertisements:	102-4/13/20, 256/66/81, 304.
Scottish Citylink:	PSU629.

Named vehicle:

E182DBB *Pride of the Glens*

HIGHLAND

Highland Scottish Omnibuses Ltd, 1 Seafield Road, Inverness, IV1 1TN

Highland Omnibuses Ltd was formed in 1952 by the British Transport Commission to consolidate the activities of a number of firms in Inverness and the north. Over the years, a large number of small operators was absorbed, as was the majority of the operations of David MacBrayne Ltd.

Highland had always had something of a Cinderella image, often having to make do with other operator's hand-me-down vehicles. There was some improvement in the late seventies and early eighties with an influx of new vehicles.

The company was renamed Highland Scottish Omnibuses in 1985. Deregulation inevitably brought competition, not only on the remunerative routes around Inverness and Fort William, but also on tendered work, further weakening the company's position.

When the company was offered for sale in 1991, the bid from the management and employees was rejected in favour of that from a consortium of Scottish Citylink and local independent Rapson of Alness. The new owners immediately embarked on a cost cutting exercise which was not to the liking of many of the drivers who defected overnight to Stagecoach's Inverness Traction. There followed a brief bitter bus war which resulted in Highland withdrawing almost entirely from Inverness, closing Tain depot and selling many of the more modern vehicles in the fleet.

Some experimental liveries have been tried since privatisation, but the foregoing events have distracted from a decision on this as yet.

Depots are at Aviemore, Fort William, Nairn, Portree, Inverness, Thurso and Wick and the liveries are red and grey or red and cream.

Daimler Fleetline D930 is seen in Thurso on a Dounreay service. The company provides many services to the Atomic Energy site. Stewart Brown

Daimler Fleetline 314, photographed in Inverness, is in the latest livery style. It is about to head out past the shores of Loch Ness on route for Urquhart Castle. Murdoch Currie

The reduction in Highland's presence in Inverness has severely reduced the Olympian fleet with many being sold to Ribble and Chester. The six with coach seats, however, still remain and 374 is seen in Inverness in Highland Coaches livery. Max Fowler

One of several 62-seat Leopards on the Isle of Skye, L251 came from the Fife Scottish fleet early in its career. It carries the latest fleetname. *Murdoch Currie*

The Duple Dominant-bodied Leopards that came from Fife in 1988 are in a variety of liveries. L825 is one in full coach livery and was photographed as it was about to leave Portree for the north of Skye. *Murdoch Currie*

The service to Inverness Airport is usually operated by a minibus, and on the occasion of this picture it was a Carlyle-bodied Sherpa that originated in the Bee Buzz operation in Altrincham. Stewart Brown

Former MetroRider demonstrator P7 is seen in Farraline Park bus station, Inverness. At present it is the only MetroRider in the fleet. Stewart Brown

Van Hool-bodied Volvo V880 has recently received the latest Citylink livery for service between Glasgow and Skye in competition with Clan Coaches. Murdoch Currie

HIGHLAND Fleet List

P1	E911AFM	Mercedes-Benz 609D	PMT	C24F	1988	Ex Whitelaw, Stonehouse, 1989
P2	E434YSU	Mercedes-Benz 609D	Scott	C24F	1988	Ex Whitelaw, Stonehouse, 1989
P3	D153NON	Freight Rover Sherpa 365	Carlyle	B20F	1987	Ex Bournemouth, 1989
P4	D154NON	Freight Rover Sherpa 365	Carlyle	B20F	1987	Ex Bournemouth, 1989
P6	D246OOJ	Freight Rover Sherpa 365	Carlyle	B20F	1987	Ex Bournemouth, 1989
P7	E77TDA	MCW MetroRider MF151/2	MCW	B25F	1987	Ex MCW demonstrator, 1987
E182	PRN125X	Leyland Tiger TRCTL11/3R	Duple Dominant IV	C49FT	1982	Ex Duple demonstrator, 1982
E189	B873UST	Leyland Tiger TRCTL11/3RH	Duple Laser 2	C46FT	1985	
E191	B875UST	Leyland Tiger TRCTL11/3RH	Duple Laser 2	C46FT	1985	
L212	GSO77V	Leyland Leopard PSU3E/4R	Alexander AYS	B62F	1979	Ex Alexander (Northern), 1981
L213	GSO78V	Leyland Leopard PSU3E/4R	Alexander AYS	B62F	1979	Ex Alexander (Northern), 1981
L214	GSO79V	Leyland Leopard PSU3E/4R	Alexander AYS	B62F	1979	Ex Alexander (Northern), 1981

L217-224

		Leyland Leopard PSU3G/4R	Alexander AY	DP49F	1981

L217	CAS511W	L219	CAS513W	L221	CAS515W	L223	CAS517W	L224	CAS518W
L218	CAS512W	L220	CAS514W	L222	CAS516W				

L227-231

		Leyland Leopard PSU3F/4R*	Alexander AYS	B62F	1982	*L227 is PSU3G/4R

L227	FAS372X	L228	FAS373X	L229	FAS374X	L230	FAS375X	L231	FAS376X

L246	CFS107S	Leyland Leopard PSU3E/4R	Duple Dominant I	C44F	1978	Ex Alexander (Fife), 1982
L251	WFS152W	Leyland Leopard PSU3F/4R	Alexander AYS	B62F	1980	Ex Alexander (Fife), 1983
L252	WFS153W	Leyland Leopard PSU3F/4R	Alexander AYS	B62F	1980	Ex Alexander (Fife), 1983

D313-327

		Leyland Fleetline FE30AGR	Eastern Coach Works	H43/32F	1978-79

D313	SAS855T	D316	SAS858T	D319	UAS63T	D322	UAS66T	D325	UAS69T
D314	SAS856T	D317	SAS859T	D320	UAS64T	D323	UAS67T	D326	UAS70T
D315	SAS857T	D318	SAS860T	D321	UAS65T	D324	UAS68T	D327	UAS71T

F375	C375CAS	Leyland Olympian ONLXB/1R	Alexander RL	DPH47/25F	1986	
F376	C376CAS	Leyland Olympian ONLXB/1R	Alexander RL	DPH47/25F	1986	
F377	C377CAS	Leyland Olympian ONLXB/1R	Alexander RL	DPH47/25F	1986	
Q401	E401TBS	Renault S56	Alexander AM	B25F	1988	
Q404	E404TBS	Renault S56	Alexander AM	B25F	1988	
Q405	E405TBS	Renault S56	Alexander AM	B25F	1988	
Q406	D316MHS	Dodge S56	Alexander AM	B21F	1986	Ex Kelvin Central, 1990
Q407u	D317MHS	Dodge S56	Alexander AM	B21F	1986	Ex Kelvin Central, 1990

Q408-412

		Dodge S56	Alexander AM	B25F	1987	Ex Kelvin Central, 1990

Q408u	D818RYS	Q409u	D819RYS	Q410u	D820RYS	Q411u	D821RYS	Q412u	D822RYS

L803	LMS383W	Leyland Leopard PSU3F/4R	Alexander AYS	B53F	1980	Ex Kelvin Scottish, 1986
L813	YSF83S	Leyland Leopard PSU3D/4R	Alexander AYS	B53F	1977	Ex Fife Scottish, 1988
L814	YSF104S	Leyland Leopard PSU3E/4R	Alexander AYS	B53F	1977	Ex Midland Scottish, 1988
V816	B216FJS	Volvo B10M-61	Van Hool Alizée	C52FT	1984	Ex Newton, Dingwall, 1985
V817	B217FJS	Volvo B10M-61	Van Hool Alizée	C52FT	1984	Ex Newton, Dingwall, 1985
L825	GSG125T	Leyland Leopard PSU3E/4R	Duple Dominant II Express	C49F	1978	Ex Fife Scottish, 1988
L828	GSG128T	Leyland Leopard PSU3E/4R	Duple Dominant II Express	C49F	1978	Ex Fife Scottish, 1988
L830	GSG120T	Leyland Leopard PSU3E/4R	Duple Dominant II Express	C49F	1978	Ex Fife Scottish, 1988
L833	ULS333T	Leyland Leopard PSU3E/4R	Alexander AYS	B53F	1979	Ex Kelvin Scottish, 1986
V834	4234NT	Volvo B10M-61	Van Hool Alizée	C52FT	1984	Ex Newton, Dingwall, 1985
L836	GCS36V	Leyland Leopard PSU3E/4R	Alexander AY	B53F	1980	Ex Clydeside Scottish, 1988
L837	ULS337T	Leyland Leopard PSU3E/4R	Alexander AYS	B53F	1979	Ex Kelvin Scottish, 1986
L843	GCS43V	Leyland Leopard PSU3E/4R	Alexander AY	B53F	1980	Ex Clydeside Scottish, 1988
L852	GCS52V	Leyland Leopard PSU3E/4R	Alexander AY	B53F	1980	Ex Clydeside Scottish, 1988
L857	DLS357V	Leyland Leopard PSU3E/4R	Alexander AYS	B53F	1979	Ex Kelvin Scottish, 1986
L863	GCS63V	Leyland Leopard PSU3E/4R	Alexander AY	B53F	1980	Ex Clydeside Scottish, 1988
L867	XSG67R	Leyland Leopard PSU3E/4R	Alexander AYS	B53F	1977	Ex Midland Scottish, 1988
L868	XSG68R	Leyland Leopard PSU3E/4R	Alexander AYS	B53F	1977	Ex Midland Scottish, 1988
L869	XSG69R	Leyland Leopard PSU3E/4R	Alexander AYS	B53F	1977	Ex Midland Scottish, 1988
L872	LMS372W	Leyland Leopard PSU3F/4R	Alexander AYS	DP49F	1980	Ex Kelvin Scottish, 1986
L873	LMS373W	Leyland Leopard PSU3F/4R	Alexander AYS	B53F	1980	Ex Kelvin Scottish, 1986
L875	LMS375W	Leyland Leopard PSU3F/4R	Alexander AYS	DP49F	1980	Ex Kelvin Scottish, 1986
L876	YSF76S	Leyland Leopard PSU3D/4R	Alexander AYS	B53F	1977	Ex Fife Scottish, 1986
L877	YSF77S	Leyland Leopard PSU3D/4R	Alexander AYS	B53F	1977	Ex Fife Scottish, 1986
L878	YSF78S	Leyland Leopard PSU3D/4R	Alexander AYS	B53F	1977	Ex Fife Scottish, 1986
V880	2080NT	Volvo B10M-61	Van Hool Alizée	C52FT	1984	Ex Newton, Dingwall, 1985
Z882	A182UGB	Leyland Tiger TRCLXC/2RH	Plaxton Paramount 3200 Ex	C49F	1984	Ex Western Scottish, 1986
V883	1983NT	Volvo B10M-61	Van Hool Alizée	C52FT	1984	Ex Newton, Dingwall, 1985
L884	YSF84S	Leyland Leopard PSU3D/4R	Alexander AYS	B53F	1977	Ex Fife Scottish, 1986
L890	YSF90S	Leyland Leopard PSU3D/4R	Alexander AYS	B53F	1977	Ex Fife Scottish, 1986
L891	YSF91S	Leyland Leopard PSU3E/4R	Alexander AYS	B53F	1977	Ex Fife Scottish, 1986
V892	3692NT	Volvo B10M-61	Van Hool Alizée	C52FT	1984	Ex Newton, Dingwall, 1985
L893	YSF103S	Leyland Leopard PSU3E/4R	Alexander AYS	B53F	1977	Ex Fife Scottish, 1986
L894	YSF94S	Leyland Leopard PSU3E/4R	Alexander AYS	B53F	1977	Ex Fife Scottish, 1986
L895	YSF95S	Leyland Leopard PSU3D/4R	Alexander AYS	B53F	1977	Ex Fife Scottish, 1986
L896	YSF96S	Leyland Leopard PSU3D/4R	Alexander AYS	B53F	1977	Ex Fife Scottish, 1986

D920-930

		Daimler Fleetline CRG6LXB	Alexander AD	H44/31F	1976	Ex Fife Scottish, 1988/90

D920	SMS120P	D924	SMS124P	D928	SMS128P	D929u	SMS129P	D930	SMS130P
D923	SMS123P	D925	SMS125P				

Previous Registrations:

1983NT	A639EJS	3692NT	A638EJS
2080NT	A637EJS	4234NT	A640EJS

Special Liveries:
Scottish Citylink: V834/80/92.

KELVIN CENTRAL

Kelvin Central Buses Ltd, Traction House, Motherwell, ML1 3DS

In 1989, the Scottish Bus Group merged Central Scottish and Kelvin Scottish to create Kelvin Central. Central's history dated back to 1926, whereas Kelvin Scottish had been a creation of 1985 incorporating some Central and some Midland Scottish territory.

The company was sold in 1991 to the new Kelvin Central company owned wholly by its employees.

The operating area extends from West Dunbartonshire to Lanarkshire in the east. Under SGB ownership there has been some retrenchment, notably on the East Kilbride to Glasgow corridor following a long strike in 1989. However, since being purchased by its employees substantial market consolidation has been achieved despite intensive competition, partly through acquisition of of the local services of other operators including Green of Kirkintilloch, McKenna of Uddingston and Beaton of Blantyre.

Although no new vehicles have been purchased since privatisation, numerous second-hand acquisitions have been made to meet increased commitments. Crew operation survives on the fleet of Routemasters which continue to ply to Glasgow from Clydebank and Easterhouse, though the service has now been split in the city centre.

The multitude of liveries proposed at one time has given way to universal adoption of the red and cream used originally for Lanarkshire Bus, though some vehicles are still in Central's dark red and cream or the Kelvin Scottish blue and yellow.

Depots are at Airdrie, Cumbernauld, Kirkintilloch, Motherwell, Old Kilpatrick and Stepps.

The Ailsa model has been threatened with withdrawal from the Kelvin fleet more than once, but has then been reinstated. Several are now in the current livery, though 1967 was still in central SMT colours when photographed leaving Anderston bus station, Glasgow. Max Fowler

Eastern Coach Works-bodied Olympian 1803 is seen in Hamilton bus station on one of the few remaining services that take Kelvin Central into East Kilbride. Murdoch Currie

Dennis Dominator 1718 is seen in the third of Kelvin Scottish's four liveries as it crosses Kelvin Bridge, Glasgow, in the winter sun. Max Fowler

1989 saw the acquisition of four Leyland Olympians from Strathtay and a further four from Fife Scottish. No. 1821 is one from the Strathtay fleet. S.J. MacDonald

The mainstay of the Scottish Bus Group's stage service requirement was the Alexander-bodied Leyland Leopard, and many have been transferred between fleets over the years. Kelvin 1544 came into the fleet from Midland Scottish via Kelvin Scottish.

Above **Former Highland Scottish Leyland National 1144, is seen in the latest livery in a damp Argyle Street, Glasgow.** Max Fowler

Leyland Leopard 2454 started operations with the Midland Scottish fleet. Fitted with the Alexander AT-type bodywork, it was photographed while on layover at Clydebank. Murdoch Currie

Dennis Dorchester 2186 is seen in Airdrie complete with Lanarkshire Bus lettering in addition to the first KCB fleetname style. Stewart Brown

Kelvin Central **53**

Leyland Tiger 3230 was new to the Alexander (Midland) fleet as MPT120 and was the prototype for the Alexander TC type. Despite the Kelvin Central Charter livery, it can be found on bus duties in and around Clydebank.
Murdoch Currie

Early in 1992, Whitelaw's provided some new styles of bus into the Kelvin fleet. In addition to two Plaxton Derwent buses was 1281, an example with Duple 300 style bodywork. It is seen leaving Anderston bus station shortly after acquisition.
Murdoch Currie

The Duple Dominant/Leyland Leopard combination was prolific through both state operators, SBG and NBC purchasing large numbers. Kelvin 2559, seen at Buchanan bus station in Glasgow, typified the type. New to Midland it is now in full Kelvin Central livery.
Murdoch Currie

Left **The Alexander-bodied Mercedes-Benz are often used on competitive services. No.1059 was photographed as it left Hamilton ahead of a Whitelaw's service to Stonehouse.** Max Fowler

Right **Purchased for the town service in Kilsyth, 1067 was personalised in favour of the regular driver. This vehicle was purchased from Duncan of Kinloch Rannoch in 1991.** Murdoch Currie

KELVIN CENTRAL Fleet List

1001	C546TJF	Ford Transit 190	Rootes	B16F	1986	Ex Stevenson, Uttoxeter, 1991
1002	C556TUT	Ford Transit 190	Rootes	B16F	1986	Ex Stevenson, Uttoxeter, 1991
1003	C193KBH	Ford Transit 190	Carlyle	B16F	1986	Ex Luton & District, 1992
1004	C194KBH	Ford Transit 190	Carlyle	B16F	1986	Ex Luton & District, 1992
1021	F914KRJ	Peugeot-Talbot Pullman	Talbot	DP22F	1989	Ex McKenna, Uddingston, 1992
1022	H315BGD	Peugeot-Talbot Pullman	Talbot	B22F	1991	Ex McKenna, Uddingston, 1992

1051-1065

		Mercedes-Benz L608D	Alexander AM	B21F	1986

1051	D125NUS	1055	D132NUS	1058	D135NUS	1062	D140NUS	1064	D142NUS
1052	D126NUS	1056	D133NUS	1059	D137NUS	1063	D141NUS	1065	D143NUS
1054	D131NUS	1057	D134NUS	1061	D139NUS				

1067	F349TSX	Mercedes-Benz 811D	Alexander AM	DP31F	1988	Ex Duncan, Kinloch Rannoch, 1991
1068	H255XDS	Mercedes-Benz 811D	Scott	DP33F	1990	Ex Whitelaw, Stonehouse, 1992
2069	E511YSU	Mercedes-Benz 709D	Alexander AM	C25F	1988	Ex McKenna, Uddingston, 1992
2070	F94KDS	Mercedes-Benz 811D	Alexander AM	C33F	1989	Ex McKenna, Uddingston, 1992
2071	F126HGD	Mercedes-Benz 609D	Reeve Burgess Beaver	C23F	1989	Ex Coakley, New Stevenston, 1992
2072	F852LHS	Mercedes-Benz 811D	Alexander AM	C33F	1989	Ex McKenna, Uddingston, 1992
2073	H125YGG	Mercedes-Benz 609D	Rapier	C24F	1990	Ex Coakley, New Stevenston, 1992
2074	H907XGA	Mercedes-Benz 811D	Reeve Burgess Beaver	C33F	1990	Ex Coakley, New Stevenston, 1992
1091	G727RGA	Leyland Swift LBM6T/2RS	Reeve Burgess Harrier	B39F	1989	Ex McKenna, Uddingston, 1992

1122-1129

		Leyland National 11351A/1R		B49F*	1978-79 Ex Green, Kirkintilloch, 1991
					*1129 is B52F

1122	CCL779T	1124	DPW783T	1126	WBN463T	1128	WBN476T	1129	XNG761S
1123	CCL780T	1125	DPW784T	1127	WBN467T				

1130-1160   Leyland National 2 NL116L11/1R   B52F   1980-81 *1151/3-60 are B49F

1130	DMS27V	1138	MDS862V	1144	WAS769V	1150	YFS307W	1156	AST156W
1131	MDS855V	1139	MDS863V	1145	MSO16W	1151	AST151W	1157	AST157W
1132	MDS856V	1140	MDS864V	1147	SNS827W	1153	AST153W	1158	AST158W
1133	MDS857V	1141	MDS867V	1148	YFS301W	1154	AST154W	1159	AST159W
1136	MDS860V	1142	MDS868V	1149	YFS306W	1155	AST155W	1160	AST160W
1137	MDS861V	1143	WAS766V						

1181-1185   Dennis Dorchester SDA806   Alexander TS   B53F   1983

1181	A101RGE	1182	A102RGE	1183	A103RGE	1184	A104RGE	1185	A105RGE

2186-2190   Dennis Dorchester SDA806   Alexander TE   C49F   1984

2186	A106UYS	2187	A107UYS	2188	A108UYS	2189	A109UYS	2190	A110UYS

3191-3195   Dennis Dorchester SDA806   Alexander TC   C47F   1984

3191	A206UYS	3192	A202UYS	3193	A203UYS	3194	A204UYS	3195	A205UYS

3201	WLT760	Leyland Tiger TRCTL11/3R	Duple Dominant III	C46FT	1981

2202-2207   Leyland Tiger TRBTL11/2R   Alexander AT   C49F   1982-83

2202	FGG602X	2204	FGG604X	2205	FGG605X	2206	FGG601X	2207	ALS104Y
2203	FGG603X								

3208	WLT910	Leyland Tiger TRBTL11/2R	Duple Dominant II Express	C47F	1983	
3209	WLT357	Leyland Tiger TRCTL11/2R	Plaxton Paramount 3200 Ex	C49F	1983	
3210	WLT741	Leyland Tiger TRCTL11/2R	Plaxton Paramount 3200 Ex	C49F	1983	
3212	WLT408	Leyland Tiger TRCTL11/2R	Plaxton Paramount 3200 Ex	C49F	1983	
3213	WLT770	Leyland Tiger TRCTL11/3R	Plaxton Paramount 3200 Ex	C52F	1983	Ex Luton & District, 1991
3214	NBD107Y	Leyland Tiger TRCTL11/3R	Plaxton Paramount 3200 Ex	C53F	1983	Ex Luton & District, 1991
3215	A104EPA	Leyland Tiger TRCTL11/2R	Plaxton Paramount 3200 Ex	C53F	1983	Ex Luton & District, 1991
3216	B287KPF	Leyland Tiger TRCTL11/3RH	Plaxton Paramount 3200 Ex	C50FT	1985	Ex Luton & District, 1991

1218-1227   Leyland Tiger TRBL11/2R   Alexander TS   B53F   1983

1218	OUS18Y	1220	OUS20Y	1222	OUS12Y	1224	OUS14Y	1226	OUS16Y
1219	OUS19Y	1221	OUS11Y	1223	OUS13Y	1225	OUS15Y	1227	OUS17Y

3228	WLT388	Leyland Tiger TRCTL11/3R	Plaxton Paramount 3200	C49FT	1983	Ex Leyland demonstrator, 1984
3229	A9KCB	Leyland Tiger TRBTL11/2RP	Alexander TE	C47F	1983	
3230	WLT976	Leyland Tiger TRBTL11/2RP	Alexander TE	C47F	1983	
3231	WLT677	Leyland Tiger TRCTL11/3RH	Duple Laser	C47FT	1984	
3232	WLT678	Leyland Tiger TRCTL11/3RH	Duple Laser	C46FT	1984	

1233-1275   Leyland Tiger TRBLXB/2RH   Alexander TS   B53F   1984-85

1233	A33VDS	1242	A22VDS	1251	A31VDS	1260	B260BYS	1268	B248BYS
1234	A34VDS	1243	A23VDS	1252	A32VDS	1261	B261BYS	1269	B249BYS
1235	A35VDS	1244	A24VDS	1253	B253BYS	1262	B262BYS	1270	B250BYS
1236	A36VDS	1245	A25VDS	1254	B254BYS	1263	B263BYS	1271	B251BYS
1237	A37VDS	1246	A26VDS	1255	B255BYS	1264	B244BYS	1272	B252BYS
1238	A38VDS	1247	A27VDS	1256	B256BYS	1265	B245BYS	1273	B241BYS
1239	A39VDS	1248	A28VDS	1257	B257BYS	1266	B246BYS	1274	B242BYS
1240	A40VDS	1249	A29VDS	1258	B258BYS	1267	B247BYS	1275	B243BYS
1241	A21VDS	1250	A30VDS	1259	B259BYS				

1281	F311RMH	Leyland Tiger TRBTL11/2RP	Duple 300	B55F	1988	Ex Whitelaw, Stonehouse, 1992
1282	F604CET	Leyland Tiger TRBTL11/2RP	Plaxton Derwent	B54F	1988	Ex Whitelaw, Stonehouse, 1992
1283	F603CET	Leyland Tiger TRBTL11/2RP	Plaxton Derwent	B54F	1988	Ex Whitelaw, Stonehouse, 1992

1284-1298   Leyland Tiger TRBLXB/2RH   Alexander TS   B53F   1987

1284	D369OSU	1287	D372OSU	1290	D375OSU	1293	D378OSU	1296	D381OSU
1285	D370OSU	1288	D373OSU	1291	D376OSU	1294	D379OSU	1297	D382OSU
1286	D371OSU	1289	D374OSU	1292	D377OSU	1295	D380OSU	1298	D383OSU

1391	LGE724Y	Volvo B58-56		Duple Dominant		B55F	1982	Ex McKenna, Uddingston, 1992

1406-1430

Leyland Leopard PSU3C/3R — Alexander AYS — B53F — 1976-77

1406	MHS23P	1410	MHS28P	1413	MHS31P	1421	MHS39P	1425	MHS43P
1407	MHS24P	1411	MHS29P	1418	MHS36P	1422	MHS40P	1426	WSU454S
1409	MHS27P	1412	MHS30P	1420	MHS38P	1424	MHS42P	1430	WSU430S

1431	GMS281S	Leyland Leopard PSU3E/4R	Alexander AYS	B53F	1978	Ex Midland Scottish, 1992
1432	YFS92S	Leyland Leopard PSU3E/4R	Alexander AYS	B53F	1977	Ex Fife Scottish, 1990

1437-1453

Leyland Leopard PSU3C/3R — Alexander AYS — B53F — 1977

1437	WSU437S	1441	WSU441S	1444	WSU444S	1447	WSU447S	1450	WSU450S
1438	WSU438S	1442	WSU442S	1445	WSU445S	1448	WSU448S	1451	WSU451S
1439	WSU439S	1443	WSU443S	1446	WSU446S	1449	WSU449S	1453	WSU453S
1440	WSU440S								

1452	YHS282S	Leyland Leopard PSU3E/4R	Duple Dominant	DP55F	1977	Ex Midland Scottish, 1992
2454	GLS274S	Leyland Leopard PSU3E/4R	Alexander AT	C49F	1978	
1455	GMS288S	Leyland Leopard PSU3D/4R	Alexander AYS	B53F	1978	
1456	GMS290S	Leyland Leopard PSU3D/4R	Alexander AYS	B53F	1978	
1457	GMS293S	Leyland Leopard PSU3D/4R	Alexander AYS	B53F	1978	

1458-1489

Leyland Leopard PSU3C/3R — Alexander AYS — B53F — 1978-79 — 1458-64/77-89 built in Belfast.

1458	EGB58T	1465	EGB65T	1472	EGB72T	1478	EGB48T	1484	EGB54T
1459	EGB59T	1466	EGB66T	1473	EGB73T	1479	EGB49T	1485	EGB55T
1460	EGB60T	1467	EGB67T	1474	EGB74T	1480	EGB50T	1486	EGB56T
1461	EGB61T	1468	EGB68T	1475	EGB75T	1481	EGB51T	1487	EGB57T
1462	EGB62T	1469	EGB69T	1476	EGB76T	1482	EGB52T	1488	EGB45T
1463	EGB63T	1470	EGB70T	1477	EGB47T	1483	EGB53T	1489	EGB46T
1464	EGB64T	1471	EGB71T						

1490	ULS317T	Leyland Leopard PSU3E/4R	Alexander AYS	B53F	1979

1491-1498

Leyland Leopard PSU3C/3R — Alexander AYS — B53F — 1979

1491	GSU831T	1493	GSU833T	1495	GSU835T	1497	GSU837T	1498	GSU838T
1492	GSU832T	1494	GSU834T	1496	GSU836T				

1499	MGR912T	Leyland Leopard PSU3E/4R	Duple Dominant	B55F	1979	Ex McKenna, Uddingston, 1992

1500-1509

Leyland Leopard PSU3C/3R — Alexander AYS — B53F — 1979

1500	GSU840T	1502	GSU842T	1504	GSU844T	1506	GSU846T	1508	GSU848T
1501	GSU841T	1503	GSU843T	1505	GSU845T	1507	GSU847T	1509	GSU849T

2510-2514

Leyland Leopard PSU3C/3R — Alexander AT — C49F — 1979

2510	GSU850T	2511	GSU851T	2512	GSU852T	2513	GSU853T	2514	GSU854T

1515-1530

Leyland Leopard PSU3C/3R — Alexander AYS — B53F — 1979 — 1515-26 built in Belfast.

1515	GSU855T	1519	GSU859T	1522	GSU862T	1525	GSU865T	1528	GSU828T
1516	GSU856T	1520	GSU860T	1523	GSU863T	1526	GSU866T	1529	GSU829T
1517	GSU857T	1521	GSU861T	1524	GSU864T	1527	GSU827T	1530	GSU830T
1518	GSU858T								

2531	EMS359V	Leyland Leopard PSU3E/4R	Alexander AT	C49F	1980

2533-2539

Leyland Leopard PSU3F/4R — Alexander AT — C49F — 1980

2533	PGA833V	2535	PGA825V	2537	PGA827V	2538	PGA830V	2539	PGA832V
2534	PGA834V	2536	PGA826V						

1540-1546

Leyland Leopard PSU3F/4R — Alexander AYS — B53F — 1981

1540	PUS150W	1542	PUS152W	1544	PUS154W	1545	PUS155W	1546	PUS156W
1541	PUS151W	1543	PUS153W						

1547-1557 — Leyland Leopard PSU3G/4R, Alexander AYS, B53F, 1981

1547	TSU647W	1550	TSU650W	1552	TSU652W	1554	TSU644W	1556	TSU646W
1548	TSU648W	1551	TSU651W	1553	TSU653W	1555	TSU645W	1557	TSU643W
1549	TSU649W								

2558	WGB497W	Leyland Leopard PSU3G/4R	Duple Dominant II Express	C47F	1981
2559	RMS395W	Leyland Leopard PSU3G/4R	Duple Dominant II Express	C47F	1981
2560	RMS396W	Leyland Leopard PSU3G/4R	Duple Dominant II Express	C47F	1981
2561	RMS401W	·Leyland Leopard PSU3G/4R	Alexander AT	C49F	1981
2562	RMS402W	Leyland Leopard PSU3G/4R	Alexander AT	C49F	1981

1563-1572 — Leyland Leopard PSU3G/4R, Alexander AYS, B53F, 1982-83

1563	LUS433Y	1565	LUS435Y	1567	LUS437Y	1569	LUS439Y	1571	LUS431Y
1564	LUS434Y	1566	LUS436Y	1568	LUS438Y	1570	LUS440Y	1572	LUS432Y

2573-2577 — Leyland Leopard PSU3F/4RT, Duple Dominant IV Express, C49F, 1981, Ex Green, Kirkintilloch, 1991

2573	VNH158W	2574	VNH160W	2575	VNH162W	2576	VNH164W	2577	VNH165W

2578	NNH190Y	Leyland Leopard PSU5C/4R	Duple Dominant IV	C57F	1983	Ex Luton & District, 1991
2579	NNH189Y	Leyland Leopard PSU5C/4R	Duple Dominant IV	C57F	1983	Ex Luton & District, 1991
2580	VNH168W	Leyland Leopard PSU3F/4RT	Duple Dominant IV Express	C49F	1981	Ex Green, Kirkintilloch, 1991
2581	HVG801V	Leyland Leopard PSU3E/4R	Duple Dominant II Express	C49F	1979	Ex Green, Kirkintilloch, 1991
2582	HVG803V	Leyland Leopard PSU3E/4R	Duple Dominant II Express	C49F	1979	Ex Green, Kirkintilloch, 1991
2583	LCL805V	Leyland Leopard PSU3E/4R	Duple Dominant II Express	C49F	1980	Ex Green, Kirkintilloch, 1991
2584	LCL806V	Leyland Leopard PSU3E/4R	Duple Dominant II Express	C49F	1980	Ex Green, Kirkintilloch, 1991
2585	MRP242V	Leyland Leopard PSU3E/4RT	Plaxton Supreme IV	C45F	1980	Ex United Counties, 1991
2586	MRP243V	Leyland Leopard PSU3E/4RT	Plaxton Supreme IV	C45F	1980	Ex United Counties, 1991
2587	VNH163W	Leyland Leopard PSU3F/4RT	Duple Dominant IV Express	C49F	1981	Ex United Counties, 1991
2588	VNH166W	Leyland Leopard PSU3F/4RT	Duple Dominant IV Express	C49F	1981	Ex United Counties, 1991
2589	VNH167W	Leyland Leopard PSU3F/4RT	Duple Dominant IV Express	C49F	1981	Ex United Counties, 1991
2590	WGA644V	Leyland Leopard PSU3E/4R	Plaxton Supreme IV Exp	C53F	1979	Ex Marbill, Beith, 1992
2591	VUD28X	Leyland Leopard PSU3G/4R	Eastern Coach Works	C49F	1982	Ex Whitelaw, Stonehouse, 1992
2592	VUD32X	Leyland Leopard PSU3G/4R	Eastern Coach Works	C49F	1982	Ex Whitelaw, Stonehouse, 1992
1603	BLS672V	MCW Metrobus DR102/3	Alexander AD	H43/30F	1979	

1612-1667 — MCW Metrobus DR102*, Alexander RL, H45/33F, 1982-84 *1612/3/32 are DR104, 1638 has a 1985 body.

1612	CKS392X	1633	BLS422Y	1642	BLS435Y	1650	BLS445Y	1658	A478GMS
1613	CKS393X	1634	BLS425Y	1643	BLS436Y	1651	A469GMS	1659	B579MLS
1619	ULS619X	1635	BLS426Y	1644	BLS438Y	1652	A471GMS	1660	B580MLS
1625	ULS625X	1636	BLS427Y	1645	BLS439Y	1653	A472GMS	1662	B586MLS
1626	ULS626X	1637	BLS428Y	1646	BLS440Y	1654	A473GMS	1664	B89PKS
1627	ULS629X	1638	BLS429Y	1647	BLS441Y	1655	A474GMS	1665	B90PKS
1628	ULS634X	1639	BLS430Y	1648	BLS442Y	1656	A475GMS	1666	B91PKS
1629	ULS635X	1640	BLS431Y	1649	BLS444Y	1657	A476GMS	1667	B92PKS
1632	ULS640X								

2674-2683 — MCW Metrobus DR102/52, Alexander RL, DPH45/33F 1986

2674	D674MHS	2676	D676MHS	2678	D678MHS	2680	D680MHS	2682	D682MHS
2675	D675MHS	2677	D677MHS	2679	D679MHS	2681	D681MHS	2683	D683MHS

1701	EGB77T	Dennis Dominator DD110	Alexander AD	H43/31F	1978

1702-1744 — Dennis Dominator DD137B*, Alexander RL, H45/34F, 1981-83 *1735-44 are DD162

1702	TYS260W	1711	TYS271W	1720	FGE440X	1729	FGE429X	1737	MNS47Y
1703	TYS262W	1712	TYS272W	1721	FGE441X	1730	FGE430X	1738	MNS48Y
1704	TYS263W	1713	TYS273W	1722	FGE422X	1731	FGE431X	1739	MNS49Y
1705	TYS265W	1714	TYS274W	1723	FGE423X	1732	WLT367	1740	MNS50Y
1706	TYS266W	1715	FGE435X	1724	FGE424X	1733	FGE433X	1741	MNS51Y
1707	TYS267W	1716	FGE436X	1725	FGE425X	1734	FGE434X	1742	MNS42Y
1708	TYS268W	1717	FGE437X	1726	FGE426X	1735	MNS45Y	1743	MNS43Y
1709	TYS269W	1718	FGE438X	1727	FGE427X	1736	MNS46Y	1744	MNS44Y
1710	TYS270W	1719	FGE439X	1728	FGE428X				

1791	FFR165S	Bristol VRT/SL3/6LXB	Eastern Coach Works	H43/31F	1978	Ex Green, Kirkintilloch, 1991
2792	FFR169S	Bristol VRT/SL3/6LXB	Eastern Coach Works	DPH43/31F	1978	Ex Green, Kirkintilloch, 1991
1801	ULS96X	Leyland Olympian ONLXB/1R	Eastern Coach Works	H45/32F	1982	
1802	ULS97X	Leyland Olympian ONLXB/1R	Eastern Coach Works	H45/32F	1982	
1803	ULS98X	Leyland Olympian ONLXB/1R	Eastern Coach Works	H45/32F	1982	
1804	ULS99X	Leyland Olympian ONLXB/1R	Eastern Coach Works	H45/32F	1982	
1805	ALS120Y	Leyland Olympian ONLXB/1R	Alexander RL	H45/32F	1983	
1806	ALS121Y	Leyland Olympian ONLXB/1R	Alexander RL	H45/32F	1983	
1807	ALS130Y	Leyland Olympian ONLXB/1R	Alexander RL	H45/32F	1983	
1808	ALS131Y	Leyland Olympian ONLXB/1R	Alexander RL	H45/32F	1983	

2809-2818

Leyland Olympian ONLXB/1RH Alexander RL DPH47/27F 1986

| 2809 | C809KHS | 2811 | C801KHS | 2813 | C803KHS | 2815 | C805KHS | 2817 | C807KHS |
| 2810 | C810KHS | 2812 | C802KHS | 2814 | C804KHS | 2816 | C806KHS | 2818 | C808KHS |

1819	C112BTS	Leyland Olympian ONLXB/1RV	Alexander RL	H47/32F	1986	Ex Strathtay, 1989
1820	C113BTS	Leyland Olympian ONLXB/1RV	Alexander RL	H47/32F	1986	Ex Strathtay, 1989
1821	C114BTS	Leyland Olympian ONLXB/1RV	Alexander RL	H47/32F	1986	Ex Strathtay, 1989
1822	C115BTS	Leyland Olympian ONLXB/1RV	Alexander RL	H47/32F	1986	Ex Strathtay, 1989
1823	A981FLS	Leyland Olympian ONLXB/1R	Alexander RL	H45/32F	1983	Ex Fife Scottish, 1989
1824	A982FLS	Leyland Olympian ONLXB/1R	Alexander RL	H45/32F	1983	Ex Fife Scottish, 1989
1825	A983FLS	Leyland Olympian ONLXB/1R	Alexander RL	H45/32F	1983	Ex Fife Scottish, 1989
1826	A984FLS	Leyland Olympian ONLXB/1R	Alexander RL	H45/32F	1983	Ex Fife Scottish, 1989

1902-1946

AEC Routemaster 5RM Park Royal H36/28R 1959-64 1941-6 ex Western Scottish, 1990

1902	EDS128A	1911	EDS300A	1918	EDS395A	1932	EDS98A	1940	ALM35B
1903	EDS117A	1912	EDS282A	1919	EDS320A	1933	EDS221A	1941	LDS281A
1904	EDS130A	1913	EDS285A	1920	WTS164A	1935	EDS107A	1942	ALM83B
1905	EDS134A	1914	EDS393A	1926	EDS312A	1936	WTS163A	1943	LDS317A
1906	EDS125A	1915	EDS392A	1927	EDS396A	1937	EDS537B	1944	LDS282A
1908	YTS824A	1916	EDS394A	1929	EDS288A	1938	ALM81B	1945	LDS283A
1909	EDS278A	1917	EDS381A	1931	EDS352A	1939	ALM73B	1946	LDS475A
1910	WLT371								

1951-1969

Ailsa B55-10 MkII Alexander AV H44/35F 1979

1951	LHS751V	1959	LHS739V	1962	LHS742V	1965	LHS745V	1968	LHS748V
1957	LHS737V	1960	LHS740V	1963	LHS743V	1967	LHS747V	1969	LHS749V
1958	LHS738V	1961	LHS741V	1964	LHS744V					

1970-1981

Ailsa B55-10 Alexander AV H44/35F 1977 1970/80/1 ex Strathtay, 1991
1971-7 ex Midland Scottish, 1990

| 1970 | YMS704R | 1972 | YMS707R | 1975 | YMS710R | 1977 | YMS712R | 1981 | YMS703R |
| 1971 | YMS705R | 1973 | YMS708R | 1976 | YMS711R | 1980 | YMS701R | | |

| 1999 | JTF218F | Leyland Titan PD2/47 | East Lancashire | O36/28F | 1968 | Ex Kelvin Scottish, 1989 |

Previous Registrations:

A9KCB	A119GLS, WLT770	EDS320A	WLT606	WGB497W	RMS394W, 630DYE
EDS98A	6CLT	EDS352A	WLT987	WLT357	TFS318Y
EDS107A	53CLT	EDS381A	WLT480	WLT367	FGE432X
EDS117A	VLT149	EDS392A	WLT439	WLT388	VTY131Y
EDS125A	VLT288	EDS393A	WLT419	WLT408	TFS321Y
EDS128A	VLT55	EDS394A	WLT471	WLT677	A125ESG
EDS130A	VLT177	EDS395A	WLT538	WLT678	A128ESG
EDS134A	VLT229	EDS396A	WLT809	WLT741	TFS319Y,WLT371,PGE442Y
EDS221A	10CLT	EDS537B	630DYE	WLT760	BSG548W
EDS278A	VLT357	LDS281A	VLT219	WLT770	NBD106Y
EDS282A	WLT408	LDS282A	VLT245	WLT910	BLS106Y
EDS285A	WLT415	LDS283A	WLT447	WLT976	A120GLS
EDS288A	WLT910	LDS317A	WLT367	WTS163A	149CLT
EDS300A	WLT388	LDS475A	134CLT	WTS164A	WLT677
EDS312A	WLT799	WGA644V	OTU582V, 728AUK	YTS824A	WLT321

Special Liveries:
Overall Advertisements: 1545, 1659, 1732/3, 1910/5.

LOTHIAN

Lothian Region Transport plc, 14 Queen Street, Edinburgh, EH2 1JL

As successor to Edinburgh Corporation Transport, Lothian is still the principal provider
of public transport in Edinburgh, though Eastern Scottish also now makes a significant
contribution. In turn, Lothian buses can be found far from the city centre in what was
once Eastern's traditional operating area.

Lothian also operate an extensive programme of local, British and Continental tours.
Following the arrival of Guide Friday with its distinctive regular interval hop-on/hop-off
style of tourist service using open top vehicles, Lothian introduced the Edinburgh Classic
Tour in similar vein. A similar competing venture sees several Lothian vehicles now
operating in Oxford.

Lothian is one of the few Scottish operators investing in a quantity of new vehicles,
continuing an annual intake of Olympians. 1991 also saw the arrival of the only two door
examples of the Leyland Lynx to be delivered to an operator.

There are, so far, no proposals by Lothian Regional Council to sell the company which
therefore is likely to be the last local authority-owned bus company in Scotland.

Liveries are madder and white for buses, with black and white for coaches. The open-top
buses are blue, black and white. Depots are located at Central, Longstone and Marine.

**Typical of the still sizeable Leyland Atlantean fleet is 510, seen climbing the Mound. The majority
of stage vehicles in the Lothian fleet are of the dual-door configuration.** Stewart Brown

The survivor of a pair of Leyland Olympians received in 1982, No.667 lost its twin in a fire in 1987. This vehicle is now the only standard length Olympian in the fleet, the later deliveries being of the longer version. David Little

After receiving tenders for double deck vehicles for 1983, the ECW-bodied Leyland Olympian was chosen. Representing the type is 746, seen travelling along Princes Street, Edinburgh. David Little

Following four batches of the all-Leyland group product Lothian has reverted to Alexander for bodywork for deliveries since 1988. The 1990/91 vehicles feature two-leaf doors, and the 1991 batch also have marker lights on the roof. Murdoch Currie

The Airport service uses single door Leyland Olympian coaches painted in the coach livery. No.366 is seen on Waverley Bridge, the terminus for this service. Murdoch Currie

The Edinburgh Classic Tour provides a hop-on hop-off facility for those wishing to visit Edinburgh's many historical locations and operates in competition with Guide Friday. Leyland Atlantean 45 is on Waverley Bridge. Max Fowler

The Leyland Nationals are now in a simplified livery. Representing the type is 148, photographed in Princes Street. David Little

With the cessation of Leyland Lynx production during the middle of 1992, the Lothian examples will probably remain the only batch still having two doors. The original dual-doored example was converted to single door for West Riding. Mike Fowler

Of the few remaining Leyland Cubs, 169 carries MAXItaxi lettering for a service in Musselburgh, where it was seen in August 1991. Mike Fowler

LOTHIAN Fleet List

14-50

		Leyland Atlantean AN68/1R	Alexander AL		O45/33F	1972		
14	BFS14L	40	BFS40L	43	BFS43L	45	BFS45L	49	BFS49L
34	BFS34L	41	BFS41L	44	BFS44L	48	BFS48L	50	BFS50L
39	BFS39L	42	BFS42L						

51	USX51V	Leyland Leopard PSU3F/4R	Duple Dominant II Express	C53F	1980
52	USX52V	Leyland Leopard PSU3F/4R	Duple Dominant II Express	C53F	1980
53	USX53V	Leyland Leopard PSU3F/4R	Duple Dominant II Express	C53F	1980
54	USX54V	Leyland Leopard PSU3F/4R	Duple Dominant II Express	C53F	1980
55	PSC55Y	Leyland Tiger TRCTL11/2R	Duple Dominant II	C49F	1982
56	PSC56Y	Leyland Tiger TRCTL11/2R	Duple Dominant II	C49F	1982
57	PSC57Y	Leyland Tiger TRCTL11/2R	Duple Dominant II	C49F	1982
58	PSC58Y	Leyland Tiger TRCTL11/2R	Duple Dominant II	C49F	1982
59	A59AFS	Leyland Tiger TRCTL11/3RH	Duple Caribbean	C51F	1983
60	A60AFS	Leyland Tiger TRCTL11/3RH	Duple Caribbean	C51F	1983
61	B61GSC	Leyland Tiger TRCTL11/3RH	Duple Laser 2	C53F	1984
62	B62GSC	Leyland Tiger TRCTL11/3RH	Duple Laser 2	C53F	1984
63	C63PSG	Leyland Tiger TRCTL11/3RH	Duple Laser 2	C53F	1985
64	C64PSG	Leyland Tiger TRCTL11/3RH	Duple Laser 2	C53F	1985
65	D65BSC	Leyland Tiger TRCTL11/3RH	Duple 340	C55F	1986
66	D66BSC	Leyland Tiger TRCTL11/3RH	Duple 340	C55F	1986

67	G67DFS	Leyland Tiger TRCL10/3ARZA	Plaxton Paramount 3500 III	C53F	1989
68	G68DFS	Leyland Tiger TRCL10/3ARZA	Plaxton Paramount 3500 III	C53F	1989
71	H71NFS	Leyland Tiger TRCL10/3ARZA	Plaxton Paramount 3500 III	C53F	1991
72	H72NFS	Leyland Tiger TRCL10/3ARZA	Plaxton Paramount 3500 III	C53F	1991
102	KSX102X	Leyland National 2 NL116AL11/2R		B45D	1982
103	KSX103X	Leyland National 2 NL116AL11/2R		B45D	1982
104	KSX104X	Leyland National 2 NL116AL11/2R		B45D	1982
105	KSX105X	Leyland National 2 NL116AL11/2R		B45D	1982

106-149

Leyland National 2 NL116TL11/1R — B45D — 1983-85

106	TFS106Y	138	B138KSF	141	B141KSF	144	B144KSF	147	B147KSF
107	TFS107Y	139	B139KSF	142	B142KSF	145	B145KSF	148	B148KSF
108	A108CFS	140	B140KSF	143	B143KSF	146	B146KSF	149	B149KSF
109	A109CFS								

159-173

Leyland Cub CU435 — Duple Dominant — B31F — 1981

| 159 | HSC159X | 163 | HSC163X | 169 | HSC169X | 170 | HSC170X | 173 | HSC173X |

177-188

Leyland Lynx LX2R11C15Z4S — Leyland Lynx 2 — B43D — 1991

177	H177OSG	180	H180OSG	183	H183OSG	185	H185OSG	187	H187OSG
178	H178OSG	181	H181OSG	184	H184OSG	186	H186OSG	188	H188OSG
179	H179OSG	182	H182OSG						

248	NSX248T	Leyland Leopard PSU3E/4R	Duple Dominant I	C53F	1979
249	NSX249T	Leyland Leopard PSU3E/4R	Duple Dominant I	C53F	1979
250	NSX250T	Leyland Leopard PSU3E/4R	Duple Dominant I	C53F	1979

300-335

Leyland Olympian ONCL10/2RZ Alexander RH — H51/30D — 1988

300	E300MSG	308	E308MSG	315	E315MSG	322	E322MSG	329	E329MSG
301	E301MSG	309	E309MSG	316	E316MSG	323	E323MSG	330	E330MSG
302	E302MSG	310	E310MSG	317	E317MSG	324	E324MSG	331	E331MSG
303	E303MSG	311	E311MSG	318	E318MSG	325	E325MSG	332	E332MSG
304	E304MSG	312	E312MSG	319	E319MSG	326	E326MSG	333	E333MSG
305	E305MSG	313	E313MSG	320	E320MSG	327	E327MSG	334	E334MSG
306	E306MSG	314	E314MSG	321	E321MSG	328	E328MSG	335	E335MSG
307	E307MSG								

336-365

Leyland Olympian ONCL10/2RZ Alexander RH — H51/30D — 1989

336	G336CSG	342	G342CSG	348	F348WSC	354	F354WSC	360	F360WSC
337	G337CSG	343	G343CSG	349	F349WSC	355	F355WSC	361	F361WSC
338	G338CSG	344	G344CSG	350	F350WSC	356	F356WSC	362	F362WSC
339	G339CSG	345	G345CSG	351	F351WSC	357	F357WSC	363	F363WSC
340	G340CSG	346	F346WSC	352	F352WSC	358	F358WSC	364	F364WSC
341	G341CSG	347	F347WSC	353	F353WSC	359	F359WSC	365	F365WSC

366-371

Leyland Olympian ONCL10/2RZ Alexander RH — DPH47/31F — 1989

| 366 | F366WSC | 368 | F368WSC | 369 | F369WSC | 370 | F370WSC | 371 | F371WSC |
| 367 | F367WSC | | | | | | | | |

401-464

Leyland Atlantean AN68/1R — Alexander AL — H45/30D — 1975

401u	GFS401N	416	GFS416N	430u	GFS430N	442	GFS442N	454	JSG454N
402	GFS402N	417u	GFS417N	431u	GFS431N	443	GFS443N	455	JSG455N
403u	GFS403N	418u	GFS418N	432	GFS432N	444	GFS444N	456	JSG456N
404u	GFS404N	420u	GFS420N	433	GFS433N	445	GFS445N	457	JSG457N
405u	GFS405N	421u	GFS421N	434u	GFS434N	446	GFS446N	458	JSG458N
407	GFS406N	422u	GFS422N	435	GFS435N	447	GFS447N	459	JSG459N
408	GFS407N	423	GFS423N	436u	GFS436N	448	GFS448N	460	JSG460N
410	GFS410N	424	GFS424N	437u	GFS437N	450	GFS450N	461	JSG461N
412u	GFS412N	425u	GFS425N	438	GFS438N	451	GFS451N	462	JSG462N
413u	GFS413N	426	GFS426N	439	GFS439N	452	GFS452N	463	JSG463N
414	GFS414N	427	GFS427N	440	GFS440N	453	GFS453N	464	JSG464N
415u	GFS415N	428u	GFS428N	441	GFS441N				

465-500

Leyland Atlantean AN68A/1R — Alexander AL — H45/30D — 1976

465	MSF465P	473	MSF473P	480	MSF480P	487	MSF487P	494	MSF494P
466	MSF466P	474	MSF474P	481	MSF481P	488	MSF488P	495	MSF495P
467	MSF467P	475	MSF475P	482	MSF482P	489	MSF489P	496	MSF496P
468	MSF468P	476	MSF476P	483	MSF483P	490	MSF490P	497	MSF497P
469	MSF469P	477	MSF477P	484	MSF484P	491	MSF491P	498	MSF498P
470	MSF470P	478	MSF478P	485	MSF485P	492	MSF492P	499	MSF499P
471	MSF471P	479	MSF479P	486	MSF486P	493	MSF493P	500	MSF500P
472	MSF472P								

501-560

Leyland Atlantean AN68A/1R — Alexander AL — H45/30D — 1976-77

501	SSG501R	513	SSG513R	525	SSG525R	537	SSG537R	549	SSG549R
502	SSG502R	514	SSG514R	526	SSG526R	538	SSG538R	550	SSG550R
503	SSG503R	515	SSG515R	527	SSG527R	539	SSG539R	551	SSG551R
504	SSG504R	516	SSG516R	528	SSG528R	540	SSG540R	552	SSG552R
505	SSG505R	517	SSG517R	529	SSG529R	541	SSG541R	553	SSG553R
506	SSG506R	518	SSG518R	530	SSG530R	542	SSG542R	554	SSG554R
507	SSG507R	519	SSG519R	531	SSG531R	543	SSG543R	555	SSG555R
508	SSG508R	520	SSG520R	532	SSG532R	544	SSG544R	556	SSG556R
509	SSG509R	521	SSG521R	533	SSG533R	545	SSG545R	557	SSG557R
510	SSG510R	522	SSG522R	534	SSG534R	546	SSG546R	558	SSG558R
511	SSG511R	523	SSG523R	535	SSG535R	547	SSG547R	559	SSG559R
512	SSG512R	524	SSG524R	536	SSG536R	548	SSG548R	560	SSG560R

561-575

Leyland Atlantean AN68A/1R — Alexander AL — H45/30D — 1978

561	YSF561S	565	YSF565S	568	YSF568S	572	YSF572S	574	YSF574S
562	YSF562S	566	YSF566S	569	YSF569S	573	YSF573S	575	YSF575S
563	YSF563S	567	YSF567S	571	YSF571S				

576-620

Leyland Atlantean AN68A/1R — Alexander AL — H45/30D — 1979 — *583 is O45/33F

576	JSX576T	585	JSX585T	594	JSX594T	605	OSC605V	613	OSC613V
577	JSX577T	586	JSX586T	595	JSX595T	606	OSC606V	614	OSC614V
578	JSX578T	587	JSX587T	596	JSX596T	607	OSC607V	615	OSC615V
579	JSX579T	588	JSX588T	597	JSX597T	608	OSC608V	616	OSC616V
580	JSX580T	589	JSX589T	598	JSX598T	609	OSC609V	617	OSC617V
581	JSX581T	590	JSX590T	601	OSC601V	610	OSC610V	618	OSC618V
582	JSX582T	591	JSX591T	602	OSC602V	611	OSC611V	619	OSC619V
583	JSX583T	592	JSX592T	603	OSC603V	612	OSC612V	620	OSC620V
584	JSX584T	593	JSX593T	604	OSC604V				

621-659

Leyland Atlantean AN68C/1R — Alexander AL — H45/30D — 1981

621	GSC621X	629	GSC629X	637	GSC637X	645	GSC645X	653	GSC653X
622	GSC622X	630	GSC630X	638	GSC638X	646	GSC646X	654	GSC654X
623	GSC623X	631	GSC631X	639	GSC639X	647	GSC647X	655	GSC655X
624	GSC624X	632	GSC632X	640	GSC640X	648	GSC648X	656	GSC656X
625	GSC625X	633	GSC633X	641	GSC641X	649	GSC649X	657	GSC657X
626	GSC626X	634	GSC634X	642	GSC642X	650	GSC650X	658	GSC658X
627	GSC627X	635	GSC635X	643	GSC643X	651	GSC651X	659	GSC659X
628	GSC628X	636	GSC636X	644	GSC644X	652	GSC652X		

660-665

Leyland Atlantean AN68C/1R — Alexander AL — H45/31F — 1981

660	GSC660X	662	GSC662X	663	GSC663X	664	GSC664X	665	GSC665X
661	GSC661X								

667	GSC667X	Leyland Olympian ONTL11/1R	Alexander RH	H47/28D	1982

668-702

Leyland Olympian ONTL11/2R — Eastern Coach Works — H50/31D — 1983

668	OFS668Y	675	OFS675Y	682	OFS682Y	689	OFS689Y	696	OFS696Y
669	OFS669Y	676	OFS676Y	683	OFS683Y	690	OFS690Y	697	OFS697Y
670	OFS670Y	677	OFS677Y	684	OFS684Y	691	OFS691Y	698	OFS698Y
671	OFS671Y	678	OFS678Y	685	OFS685Y	692	OFS692Y	699	OFS699Y
672	OFS672Y	679	OFS679Y	686	OFS686Y	693	OFS693Y	700	OFS700Y
673	OFS673Y	680	OFS680Y	687	OFS687Y	694	OFS694Y	701	OFS701Y
674	OFS674Y	681	OFS681Y	688	OFS688Y	695	OFS695Y	702	OFS702Y

703-736

Leyland Olympian ONTL11/2R Eastern Coach Works H51/32D 1983

703	A703YFS	710	A710YFS	717	A717YFS	724	A724YFS	731	A731YFS
704	A704YFS	711	A711YFS	718	A718YFS	725	A725YFS	732	A732YFS
705	A705YFS	712	A712YFS	719	A719YFS	726	A726YFS	733	A733YFS
706	A706YFS	713	A713YFS	720	A720YFS	727	A727YFS	734	A734YFS
707	A707YFS	714	A714YFS	721	A721YFS	728	A728YFS	735	A735YFS
708	A708YFS	715	A715YFS	722	A722YFS	729	A729YFS	736	A736YFS
709	A709YFS	716	A716YFS	723	A723YFS	730	A730YFS		

737-769

Leyland Olympian ONTL11/2R Eastern Coach Works H51/32D 1984

737	B737GSC	744	B744GSC	751	B751GSC	758	B758GSC	764	B764GSC
738	B738GSC	745	B745GSC	752	B752GSC	759	B759GSC	765	B765GSC
739	B739GSC	746	B746GSC	753	B753GSC	760	B760GSC	766	B766GSC
740	B740GSC	747	B747GSC	754	B754GSC	761	B761GSC	767	B767GSC
741	B741GSC	748	B748GSC	755	B755GSC	762	B762GSC	768	B768GSC
742	B742GSC	749	B749GSC	756	B756GSC	763	B763GSC	769	B769GSC
743	B743GSC	750	B750GSC	757	B757GSC				

770-794

Leyland Olympian ONTL11/2R Eastern Coach Works H51/32D 1985-86

770	C770SFS	775	C775SFS	780	C780SFS	785	C785SFS	790	C790SFS
771	C771SFS	776	C776SFS	781	C781SFS	786	C786SFS	791	C791SFS
772	C772SFS	777	C777SFS	782	C782SFS	787	C787SFS	792	C792SFS
773	C773SFS	778	C778SFS	783	C783SFS	788	C788SFS	793	C793SFS
774	C774SFS	779	C779SFS	784	C784SFS	789	C789SFS	794	C794SFS

800-871

Leyland Olympian ON2R56C13Z4 Alexander RH H51/30D 1990/91

800	G800GSX	815	G815GSX	830	G830GSX	844	J844TSC	858	J858TSC
801	G801GSX	816	G816GSX	831	G831GSX	845	J845TSC	859	J859TSC
802	G802GSX	817	G817GSX	832	G832GSX	846	J846TSC	860	J860TSC
803	G803GSX	818	G818GSX	833	G833GSX	847	J847TSC	861	J861TSC
804	G804GSX	819	G819GSX	834	G834GSX	848	J848TSC	862	J862TSC
805	G805GSX	820	G820GSX	835	G835GSX	849	J849TSC	863	J863TSC
806	G806GSX	821	G821GSX	836	J836TSC	850	J850TSC	864	J864TSC
807	G807GSX	822	G822GSX	837	J837TSC	851	J851TSC	865	J865TSC
808	G808GSX	823	G823GSX	838	J838TSC	852	J852TSC	866	J866TSC
809	G809GSX	824	G824GSX	839	J839TSC	853	J853TSC	867	J867TSC
810	G810GSX	825	G825GSX	840	J840TSC	854	J854TSC	868	J868TSC
811	G811GSX	826	G826GSX	841	J841TSC	855	J855TSC	869	J869TSC
812	G812GSX	827	G827GSX	842	J842TSC	856	J856TSC	870	J870TSC
813	G813GSX	828	G828GSX	843	J843TSC	857	J857TSC	871	J871TSC
814	G814GSX	829	G829GSX						

900	JSC900E	Leyland Atlantean PDR2/1	Alexander J	O47/35F	1968

911-942

Leyland Atlantean AN68/1R Alexander AL O45/33F 1974

911u	OFS911M	925u	OSF925M	928u	OSF928M	939	OSF939M	942	OSF942M
912u	OFS912M								

Named vehicles:
14 *The Oxford Student*, 34 *The Oxford Graduate*, 39 *Dunedin Star*, 40 *Edinburgh Star*, 41 *Scottish Star*, 42 *Highland Star*,
43 *Lowland Star*, 44 *Gaelic Star*, 45 *Celtic Star*, 48 *The Oxford Professor*, 49 *The Oxford Don*, 50 *The Oxford Blue*,
583 *Caledonian Star*, 900 *Northern Star*, 939 *The Oxford Bulldog*, 942 *Pentland Star*.

Special Liveries:
Overall Advertisements: 658/77, 710/22/52/4/6/8/68/75/90.

LOWLAND

Lowland Omnibuses Ltd, Duke Street, Galashiels, TD1 1QA

Formed in 1985 out of the Borders and East Lothian areas of Eastern Scottish, Lowland was the first Scottish Bus Group company to be sold when, in August 1990, it was purchased by its management and employees, the word Scottish being dropped from the name at that time.

In 1991, the business of Ian Glass of Haddington was acquired. While this will allow some rationalisation of services, the respected name of Ian Glass has been retained for use on coaches.

Lowland is one of the few former SBG companies to have added full-size new vehicles to its fleet since privatisation. These consist of five Scania coaches and four Alexander Q-type style Leyland Tigers, built at the Belfast factory.

The livery of dark green and yellow for service vehicles remains unaltered apart from the application of a new logo. Coaches are cream, light green and yellow. Depots are at Berwick, Dunbar, Galashiels, Haddington, Hawick, Kelso and Peebles.

Peebles depot is the home of Daimler Fleetline 813, an example of the type with Eastern Coach Works body style. It is seen pulling out from its Edinburgh terminus.
Stewart Brown

A source of secondhand double-deckers has been found on the Isle of Wight in Southern Vectis, from where three Bristol VRTs for the fleet have been acquired.
C.M. Anderson

One of three Dennis Dominators in the fleet, 661 is seen in Galashiels depot. The trio originated with Central Scottish.
Murdoch Currie

Coach-seated Leyland Olympian 901 is seen approaching Haymarket, in Edinburgh, to take up a limited stop service to North Berwick.
David Little

The open-top Fleetline, 1014, was new to Fife Scottish as FRF51. It is seen at Berwick bus station when participating in 'Telethon '90'.
M.M. Fowler

Lowland   **69**

The Seddon Pennine continues to play an important part in Lowland's operations. Alexander AYS-bodied 9 is about to enter the bus station in Edinburgh on a service to North Berwick on the East Lothian coast. Murdoch Currie

In the midst of the Borders, 229 with Alexander's AT bodywork turns into Jedburgh bus station. Mike Fowler

In 1987, a trio of the bus version of the Leyland Tiger arrived complete with Alexander's TE-type dual purpose body. First of the three, 328, is seen approaching the halfway stop, Southwaite motorway service area, on an express service to Blackpool. David Little

Four Volvo-engined Leyland Tigers with Alexander Q-type bodywork joined the fleet in 1991. The Q-type is one of the styles built in Belfast rather than Falkirk. Carlisle railway station is the southern terminus for rail replacement service 95, where 301 was seen early in 1992. Murdoch Currie

Pride of the fleet are five Plaxton-bodied Scanias purchased just after privatisation in 1990. Standing at Balloch is 102, the revised style of the Plaxton Paramount 3500 3. M. Currie

This vehicle was built as an AT-type for Western. It later joined the SBG Engineering hire fleet and was extensively refurbished including the grafting on of a TE front end. Since being photographed at Beamish Museum, it has gained a cherished index mark. David Little

Duple-bodied Bedford YNT 615 was acquired with the Ian Glass business and is seen on a former Glass service. It is intended to keep the name and livery for certain coach work. Stewart Brown

The Berwick Beavers operate around the Berwick area in competition with Northumbria. Of the seven operated one has high-back seating. Seen in the bus station at Berwick is 754, fitted with service bus seating. Mick Fowler

All vehicles are formerly Eastern Scottish in 1985 unless otherwise stated.

2-39

								Seddon Pennine 7		Alexander AYS		DP49F*	1979-81	*5/7/9/31/2/9 are B53F
2	SSX602V	6	SSX606V	9	SSX609V	32	YSG632W	37	LSC937T					
3	SSX603V	7	SSX607V	10	SSX610V	36	LSC936T	39	YSG639W					
5	SSX605V	8	SSX608V	31	YSG631W									

43-59

								Seddon Pennine 7		Alexander AY		B60F	1977-78	53/5/7 ex Eastern Scottish, 1987
43	ESC843S	48	ESC848S	53	VSX753R	56	VSX756R	58	VSX758R					
46	ESC846S	49	ESC849S	55	VSX755R	57	VSX757R	59	VSX759R					

60	YSG660W	Seddon Pennine 7	Alexander AYS	DP49F	1981
84	JFS984X	Seddon Pennine 7	Alexander AYS	B53F	1982
85	JFS985X	Seddon Pennine 7	Alexander AYS	DP49F	1982
86	JFS986X	Seddon Pennine 7	Alexander AYS	B53F	1982

101-105

										Scania K113CRB	Plaxton Paramount 3500 III	C53F	1990	Variable seating
101	G101RSH	102	G102RSH	103	H103TSH	104	H104TSH	105	H105TSH					

159	TVF619R	Leyland National 11351A/1R		B49F	1977	Ex Glass, Haddington, 1991

161-173

								Leyland National 11351A/1R			B52F*	1977-78	*161/2/72 are B51F
161	BSF771S	165	BSF765S	169	GSX869T	172	BSF772S	173	BSF763S				
162	GSX862T	168	GSX868T	170	GSX870T								

212-299

								Seddon Pennine 7		Alexander AT		C49F	1978-79	212/3 ex Kelvin Scottish, 1986
														258-68 ex SBG Engineering, 1990
212	JSF912T	227	JSF927T	230	JSF930T	267	DSD967V	291	GSX891T					
213	JSF913T	228	JSF928T	258	DSD958V	268	DSD968V	292	GSX892T					
220	JSF920T	229	JSF929T	265	DSD965V	289	GSX889T	299	GSX899T					
224	JSF924T													

301	J301ASH	Leyland Tiger TR2R56V16Z4	Alexander Q	DP49F	1991
302	J302ASH	Leyland Tiger TR2R56V16Z4	Alexander Q	DP49F	1991
303	J303ASH	Leyland Tiger TR2R56V16Z4	Alexander Q	DP49F	1991
304	J304ASH	Leyland Tiger TR2R56V16Z4	Alexander Q	DP49F	1991
313	PSF313Y	Leyland Tiger TRBTL11/2R	Alexander AT	C49F	1982
314	PSF314Y	Leyland Tiger TRBTL11/2R	Alexander AT	C49F	1982
315	PSF315Y	Leyland Tiger TRBTL11/2R	Alexander AT	C49F	1982
316	PSF316Y	Leyland Tiger TRBTL11/2R	Alexander AT	C49F	1982

322-327

										Leyland Tiger TRBTL11/2RP	Alexander TE	C49F	1983
322	A322BSC	324	A324BSC	325	A325BSC	326	A326BSC	327	A327BSC				
323	A323BSC												

328	D328DKS	Leyland Tiger TRBTL11/2RH	Alexander TE	C49F	1987	
329	D329DKS	Leyland Tiger TRBTL11/2RH	Alexander TE	C49F	1987	
330	D330DKS	Leyland Tiger TRBTL11/2RH	Alexander TE	C49F	1987	
376	D276FAS	Leyland Tiger TRCTL11/3RH	Alexander TE	C53F	1987	Ex Highland Scottish, 1987
402	DFS802S	Seddon Pennine 7	Plaxton Supreme III Exp	C49F	1978	
406	DFS806S	Seddon Pennine 7	Plaxton Supreme III Exp	C49F	1978	
407	DFS807S	Seddon Pennine 7	Plaxton Supreme III Exp	C49F	1978	
409	DFS809S	Seddon Pennine 7	Plaxton Supreme III Exp	C49F	1978	Ex Eastern Scottish, 1988
415	PSU315	Seddon Pennine 7	Plaxton Supreme IV Exp	C49F	1978	
416	PSU316	Seddon Pennine 7	Plaxton Supreme IV Exp	C45F	1978	
417	PSU317	Seddon Pennine 7	Plaxton Supreme IV Exp	C45F	1978	Ex Kelvin Scottish, 1986
418	PSU318	Seddon Pennine 7	Plaxton Supreme IV Exp	C45F	1978	Ex Kelvin Scottish, 1986
422	PSU322	Seddon Pennine 7	Plaxton Supreme IV Exp	C49F	1978	
433	PSU319	Seddon Pennine 7	Alexander AT	C45F	1979	Ex SBG Engineering, 1990
492	CSG792S	Seddon Pennine 7	Plaxton Supreme III Exp	C49F	1978	
494	CSG794S	Seddon Pennine 7	Plaxton Supreme III Exp	C45F	1978	Ex Eastern Scottish, 1990
495	DFS795S	Seddon Pennine 7	Plaxton Supreme III Exp	C49F	1978	
519	NSC413X	Leyland Tiger TRCTL11/3R	Duple Goldliner III	C46FT	1982	Ex Kelvin Scottish, 1988
520	PSU320	Leyland Royal Tiger B50	Roe Doyen	C44FT	1984	Ex Eastern Scottish, 1989
521	PSU321	Leyland Royal Tiger B50	Roe Doyen	C46FT	1984	Ex Eastern Scottish, 1988
522	KSU388	Leyland Tiger TRCTL11/3RH	Duple 340	C46FT	1987	Ex Kelvin Scottish, 1989

567	B267KPF	Leyland Tiger TRCTL11/2R	Plaxton Paramount 3200 Ex	C53F	1985	Ex Glass, Haddington, 1991
588	NSC411X	Leyland Tiger TRCTL11/3R	Duple Goldliner III	C46FT	1982	Ex Kelvin Scottish, 1988
589	KSU389	Leyland Tiger TRCTL11/3R	Duple Goldliner IV	C50FT	1982	Ex Kelvin Scottish, 1988
590	KSU390	Leyland Tiger TRCTL11/2R	Plaxton Paramount 3200 Ex	C49F	1983	
591	KSU391	Leyland Tiger TRCLXC/2RH	Plaxton Paramount 3200 Ex	C49F	1984	Ex Western Scottish, 1986
592	KSU392	Leyland Tiger TRCTL11/2RH	Plaxton Paramount 3200	C49F	1985	Ex Eastern Scottish, 1987
593	KSU393	Leyland Tiger TRCTL11/2RH	Plaxton Paramount 3200	C49F	1985	
594	KSU394	Leyland Tiger TRCTL11/2RH	Plaxton Paramount 3200	C48FT	1987	
604	DSX400S	Bedford YMT	Plaxton Supreme III	C44DLT	1978	Ex Glass, Haddington, 1991
605	MGR658T	Bedford YMT	Plaxton Supreme IV	C53F	1979	Ex Glass, Haddington, 1991
606	WOV582T	AEC Reliance 6U3ZR	Plaxton Supreme IV	C53F	1979	Ex Glass, Haddington, 1991
607	APH528T	Bedford YLQ/S	Duple Dominant II	C35F	1979	Ex Glass, Haddington, 1991
612	VSC550V	Bedford CFL	Plaxton Mini Supreme	C17F	1980	Ex Glass, Haddington, 1991
614	NUD801W	Leyland Leopard PSU3F/4R	Duple Dominant II	C53F	1981	Ex Glass, Haddington, 1991
615	KUX233W	Bedford YNT	Duple Dominant IV	C53F	1981	Ex Glass, Haddington, 1991
616	PNT803X	Bedford YNT	Duple Dominant IV	C55F	1982	Ex Glass, Haddington, 1991
617	MVK332X	Leyland Leopard PSU3E/4R	Plaxton Supreme IV	C53F	1982	Ex Glass, Haddington, 1991
618	JFS166X	Leyland Tiger TRCTL11/3R	Plaxton Supreme V	C51F	1982	Ex Glass, Haddington, 1991
619	NDS838Y	Mercedes-Benz L608D	Reeve Burgess	C25F	1983	Ex Glass, Haddington, 1991
620	TSF895Y	Fiat 60F10	Caetano Beja	C18F	1983	Ex Glass, Haddington, 1991
621	ESX257	DAF MB200DKTL600	Van Hool Alizée	C46FT	1982	Ex Glass, Haddington, 1991
622	BSS76	Leyland Tiger TRCTL11/3R	Jonckheere Jubilee	C51FT	1984	Ex Glass, Haddington, 1991
623	B88KSF	DAF SB2300DHS585	Smit Euroliner	C53F	1985	Ex Glass, Haddington, 1991
625	C777VSC	Bedford CFL	Scott	C12F	1986	Ex Glass, Haddington, 1991
626	C700USC	DAF MB200DKFL600	Duple Caribbean	C53F	1986	Ex Glass, Haddington, 1991
627	E888MSX	Dennis Javelin 12SDA1907	Duple 320	C53F	1988	Ex Glass, Haddington, 1991
628	E900MSX	Dennis Javelin 85SDL1903	Duple 320	C35F	1988	Ex Glass, Haddington, 1991
629	F777UFS	Dennis Javelin 12SDA1907	Duple 320	C53F	1989	Ex Glass, Haddington, 1991
655	TYS255W	Dennis Dominator DD135B	Alexander RL	H45/34F	1981	Ex Central Scottish, 1987
661	TYS261W	Dennis Dominator DD137B	Alexander RL	H45/34F	1981	Ex Central Scottish, 1987
664	TYS264W	Dennis Dominator DD137B	Alexander RL	H45/34F	1981	Ex Central Scottish, 1987
706	FFS6X	Bedford VAS5	Reeve Burgess	DP17F	1981	
707	FFS7X	Bedford VAS5	Reeve Burgess	DP24F	1981	
710	FFS10X	Bedford VAS5	Reeve Burgess	DP24F	1981	
711	D711CKS	Bedford VAS5	Reeve Burgess	DP19F	1987	
712	D712CKS	Bedford VAS5	Reeve Burgess	DP19F	1987	
713	D713CSH	Bedford VAS5	Reeve Burgess	DP19F	1987	
714	D714CSH	Bedford VAS5	Reeve Burgess	DP19F	1987	
715	G715OSH	Leyland Swift LBM6T/1RS	Reeve Burgess Harrier	C21F	1989	

750-756

		Renault-Dodge S56		Alexander AM		B25F*	1987-88	*756 is DP25F
750	D750DSH	752	D752DSH	754	D754DSH	755	D755DSH	756	E756GSH
751	D751DSH	753	D753DSH						

803	KSX703N	Daimler Fleetline CRG6LXB	Eastern Coach Works	H43/32F	1975	
813	KSX713N	Daimler Fleetline CRG6LXB	Eastern Coach Works	H43/32F	1975	Ex Kelvin Central, 1989
850	MDL650R	Bristol VRT/SL3/6LXB	Eastern Coach Works	H43/31F	1976	Ex Southern Vectis, 1990
854	GSC954T	Leyland Fleetline FE30AGR	Eastern Coach Works	H43/32F	1978	
855	NDL655R	Bristol VRT/SL3/6LXB	Eastern Coach Works	H43/31F	1977	Ex Southern Vectis, 1991
856	NDL656R	Bristol VRT/SL3/6LXB	Eastern Coach Works	H43/31F	1977	Ex Southern Vectis, 1991
871	OSG71V	Leyland Fleetline FE30AGR	Eastern Coach Works	H43/32F	1979	
901	D901CSH	Leyland Olympian ONTL11/1RH	Alexander RL	DPH43/27F	1987	
902	D902CSH	Leyland Olympian ONTL11/1RH	Alexander RL	DPH43/27F	1987	
916	ALS116Y	Leyland Olympian ONLXB/1R	Alexander RL	H45/32F	1983	
943	A143BSC	Leyland Olympian ONLXB/1R	Alexander RL	DPH45/29F	1984	
959	B159KSC	Leyland Olympian ONTL11/1RH	Alexander RL	H45/32F	1985	
960	B160KSC	Leyland Olympian ONTL11/1RH	Alexander RL	H45/32F	1985	
988	VAO488Y	Leyland Titan TNTL11/1RF	Leyland	H48/31F	1982	Ex Glass, Haddington, 1991
1014	PSU314	Daimler Fleetline CRG6LXB	Alexander AD	O44/31F	1971	Ex Fife Scottish, 1986

Previous Registrations:

BSS76	A678DSF	KSU392	B342RLS	PSU317	DSC974W
ESX257	WFR612Y	KSU393	B343RLS	PSU318	DSC975W
KSU388	D320RNS	KSU394	D501CSH	PSU319	DSD933V
KSU389	PSF559Y	PSU314	RXA51J	PSU320	A562BSX
KSU390	TFS317Y	PSU315	OSF963V	PSU321	A563BSX
KSU391	A185UGB	PSU316	USX971V	PSU322	LSC950T
NSC411X	MSC557X, KSU388	NSC413X	MSC552X, WLT741, HGD741X, PSU319		

Special Liveries:
Chieftain Tours: 101/2
Overall Advertisements: 258, 326/9.

MIDLAND BLUEBIRD

Midland Scottish Omnibuses Ltd, Carmuirs House, 300 Stirling Road, Larbert, FK5 3NJ

GRT Holdings, owners of Grampian Regional Transport, became the first outsider to buy a Scottish Bus Group company in September 1990 when it was successful in bidding for Midland Scottish.

The company can trace lineage to 1914 when Walter Alexander purchased his first bus. The Alexander empire grew to serve much of Scotland, but in 1961 was divided with W Alexander & Sons (Midland) Ltd being formed to cover the southern area of operation. The company was later renamed Midland Scottish Omnibuses Ltd. In 1985, the depots nearer Glasgow passed to Kelvin Scottish and the depots at Crieff, Perth and Pitlochry to the new Strathtay company. This left Midland with Central Region and the northern part of West Lothian together with an outpost at Oban, in Argyll. The depots which remain are at Balfron, Bannockburn, Larbert, Linlithgow and Oban. Alloa depot closed in 1991.

The Grampian influence is apparent in the new livery, a blue version of that used in the Granite City, and in the occasional appearance of Grampian vehicles on loan. Recent additions to the fleet have been a few minibuses and some vehicles transferred from the Grampian fleet.

Eastern Coach Works-bodied Leyland Fleetline 749, was photographed at Falkirk in the new livery. It has lost its front upper deck ventilators at some stage. Max Fowler

Midland Bluebird 752
has somehow
managed to retain
the original livery
style that was
peculiar to the 1980
batch of Alexander-
bodied Fleetlines.
Max Fowler

Several Leyland
Atlanteans, including
No.700 shown here,
have been transferred
from the Aberdeen-
based Grampian fleet
to Midland Bluebird.
The centre door is
not used by Midland.
Murdoch Currie

The 1986 intake of Alexander-bodied Metrobuses included five with coach seats. No.813 is seen on a special service in a wet Falkirk. Max Fowler

Operating the Bo'ness town service is the newest of the dwindling fleet of Seddons, most of which were acquired when Linlithgow depot was transferred from Eastern Scottish. Graeme Yuill

Midland Bluebird retain a few of the earlier Leyland Nationals. Now the lowest number in the fleet, 2 was photographed as it departed from Falkirk bus station. The depot code, L, can be seen on the offside front. Max Fowler

Acquired with the Oban operations of Highland, Leyland Leopard 430 passes through Ballachulish on the Oban to Fort William service. Stewart Brown

Stirling-bound Leyland Leopard 273, with Alexander T-type bodywork, is seen in the Grampian-inspired livery while it gathers passengers in Falkirk. Max Fowler

Originally acquired for services in Alloa, the MetroRiders have had a rather nomadic career. No.650 was back in Alloa when photographed in September 1991. Murdoch Currie

One of two Reeve Burgess Beaver-bodied Mercedes-Benz 709Ds that arrived in 1990 is 625. It is seen on a local service in Stirling. Murdoch Currie

Recent additions to the fleet have been ten Alexander-bodied Mercedes-Benz 709s. This one is seen in King Street, Stirling. Graeme Yuill

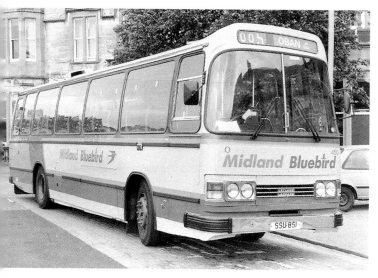

Leyland Leopard with a Duple Dominant I body, 450 was originally in the Fife fleet. It is now based in Oban where it was photographed having arrived on the Fort William service.
Murdoch Currie

MIDLAND BLUEBIRD Fleet List

| 2 | OLS802T | Leyland National 11351A/1R | | | B52F | 1978 |
| 3 | OLS803T | Leyland National 11351A/1R | | | B52F | 1978 |

10-15

Leyland National 10351B/1R   B44F*   1978   *14 is B37F, 15 B40F

| 10 | OLS810T | 12 | OLS812T | 13 | OLS813T | 14 | OLS814T | 15 | OLS815T |
| 11 | OLS811T | | | | | | | | |

16-47

Leyland National 2 NL116L11/1R   B52F*   1980-81   24, 41-7 ex Kelvin Scottish, 1987/88
                                                               *44/5/7 are B49F

16	DMS16V	28	NLS980W	41	RFS580V	44	WAS764V	46	YFS302W
24	DMS24V	29	NLS981W	42	RFS587V	45	SNS830W	47	YFS303W
26	DMS26V	32	NLS984W	43	RFS589V				

101	FSU381	Leyland Tiger TRBTL11/2R	Alexander AT	C49F	1983	
102	FSU382	Leyland Tiger TRBTL11/2R	Alexander AT	C49F	1983	
103	FSU383	Leyland Tiger TRBTL11/2R	Alexander AT	C49F	1983	
105	SSU380	Leyland Tiger TRBTL11/2R	Alexander AT	C49F	1983	
107	101ASV	Leyland Tiger TRBTL11/2R	Duple Dominant II Express	C47F	1983	Ex Kelvin Scottish, 1986
108	FSU308	Leyland Tiger TRBTL11/2R	Duple Dominant II Express	C47F	1983	Ex Kelvin Scottish, 1986
109	109ASV	Leyland Tiger TRBTL11/2R	Duple Dominant II Express	C47F	1983	Ex Kelvin Scottish, 1986
114	FSU334	Leyland Tiger TRBTL11/2R	Alexander TE	C46F	1983	
116	SSU816	Leyland Tiger TRBTL11/2RP	Alexander TE	C47F	1983	
117	BSV807	Leyland Tiger TRBTL11/2RP	Alexander TE	C47F	1983	Ex Kelvin Scottish, 1988
118	7881UA	Leyland Tiger TRBTL11/2RP	Alexander TE	C47F	1983	
121	SSU821	Leyland Tiger TRCTL11/3RH	Duple Caribbean	C51F	1984	
122	612DYM	Leyland Tiger TRCTL11/3RH	Duple Caribbean	C44FT	1984	
123	OPV239	Leyland Tiger TRCTL11/3RH	Duple Caribbean	C44FT	1984	
124	VSU715	Leyland Tiger TRCTL11/3RH	Duple Caribbean	C44FT	1984	
129	SSU859	Leyland Tiger TRCTL11/3RH	Duple Laser	C46FT	1984	
130	693AFU	Leyland Tiger TRCTL11/3RH	Duple Laser	C46FT	1984	
131	SSU831	Leyland Tiger TRCTL11/3RH	Duple Laser 2	C46FT	1985	
132	SSU837	Leyland Tiger TRCTL11/3RH	Duple Laser 2	C46FT	1985	
134	889MHX	Leyland Tiger TRCTL11/3R	Duple Laser	C46FT	1984	Ex Highland Scottish, 1985
136	SSU897	Leyland Tiger TRCLXC/2RH	Plaxton Paramount 3200 Ex	C49F	1984	Ex Clydeside Scottish, 1985
137	SSU727	Leyland Tiger TRCLXC/2RH	Plaxton Paramount 3200 Ex	C49F	1984	Ex Clydeside Scottish, 1985
138	OTV798	Leyland Tiger TRCLXC/2RH	Plaxton Paramount 3200 Ex	C49F	1984	Ex Western Scottish, 1986
139	119ASV	Leyland Tiger TRCTL11/3R	Duple Goldliner IV	C53F	1982	Ex Western Scottish, 1986
140	FSU333	Leyland Tiger TRCTL11/3R	Duple Goldliner IV	C46FT	1982	Ex Western Scottish, 1986

141-145 Leyland Tiger TRCTL11/3RH Duple 340 C49FT 1987

141	SSU841	142	SSU857	143	KSU834	144	FSV634	145	156ASV

146	9416UA	Leyland Tiger TRCTL11/3R	Duple Dominant IV	C46FT	1981	Ex Eastern Scottish, 1988
147	SSU827	Leyland Tiger TRCTL11/3R	Duple Goldliner IV	C44FT	1982	Ex Kelvin Scottish, 1988
148	SSU861	Leyland Tiger TRCTL11/3R	Duple Goldliner IV	C44FT	1982	Ex Kelvin Scottish, 1988
149	SSU829	Leyland Tiger TRCTL11/3R	Duple Goldliner III	C46FT	1982	Ex Kelvin Scottish, 1988
150	WSU487	Leyland Tiger TRCTL11/3R	Plaxton Paramount 3200 Ex	C53F	1983	Ex Grampian, 1991
151	WSU489	Leyland Tiger TRCTL11/3R	Plaxton Paramount 3200 Ex	C53F	1983	Ex Grampian, 1991
152	GSU338	Leyland Tiger TRCTL11/3R	Plaxton Paramount 3200 Ex	C57F	1983	Ex Grampian, 1991
153	GSU339	Leyland Tiger TRCTL11/3R	Plaxton Paramount 3200 Ex	C57F	1983	Ex Grampian, 1991
154	PSU625	Leyland Tiger TRCLXC/2RH	Plaxton Paramount 3200 Ex	C53F	1986	Ex Grampian, 1991
155	PSU622	Leyland Tiger TRCLXC/2RH	Plaxton Paramount 3200 Ex	C53F	1986	Ex Grampian, 1991
202	692FFC	Volvo B10M-61	Jonckheere Jubilee	C47FT	1989	Ex River Valley, S. Valence, 1991
257u	158ASV	Leyland Leopard PSU3E/4R	Duple Dominant Express	C49F	1977	

264-273 Leyland Leopard PSU3D/4R Alexander AT C49F 1978

264	GLS264S	268	HSU301	269	GLS269S	270	FSF682S	273	GLS273S
265	GLS265S								

279-338 Leyland Leopard PSU3E/4R* Alexander AYS B53F 1978-79 *296, 302 are PSU3D/4R

279	GMS279S	297	GMS297S	304	GMS304S	319	ULS319T	331	ULS331T
284	GMS284S	298	GMS298S	306	GMS306S	324	ULS324T	332	ULS332T
286u	GMS286S	300u	GMS300S	307	GMS307S	325	ULS325T	336	ULS336T
287	GMS287S	302u	GMS302S	308	GMS308S	327	ULS327T	338	ULS338T
296	GMS296S	303	GMS303S	309	GMS309S	328	ULS328T		

340	110ASV	Leyland Leopard PSU3E/4R	Duple Dominant II Express	C49F	1979
344	144ASV	Leyland Leopard PSU3E/4R	Duple Dominant II Express	C49F	1979
345u	FSU335	Leyland Leopard PSU3E/4R	Duple Dominant II Express	C49F	1979

349-356 Leyland Leopard PSU3E/4R Alexander AYS B53F 1979

349	DLS349V	351	DLS351V	353	DLS353V	355	DLS355V	356	DLS356V
350	DLS350V	352	DLS352V						

360-366 Leyland Leopard PSU3E/4R Alexander AT C49F 1980

360	EMS360V	362	EMS362V	363	EMS363V	364	EMS364V	366	EMS366V

367	FSU307	Leyland Leopard PSU3F/4R	Duple Dominant II Express	C49F	1980

374-386 Leyland Leopard PSU3F/4R Alexander AYS B53F* 1980 *378 is DP49F, 380 is B62F

374	LMS374W	377	LMS377W	379	LMS379W	381	LMS381W	384	LMS384W
376	LMS376W	378	LMS378W	380	LMS380W	382	LMS382W	386	LMS386W

393	FSU318	Leyland Leopard PSU3G/4R	Duple Dominant II Express	C49F	1981
397	FSU302	Leyland Leopard PSU3G/4R	Duple Dominant II Express	C49F	1981
398	RMS398W	Leyland Leopard PSU3G/4R	Alexander AT	C49F	1981
399	RMS399W	Leyland Leopard PSU3G/4R	Alexander AT	C49F	1981
400	RMS400W	Leyland Leopard PSU3G/4R	Alexander AT	C49F	1981

403-412 Leyland Leopard PSU3G/4R Alexander AYS DP49F* 1982 *410/1 are B53F

403	TMS403X	408	TMS408X	410	TMS410X	411	TMS411X	412	TMS412X

413-417 Leyland Leopard PSU3G/4R Alexander AT C49F 1982

413	ULS713X	414	ULS714X	415	ULS715X	416	ULS716X	417	ULS717X

418	WFS151W	Leyland Leopard PSU3F/4R	Alexander AYS	B62F	1980	Ex Alexander (Fife), 1982
419	WFS154W	Leyland Leopard PSU3F/4R	Alexander AYS	B62F	1980	Ex Alexander (Fife), 1982
421	XMS421Y	Leyland Leopard PSU3G/4R	Alexander AYS	DP49F	1982	
425	XMS425Y	Leyland Leopard PSU3G/4R	Alexander AYS	DP49F	1982	
429	FSU319	Leyland Leopard PSU3E/4R	Duple Dominant I	C49F	1978	Ex Highland Scottish, 1985
430	CAS519W	Leyland Leopard PSU3G/4R	Alexander AY	DP49F	1981	Ex Highland Scottish, 1985
431	CAS520W	Leyland Leopard PSU3G/4R	Alexander AY	DP49F	1981	Ex Highland Scottish, 1985
444	VXU444	Leyland Leopard PSU3E/4R	Duple Dominant I	C49F	1978	Ex Fife Scottish, 1987
445	SSU874	Leyland Leopard PSU3E/4R	Duple Dominant I	C49F	1978	Ex Fife Scottish, 1987

446u	YSF101S	Leyland Leopard PSU3E/4R	Alexander AYS	B53F	1977	Ex Fife Scottish, 1987
448	TSV612	Leyland Leopard PSU3E/4R	Duple Dominant I	C49F	1978	Ex Fife Scottish, 1987
449	SSU849	Leyland Leopard PSU3E/4R	Duple Dominant I	C49F	1978	Ex Fife Scottish, 1987
450	SSU851	Leyland Leopard PSU3E/4R	Duple Dominant I	C49F	1978	Ex Fife Scottish, 1987
451	GSO80V	Leyland Leopard PSU3E/4R	Alexander AYS	B53F	1980	Ex Fife Scottish, 1988
452	GSO81V	Leyland Leopard PSU3E/4R	Alexander AYS	B53F	1980	Ex Fife Scottish, 1988

453-459

Leyland Leopard PSU3F/4R · Alexander AYS · B53F · 1980-81 · Ex Fife Scottish, 1989

453	WFS145W	455	WFS143W	457	CFS155W	458	CFS156W	459	CFS157W
454	WFS146W	456	WFS144W						

467	HSU247	Leyland Leopard PSU5D/4R	Plaxton Supreme IV	C53F	1981	Ex Grampian, 1991
468	HSU273	Leyland Leopard PSU5D/4R	Plaxton Supreme IV	C53F	1981	Ex Grampian, 1991
501	365UMY	Seddon Pennine 7	Alexander AT	C24FL	1976	Ex Western Scottish, 1984
509u	GSX890T	Seddon Pennine 7	Alexander AT	C49F	1978	Ex Eastern Scottish, 1985
510	GSX894T	Seddon Pennine 7	Alexander AT	C49F	1978	Ex Eastern Scottish, 1985
511	JSF916T	Seddon Pennine 7	Alexander AT	C49F	1979	Ex Eastern Scottish, 1985
512	JSF917T	Seddon Pennine 7	Alexander AT	C49F	1979	Ex Eastern Scottish, 1985
515	FSU315	Seddon Pennine 7	Plaxton Supreme IV Exp	C49F	1979	Ex Eastern Scottish, 1985

521-527

Seddon Pennine 7 · Alexander AYS · B53F* · 1979-82 · Ex Eastern Scottish, 1985
*521/3 are B62F, 526/7 are B49F

521	LSC941T	523u	SSX614V	525	YSG633W	526	YSG634W	527	JFS983X
522	SSX604V	524	SSX615V						

531	FSU320	Seddon Pennine 7	Plaxton Supreme IV Exp	C49F	1979	Ex Kelvin Scottish, 1985
532	FSU301	Seddon Pennine 7	Plaxton Supreme IV Exp	C49F	1979	Ex Kelvin Scottish, 1985

533-537

Seddon Pennine 7 · Alexander AY · DP49F* · 1979 · Ex Clydeside Scottish, 1987
*533 is B62F

533u	ASD840T	534	BSD845T	535	BSD854T	536	BSD855T	537	BSD857T

538-542

Seddon Pennine 7 · Plaxton Supreme IV Exp · C49F* · 1979-81 · Ex Kelvin Central, 1989
*542 is C45F

538	LSC956T	539	NSX957T	540	OSF964V	541	PXI8935	542	DSC976W

601	D601FLS	Freight Rover Sherpa 350D	Elme Orion	C16F	1986	
602	D602FLS	Freight Rover Sherpa 350D	Elme Orion	C16F	1986	

603-611

Mercedes-Benz L608D · Alexander AM · B20F · 1986 · Ex Bluebird Northern, 1992

603	C805SDY	605	C817SDY	607	D226UHC	609	D229UHC	611	D424UHC
604	C812SDY	606	C821SDY	608	D227UHC				

617	D517RCK	Mercedes-Benz L608D	Reeve Burgess	DP19F	1986	Ex Cumberland, 1991
618	D532RCK	Mercedes-Benz L608D	Reeve Burgess	B20F	1986	Ex Cumberland, 1991
619	D119NUS	Mercedes-Benz L608D	Alexander AM	B21F	1986	Ex Kelvin Scottish, 1987
620	D120NUS	Mercedes-Benz L608D	Alexander AM	B21F	1986	Ex Kelvin Scottish, 1987
622	C102KDS	Mercedes-Benz L608D	Alexander AM	B21F	1986	Ex Kelvin Scottish, 1987
623	C103KDS	Mercedes-Benz L608D	Alexander AM	B21F	1986	Ex Kelvin Scottish, 1987
625	H925PMS	Mercedes-Benz 709D	Reeve Burgess Beaver	B25F	1990	
626	H926PMS	Mercedes-Benz 709D	Reeve Burgess Beaver	B25F	1990	

632-641

Mercedes-Benz 709D · Alexander AM · B25F* · 1991 · *637-641 are DP23F

632	H972RSG	634	H974RSG	636	H976RSG	638	J775WLS	640	J778WLS
633	H973RSG	635	H975RSG	637	J774WLS	639	J776WLS	641	J779WLS

647	D647GLS	MCW MetroRider MF150/1	MCW	C25F	1987	
648	D648GLS	MCW MetroRider MF150/1	MCW	C25F	1987	
649	D649GLS	MCW MetroRider MF150/1	MCW	C25F	1987	
650	D650GLS	MCW MetroRider MF150/1	MCW	C25F	1987	

700-708

Leyland Atlantean AN68A/1R · Alexander AL · H45/29D · 1977 · Ex Grampian, 1991-92

700	ORS200R	702	ORS202R	703	ORS203R	704	ORS204R	708	ORS208R
701	ORS201R							

| 721 | SMS121P | Daimler Fleetline CRG6LXB | | Alexander AD | | H44/31F | 1976 |

734-750
Leyland Fleetline FE30AGR — Eastern Coach Works — H43/32F — 1979

734	ULS659T	739	ULS664T	747	ULS672T	749	ULS674T	750	ULS675T
737	ULS662T	746	ULS671T						

751-766
Leyland Fleetline FE30AGR — Alexander AD — H44/31F — 1980

751	LMS151W	752	LMS152W	755	LMS155W	764	LMS164W	766	LMS166W

| 798 | ORS198R | Leyland Atlantean AN68A/1R | Alexander AL | H45/29D | 1977 | Ex Grampian, 1992 |
| 799 | ORS199R | Leyland Atlantean AN68A/1R | Alexander AL | H45/29D | 1977 | Ex Grampian, 1991 |

800-807
MCW Metrobus DR132 — Alexander RL — H45/33F — 1985 — 800-4 ex Kelvin Central, 1990

800	B100PKS	802	B102PKS	804	B104PKS	806	B106PKS	807	B88PKS
801	B101PKS	803	B103PKS	805	B105PKS				

808-813
MCW Metrobus DR102 — Alexander RL — H45/33F* — 1986 — *812/3 are CH47/33F

808	D108ELS	810	D110ELS	811	D111ELS	812	143ASV	813	D113ELS
809	D109ELS								

814-821
MCW Metrobus DR132 — Alexander RL — DPH45/33F* 1986-87 *817-21 CH47/33F

814	D114ELS	816	D116ELS	818	E771PSG	820	E620NLS	821	E621NLS
815	D115ELS	817	E617NLS	819	WLT724				

830-899
MCW Metrobus DR102* — Alexander RL — H45/33F — 1982-85 *887/8/98/9 are type DR132
841-3 are type DR104, 831-4/84/7/93 ex Kelvin Central, 1989-90

830	ULS630X	837	ULS637X	859	BLS437Y	882	B582MLS	893	B93PKS
831	ULS620X	841	ULS641X	865	BLS443Y	883	B583MLS	894	B94PKS
832	ULS622X	842	ULS642X	868	BLS446Y	884	B584MLS	895	B95PKS
833	ULS623X	843	ULS643X	870	A470GMS	885	B585MLS	896	B96PKS
834	ULS624X	845	BLS423Y	877	A477GMS	887	B587MLS	898	B98PKS
836	ULS636X	854	BLS432Y	881	B581MLS	888	B588MLS	899	B99PKS

Previous Registrations:

101ASV	BLS107Y	FSU318	RMS393W	SSU380	ALS105Y
109ASV	BLS109Y	FSU319	CFS111S	SSU727	A169UGB
110ASV	ULS647T	FSU320	LSC945T	SSU816	A116GLS
119ASV	SSJ132Y	FSU333	SSJ133Y	SSU821	A121ESG
143ASV	D112ELS	FSU334	BMS514Y	SSU827	MSC554X, WLT770,
144ASV	ULS651T	FSU335	ULS652T		HGD711X
156ASV	D625GSG, D145HMS,	FSU381	ALS101Y	SSU829	MSC555X, WLT760,
	692FFC	FSU382	ALS102Y		HGD745X
158ASV	YMS257R	FSU383	ALS103Y	SSU831	B131PMS
365UMY	MSJ371P	FSV634	D144HMS	SSU837	B132PMS
612DYM	A122ESG	GSU338	ERF72Y, 4327PL,	SSU841	D141HMS
692FFC	F914YNV		FEH778Y	SSU849	CFS114S
693AFU	A130ESG	GSU339	ERF73Y, 8636PL,	SSU851	CFS118S
7881UA	A118GLS		FEH780Y	SSU857	D142HMS
889MHX	A504PST	HSU247	LPN355W	SSU859	A129ESG, 692FFC
9416UA	BSG544W	HSU273	LPN357W, 411DCD,	SSU861	MSC555X
BSV807	A117GLS, WLT415,		OUF51W	SSU874	CFS117S
	A253WYS	HSU301	GLS268S	SSU897	A168UGB
E771PSG	E618NLS, FSU309	KSU834	D143HMS	TSV612	CFS112S
FSF682S	156ASV, GLS270S	OTV798	A184UGB	VSU715	A124ESG
FSU301	LSC946T	OPV239	A123ESG	VXU444	CFS113S
FSU302	RMS397W	PSU622	D51VSO	WLT724	E619NLS
FSU307	GLS947V	PSU625	D54VSO	WSU487	A21GBC
FSU308	BLS108Y	PXI8935	USX969V	WSU489	A22GBC
FSU315	LSC946T				

Special Liveries:
Bluebird Executive: 145, 202
Overall Advertisements: 534, 887
Scottish Citylink: 116/7/22-4/38/41-4/7/9.

S M T

Eastern Scottish Omnibuses Ltd, New Street, Edinburgh EH8 8DW

This company and its predecessors have served Edinburgh and the Lothians since 1905. The present company began life as Scottish Omnibuses Ltd in 1949, but the famous SMT fleetname remained in use until the early sixties. After brief experiments with 'Scottish Omnibuses' and 'Scottish', a change of livery from light green/cream to dark green/cream was followed by the adoption of the fleetname 'Eastern Scottish' very much in Tilling style.

The company name was changed to Eastern Scottish Omnibuses Ltd in 1985. However, to many people the buses continued to be 'SMT buses'. This was recognised by the management and employees when their holding company SMT Omnibuses plc was successful in September 1990 in purchasing Eastern Scottish from the Scottish Bus Group, because they have re-introduced the SMT fleetname in a reworking of the earlier diamond motif.

The main activities continue to be interurban services throughout Lothian Region and high frequency minibus services within the city of Edinburgh.

The large depot and office building in New Street, Edinburgh, will be vacated during 1992 as it was not included in the sale. A new base for City Sprinter minibuses was opened in Westfield Avenue, Edinburgh, which will also become the company's Head Office, while big buses will be dispersed to other depots.

The fleet has changed little in recent years, the only fresh blood being a batch of larger Renault minibuses delivered in 1991. Depots are located at Edinburgh, Bathgate, Dalkeith, Livingston and Musselburgh.

The liveries are dark green and cream for buses, light green and cream for minibuses with red and maroon for coaches.

The oldest Leyland Fleetlines in the SMT fleet are retained for use on school services, for which an orange patch is placed on the front. DD712 is seen at Edinburgh. Mike Fowler

Ailsa VV38 is a special livery to operate the link between Edinburgh city centre and the ferry terminal at Granton Harbour to connect with a hydrofoil service between Fife and Edinburgh that commenced in 1991. Stewart Brown

Mark III Ailsa VV87, is seen in Princes Street, Edinburgh, in the height of the 1991 summer. Mike Fowler

Freshly-painted Eastern Coach Works-bodied Leyland Olympian LL115 loads at Bathgate station.
Murdoch Currie

Alexander-bodied Leyland Olympian LL122, awaits a space in Edinburgh's St Andrew Square bus station. Murdoch Currie

Several Bathgate-based Leyland Lions have lost the 'green triangle' livery in favour of a simpler style. Seen in Princes Street, Edinburgh is LL179 in the new colours. Mike Fowler

The Seddon Pennine with Alexander bodywork is still very much the mainstay of the SMT fleet. S643 is seen in Princes Street, Edinburgh. Mike Fowler

Leyland Tiger ZL312, with two-tone green waist stripes, circumnavigates St Andrew Square, Edinburgh, bound for South Queensferry, the terminal of the car-ferry before the Forth Road Bridge was built. Stewart Brown

Most of the 1991 Renault S75s are in City Sprinter livery for service within Edinburgh. In contrast to the earlier minibuses they are fitted with Reeve Burgess bodies. Showing the Beaver-style delivery is 494, seen on one of the services that compete with Lothian. Graeme Yuill

SMT initially used an adaptation of Clansman Monarch livery for the coach fleet. Duple-bodied Leyland Tiger L345 on a tour of Fife takes a break in St Andrews. It has since been painted in Citylink colours. Murdoch Currie

Plaxton-bodied Seddons retain the green triangle livery, though the triangles are now dark green. YS960 pulls out of St Andrew Square bus station, Edinburgh as it heads for Penicuik. Mike Fowler

Once the pride of the London service, the Leyland Tigers with Duple Caribbean bodies are now used on Citylink services within Scotland. XCL566 was photographed in Edinburgh having come from Ayr through Glasgow. Murdoch Currie

Three of the Leyland Lions carry Citylink livery. ZLL186 was about to leave Bathgate on more local work when photographed in August 1991. Murdoch Currie

SMT Fleet List

YD8	J8SMT	Dennis Javelin 12SDA1907	Plaxton Paramount 3200 III	C53F	1992	
XD19	A19SMT	Dennis Javelin 12SDA1907	Duple 320	C53FT	1988	Ex Martin, Spean Bridge, 1992
B23	AWG623	AEC Regal	Alexander	C31F	1947	

VV33-41
Ailsa B55-10 — Alexander AV — H44/35F — 1978 — Ex Clydeside, 1988

VV33	TSJ593S	VV35	TSJ595S	VV37	TSJ597S	VV39	TSJ599S	VV41	TSJ601S
VV34	TSJ594S	VV36	TSJ596S	VV38	TSJ598S	VV40	TSJ600S		

VV42-50
Ailsa B55-10 — Alexander AV — H44/35F — 1978 — Ex Central Scottish, 1988

VV42	BGG252S	VV44	BGG254S	VV46	BGG256S	VV48	BGG258S	VV50	BGG260S
VV43	BGG253S	VV45	BGG255S	VV47	BGG257S	VV49	BGG259S		

DD51-75
Leyland Fleetline FE30AGR — Eastern Coach Works — H43/32F — 1979

DD51	OSG51V	DD55	OSG55V	DD63	OSG63V	DD67	OSG67V	DD72	OSG72V
DD52	OSG52V	DD60	OSG60V	DD64	OSG64V	DD68	OSG68V	DD73	OSG73V
DD53	OSG53V	DD61	OSG61V	DD65	OSG65V	DD69	OSG69V	DD74	OSG74V
DD54	OSG54V	DD62	OSG62V	DD66	OSG66V	DD70	OSG70V	DD75	OSG75V

VV76-95
Volvo-Ailsa B55-10 MkIII — Alexander RV — H44/35F — 1981

VV76	HSF76X	VV81	HSF81X	VV85	HSF85X	VV89	HSF89X	VV93	HSF93X
VV77	HSF77X	VV82	HSF82X	VV86	HSF86X	VV91	HSF91X	VV94	HSF94X
VV78	HSF78X	VV83	HSF83X	VV87	HSF87X	VV92	HSF92X	VV95	HSF95X
VV80	HSF80X	VV84	HSF84X	VV88	HSF88X				

LL100-115
Leyland Olympian ONLXB/1R — Eastern Coach Works — H45/32F* — 1982 — *ZLLs are DP45/32F

LL100	ULS100X	ZLL104	ULS104X	LL107	ULS107X	LL110	ULS110X	LL113	ULS113X
ZLL101	ULS101X	LL105	ULS105X	LL108	ULS108X	LL111	ULS111X	LL114	ULS114X
ZLL102	ULS102X	LL106	ULS106X	LL109	ULS109X	LL112	ULS112X	LL115	ULS115X
ZLL103	ULS103X								

LL117-142
Leyland Olympian ONLXB/1R — Alexander RL — H45/32F — 1983-84

LL117	ALS117Y	LL124	ALS124Y	LL129	ALS129Y	LL135	ALS135Y	LL139	A139BSC
LL118	ALS118Y	LL125	ALS125Y	LL132	ALS132Y	LL136	A136BSC	LL140	A140BSC
LL119	ALS119Y	LL126	ALS126Y	LL133	ALS133Y	LL137	A137BSC	LL141	A141BSC
LL122	ALS122Y	LL127	ALS127Y	LL134	ALS134Y	LL138	A138BSC	LL142	A142BSC
LL123	ALS123Y	LL128	ALS128Y						

LL144	B144GSC	Leyland Olympian ONTL11/2R	Alexander RLC	CH43/20F	1984
LL145	B145GSC	Leyland Olympian ONTL11/2R	Alexander RLC	CH43/20F	1984

VV149-158
Volvo-Ailsa B55-10 MkIII — Alexander RV — H44/37F — 1984

VV149	B149GSC	VV151	B151GSC	VV153	B153GSC	VV155	B155GSC	VV157	B157GSC
VV150	B150GSC	VV152	B152GSC	VV154	B154GSC	VV156	B156GSC	VV158	B158GSC

LL161	B161KSC	Leyland Olympian ONTL11/1R	Alexander RL	H45/32F	1985
LL162	B162KSC	Leyland Olympian ONTL11/1R	Alexander RL	H45/32F	1985
LL163	B163KSC	Leyland Olympian ONTL11/1R	Alexander RL	H45/32F	1985

VV169-173
Volvo Citybus B10M-50 — Alexander RV — H47/37F — 1985

VV169	B169KSC	VV170	B170KSC	VV171	B171KSC	VV172	B172KSC	VV173	B173KSC

ZLL174-186
Leyland Lion LDTL11/2R — Alexander RH — DPH49/37F* — 1986-7 — *180/4-6 are DPH43/33F 176/7 are DP5/37F

ZLL174	C174VSF	ZLL177	C177VSF	ZLL180	C180VSF	ZLL183	C183VSF	ZLL185	D185ESC
ZLL175	C175VSF	ZLL178	C178VSF	ZLL181	C181VSF	ZLL184	D184ESC	ZLL186	D186ESC
ZLL176	C176VSF	ZLL179	C179VSF	ZLL182	C182VSF				

Code	Reg	Chassis	Body	Seating	Year	Notes
ZVV187	E187HSF	Volvo Citybus B10M-50	Alexander RV	DPH45/35F	1987	
ZVV188	E188HSF	Volvo Citybus B10M-50	Alexander RV	DPH45/35F	1987	
ZVV189	E189HSF	Volvo Citybus B10M-50	Alexander RV	DPH45/35F	1987	
ZVV190	E190HSF	Volvo Citybus B10M-50	Alexander RV	DPH45/35F	1987	
ZL311	PSF311Y	Leyland Tiger TRBTL11/2R	Alexander AT	C49F	1982	
ZL312	PSF312Y	Leyland Tiger TRBTL11/2R	Alexander AT	C49F	1982	
ZL328	A328BSC	Leyland Tiger TRBTL11/2RP	Alexander TE	C45F	1983	
ZL329	A329BSC	Leyland Tiger TRBTL11/2RP	Alexander TE	C49F	1983	
YL330	WSV140	Leyland Tiger TRCTL11/2R	Plaxton Paramount 3200 Ex	C49F	1984	
YL331	WSV142	Leyland Tiger TRCTL11/2R	Plaxton Paramount 3200 Ex	C49F	1984	
YL332	WSV135	Leyland Tiger TRCTL11/2RH	Plaxton Paramount 3200 Ex	C49F	1984	
XM333	A333BSC	MCW Metroliner CR126/7	MCW	C48FT	1984	

YL335-341

		Leyland Tiger TRCTL11/2RH	Plaxton Paramount 3200	C49F	1985

YL335	GCS245	YL337	WSV137	YL339	WSV139	YL340	A10SMT	YL341	WSV141
YL336	WSV136	YL338	WSV138						

Code	Reg	Chassis	Body	Seating	Year	Notes
YL343	WSV143	Leyland Tiger TRCLT10/2RH	Duple Laser 2	C53F	1985	
YL344	A14SMT	Leyland Tiger TRCTL11/3RZ	Duple Caribbean 2	C51F	1984	Ex Duple demonstrator, 1986
CL345	A15SMT	Leyland Tiger TRCTL11/3RH	Duple 340	C53F	1987	
CL346	A16SMT	Leyland Tiger TRCTL11/3RH	Duple 340	C53F	1987	
YL347	A17SMT	Leyland Tiger TRCTL11/3RH	Duple 340	C53F	1987	
YL348	A18SMT	Leyland Tiger TRCTL11/3RH	Duple 340	C53F	1987	
ZL349	D349ESC	Leyland Tiger TRBTL11/2RP	Alexander TE	C49F	1987	
ZL350	D350ESC	Leyland Tiger TRBTL11/2RP	Alexander TE	C49F	1987	
ZL351	D351ESC	Leyland Tiger TRBTL11/2RP	Alexander TE	C49F	1987	
YL352	A12SMT	Leyland Tiger TRCL10/3RZA	Duple 340	C53F	1987	
YL353	A13SMT	Leyland Tiger TRCL10/3RZA	Duple 340	C53F	1987	
MC398	FFS8X	Bedford VAS5	Reeve Burgess	DP17F	1981	Ex Lowland Scottish, 1988

MR401-430

	Dodge S56	Alexander AM	B21F*	1986	*MR420 is B16FL

MR401	D401ASF	MR407	D407ASF	MR413	D413ASF	MR419	D419ASF	MR425	D425ASF
MR402	D402ASF	MR408	D408ASF	MR414	D414ASF	MR420	D420ASF	MR426	D426ASF
MR403	D403ASF	MR409	D409ASF	MR415	D415ASF	MR421	D421ASF	MR427	D427ASF
MR404	D404ASF	MR410	D410ASF	MR416	D416ASF	MR422	D422ASF	MR428	D428ASF
MR405	D405ASF	MR411	D411ASF	MR417	D417ASF	MR423	D423ASF	MR429	D429ASF
MR406	D406ASF	MR412	D412ASF	MR418	D418ASF	MR424	D424ASF	MR430	D430ASF

MR431-470

	Renault S56	Alexander AM	B25F*	1987	*ZMRs are DP25F

MR431	E431JSG	MR439	E439JSG	MR447	E447JSG	MR455	E455JSG	MR463	E463JSG
MR432	E432JSG	MR440	E440JSG	MR448	E448JSG	MR456	E456JSG	MR464	E464JSG
MR433	E433JSG	MR441	E441JSG	MR449	E449JSG	MR457	E457JSG	MR465	E465JSG
MR434	E434JSG	MR442	E442JSG	MR450	E450JSG	MR458	E458JSG	ZMR466	E466JSG
MR435	E435JSG	MR443	E443JSG	MR451	E451JSG	MR459	E459JSG	ZMR467	E467JSG
MR436	E436JSG	MR444	E444JSG	MR452	E452JSG	MR460	E460JSG	ZMR468	E468JSG
MR437	E437JSG	MR445	E445JSG	MR453	E453JSG	MR461	E461JSG	ZMR469	E469JSG
MR438	E438JSG	MR446	E446JSG	MR454	E454JSG	MR462	E462JSG	ZMR470	E470JSG

MR471-502

	Renault S75	Reeve Burgess Beaver	B31F	1991

MR471	H471OSC	MR477	H477OSC	MR484	H484OSC	MR490	H490OSC	MR496	H496OSC
MR472	H472OSC	MR478	H478OSC	MR485	H485OSC	MR491	H491OSC	MR497	H497OSC
MR473	H473OSC	MR479	H479OSC	MR486	H486OSC	MR492	H492OSC	MR498	H498OSC
MR474	H474OSC	MR481	H481OSC	MR487	H487OSC	MR493	H493OSC	MR499	H499OSC
MR475	H475OSC	MR482	H482OSC	MR488	H488OSC	MR494	H494OSC	MR501	H501OSC
MR476	H476OSC	MR483	H483OSC	MR489	H489OSC	MR495	H495OSC	MR502	H502OSC

M503-517

	Optare MetroRider	Optare	B25F	1992

M503	J503WSX	M506	J506WSX	M509	J509WSX	M512	J512WSX	M515	J515WSX
M504	J504WSX	M507	J507WSX	M510	J510WSX	M513	J513WSX	M516	J516WSX
M505	J505WSX	M508	J508WSX	M511	J511WSX	M514	J514WSX	M517	J517WSX

XCL550	BSG550W	Leyland Tiger TRCTL11/3R	Duple Dominant III	C46FT	1981

XCL564-569

	Leyland Tiger TRCTL11/3RH	Duple Caribbean 2	C44FT*	1985	*XCL565 is C46FT

XCL564	B564LSC	XCL566	B566LSC	XCL567	B567LSC	XCL568	B568LSC	XCL569	B569LSC

S591-659

Seddon Pennine 7 — Alexander AYS — B53F — 1979-80

S591	RSX591V	S613	SSX613V	S624	SSX624V	S638	YSG638W	S647	YSG647W
S592	RSX592V	S616	SSX616V	S625	SSX625V	S640	YSG640W	S648	YSG648W
S593	RSX593V	S617	SSX617V	S627	SSX627V	S641	YSG641W	S650	YSG650W
S594	RSX594V	S618	SSX618V	S628	SSX628V	S642	YSG642W	S654	YSG654W
S595	SSX595V	S619	SSX619V	S629	SSX629V	S643	YSG643W	S655	YSG655W
S596	SSX596V	S620	SSX620V	S630	SSX630V	S644	YSG644W	S657	YSG657W
S597	SSX597V	S621	SSX621V	S635	YSG635W	S645	YSG645W	S658	YSG658W
S611	SSX611V	S622	SSX622V	S636	YSG636W	S646	YSG646W	S659	YSG659W
S612	SSX612V	S623	SSX623V	S637	YSG637W				

DD694-716

Daimler Fleetline CRG6LXB-30 — Eastern Coach Works — H43/32F — 1975

DD694	KSX694N	DD699	KSX699N	DD711	KSX711N	DD712	KSX712N	DD716	KSX716N
DD696	KSX696N								

VV773-782

Ailsa B55-10 — Alexander AV — H44/35F — 1978

VV773	CSG773S	VV775	CSG775S	VV777	CSG777S	VV779	CSG779S	VV781	CSG781S
VV774	CSG774S	VV776	CSG776S	VV778	CSG778S	VV780	CSG780S	VV782	CSG782S

S839	ESC839S	Seddon Pennine 7	Alexander AY	B53F	1978

DD852-861

Leyland Fleetline FE30AGR — Eastern Coach Works — H43/32F — 1978

DD852	GSC852T	DD855	GSC855T	DD859	GSC859T	DD860	GSC860T	DD861	GSC861T
DD853	GSC853T	DD856	GSC856T						

ZS877-926

Seddon Pennine 7 — Alexander AT — C49F — 1978-79

ZS877	GSX877T	ZS885	GSX885T	ZS899	GSX897T	ZS902	JSF902T	ZS910	JSF910T
ZS878	GSX878T	ZS886	GSX886T	ZS899	GSX899T	ZS903	JSF903T	ZS911	JSF911T
ZS881	GSX881T	ZS893	GSX893T	ZS900	GSX900T	ZS904	JSF904T	ZS922	JSF922T
ZS884	GSX884T	ZS896	GSX896T	ZS901	GSX901T	ZS909	JSF909T	ZS926	JSF926T

S932	LSC932T	Seddon Pennine 7	Alexander AYS	B53F	1979
S933	LSC933T	Seddon Pennine 7	Alexander AYS	B53F	1979
S938	LSC938T	Seddon Pennine 7	Alexander AYS	B53F	1979
S939	LSC939T	Seddon Pennine 7	Alexander AYS	B53F	1979

YS942-973

Seddon Pennine 7 — Plaxton Supreme IV Exp — C49F* — 1979-81   *YS972/3 are C45F

YS942	WSV142	YS951	XXX001	YS958	NSX958T	YS962	XXX004	YS968	USX968V
YS943	LSC943T	YS953	LSC953T	YS959	XXX002	YS965	XXX005	YS970	USX970V
YS947	LSC947T	YS954	LSC954T	YS960	NSX960T	YS966	XXX006	YS972	XXX008
YS948	LSC948T	YS955	LSC955T	YS961	XXX003	YS967	XXX007	YS973	WSV144
YS949	LSC949T		Note: New marks are awaited from DLVA.						

S979	JFS979X	Seddon Pennine 7	Alexander AYS	B53F	1982
S980	JFS980X	Seddon Pennine 7	Alexander AYS	B53F	1982
S981	JFS981X	Seddon Pennine 7	Alexander AYS	B53F	1982
S982	JFS982X	Seddon Pennine 7	Alexander AYS	B53F	1982

Previous Registrations:

A10SMT	B340RLS	XXX001T	WSV141, LSC951T	WSV136	B336RLS
A12SMT	E352KSF	XXX002T	WSV136, NSX959T	WSV137	B337RLS
A13SMT	E353KSF	XXX003V	GCS245, OSF961V	WSV138	B338RLS
A14SMT	B446WRN	XXX004V	WSV137, OSF962V	WSV139	B339RLS
A15SMT	D345ESC	XXX005V	WSV138, OSF965V	WSV140	A330BSC
A16SMT	D346ESC	XXX006V	WSV139, OSF966V	WSV141	B341RLS
A17SMT	D347ESC	XXX007V	WSV140, USX967V	WSV142	LSC942T
A18SMT	D348ESC	XXX008W	WSV143, DSC972W	WSV143	C343WHS
A19SMT	F250OFP	WSV135	A332BSC	WSV144	DSC973W

Note: New marks for the Seddons are awaited from DLVA.

Special Liveries:

Overall Advertisements: VV37/8/78, LL132/6/61, MR440-3/65
Scottish Citylink: CL345/6, XCL564-9.
SMT coach livery: YD8, XD19, YL330-2, XM333, YL335-41/43/4.

STAGECOACH

Stagecoach Scotland Ltd, Guild Street, Aberdeen, AB9 2DP

The Stagecoach group of companies has grown in just over ten years from a one-bus operation to one of the largest bus operators in the United Kingdom. It also has considerable international interests.

The original Stagecoach company was sold in 1989 together with the Stagecoach express service network to National Express to become Tayside Travel Services. Magicbus (Scotland) Ltd, which had previously been responsible for the Glasgow-based services, was renamed Stagecoach Scotland Ltd and all Scottish local bus interests brought under its wing at the new Perth headquarters.

Stagecoach is now firmly established as a provider of services in Tayside and in 1991 established a new out-station in Crieff following Strathtay's departure from the town.

In July 1989 Alexander (North East) of Aberdeen rescued Inverness Traction, acquiring it as a going concern, but in November 1989 Alexanders itself went into receivership. Stagecoach took over the Inverness operation, re-equipped it with new Mercedes-Benz minibuses and proceeded to compete vigorously with Highland Scottish. Following SBG's disposal of Highland to Citylink and Rapson in 1991, the battle for supremacy in Inverness increased for a few weeks. Stagecoach succeeded to the extent that it was necessary to acquire extra parking land in Inverness and open additional premises in Tain. Subsequently, the Inverness Traction unit was transferred to Bluebird Northern which had been dealing with day-to-day management for some time.

The Glasgow base was moved to Hobden Street in February 1990, and the former McLennan depot at Spittalfield was closed during 1991. It is understood the operations in the Glasgow area, together with some vehicles, will be sold to Kelvin Central during April.

A large proportion of a group order for 100 Mercedes-Benz minibuses entered service with this operator. Some have subsequently been transferred to other Stagecoach companies in England, while others are now with Bluebird Northern. There are still a few active Bristol FLFs in the fleet, though most have been replaced by former English company Bristol VRTs which themselves are being displaced on Perth city services by Olympians from Bluebird.

Depots are at Crieff, Dundee, and Perth. The livery is white with orange, red and blue bands.

Originally London Transport RM1245, No.607 is typical of the AEC Routemasters still being used by Stagecoach on Perth town services. Ten of the standard Routemaster remain active.
Graeme Yuill

Only a few Bristol FLFs remain in Stagecoach service and these are restricted to school duties around Perth. A former Central SMT example is now numbered 003. Murdoch Currie

Two former East Midland Bristol VRTs are seen at the St Enoch terminus in Glasgow on the Castlemilk circular, a route once the province of former London Routemasters. Seen shortly after being transferred from Mansfield, 093 and 094 typify the design of bus now becoming the most numerous in the fleet. Stewart Brown

Most of Northern's Eastern Coach Works-bodied Leyland Olympians have been transferred to the Perth operations of Stagecoach. Parked side by side in the depot at Perth are 013 and 014. J. Burnett

Seen leaving St Enoch Square in Glasgow is 314, one of 100 Alexander-bodied Mercedes-Benz delivered to the Stagecoach group in 1990. The type was supplied in two batches mostly with PAO and TSL index marks from the Mercedes-Benz dealerships involved. Now scattered through many Stagecoach companies, 314 is one fitted with the high-back seating. Murdoch Currie

Dennis Darts fitted with Alexander's new 'Dash' body design are appearing in several Stagecoach group fleets, particularly in the south of the country. An initial allocation of eighteen can be found in Scotland including six with Magicbus in Glasgow. Photographed in February 1992 is 515. Max Fowler

STAGECOACH Fleet List

001	DGS625	Leyland Tiger PS1/2	McLennan	C37F	1951	Ex Davies, Pencader, 1987
002	HDV639E	Bristol MW6G	Eastern Coach Works	C39F	1967	Ex Western National, 1980
003	HGM335E	Bristol FLF6G	Eastern Coach Works	H44/34F	1967	Ex Central SMT, 1981
004	GRX129D	Bristol FLF6G	Eastern Coach Works	H38/32F	1966	Ex Cleverly, Cwmbran, 1987
005	GRX131D	Bristol FLF6G	Eastern Coach Works	H38/32F	1966	Ex Cleverly, Cwmbran, 1987
006	GRX132D	Bristol FLF6G	Eastern Coach Works	H38/32F	1966	Ex Cleverly, Cwmbran, 1987

012-032

		Leyland Olympian ONLXB/1R	Eastern Coach Works	H45/32F	1982	Ex Northern Scottish, 1991

012	TSO12X	014	TSO14X	019	9492SC	021	TSO21X	030	TSO30X
013	TSO13X	016	TSO16X	020	TSO20X	024	TSO24X	032	TSO32X

084	RPR716R	Bristol VRT/SL3/6LXB	Eastern Coach Works	H43/31F	1977	Ex Hampshire Bus, 1992
090	OTO149R	Bristol VRT/SL3/501	Eastern Coach Works	H39/31F	1976	Ex East Midland, 1990
091	OTO151R	Bristol VRT/SL3/501	Eastern Coach Works	H39/31F	1976	Ex East Midland, 1990

092-096

		Bristol VRT/SL3/6LXB	Eastern Coach Works	H39/31F	1976	Ex East Midland, 1991

092	MAU141P	093	MAU142P	094	MAU144P	095	MAU145P	096	MAU146P

097	JNU134N	Bristol VRT/SL2/6G	Eastern Coach Works	H39/31F	1975	Ex East Midland, 1991
098	YTU358S	Bristol VRT/SL3/501	Eastern Coach Works	H41/31F	1977	Ex East Midland, 1991
099	NEL117P	Bristol VRT/SL3/501	Eastern Coach Works	DPH41/29F	1976	Ex Hampshire Bus, 1989
100	NEL119P	Bristol VRT/SL3/501	Eastern Coach Works	DPH41/29F	1976	Ex Hampshire Bus, 1989
101	NEL120P	Bristol VRT/SL3/501	Eastern Coach Works	DPH41/29F	1976	Ex Hampshire Bus, 1989
102	HRP672N	Bristol VRT/SL2/6G	Eastern Coach Works	H43/31F	1975	Ex United Counties, 1990
103	FDV810V	Bristol VRT/SL3/6LXB	Eastern Coach Works	H43/31F	1980	Ex Devon General, 1989
104	OVV850R	Bristol VRT/SL3/501	Eastern Coach Works	H43/31F	1976	Ex United Counties, 1991
105	FDV816V	Bristol VRT/SL3/6LXB	Eastern Coach Works	H43/31F	1980	Ex Devon General, 1989
107	FDV819V	Bristol VRT/SL3/6LXB	Eastern Coach Works	H43/31F	1980	Ex Devon General, 1989
109	FDV840V	Bristol VRT/SL3/6LXB	Eastern Coach Works	H43/31F	1980	Ex Devon General, 1989
110	ONH846P	Bristol VRT/SL3/501	Eastern Coach Works	H43/31F	1976	Ex United Counties, 1991
111	XNV881S	Bristol VRT/SL3/6LXB	Eastern Coach Works	H43/31F	1978	Ex United Counties, 1991
116	VTV167S	Bristol VRT/SL3/6LXB	Eastern Coach Works	H43/31F	1978	Ex East Midland, 1990
117	LJA615P	Leyland Atlantean AN68/1R	Northern Counties	H43/32F	1976	Ex Ribble, 1990
118	LJA636P	Leyland Atlantean AN68/1R	Northern Counties	H43/32F	1976	Ex Ribble, 1990
119	KBU914P	Leyland Atlantean AN68/1R	Northern Counties	H43/32F	1975	Ex Ribble, 1990
127	RJT153R	Bristol VRT/SL3/6LXB	Eastern Coach Works	H43/31F	1977	Ex Hampshire Bus, 1992
128	RJT155R	Bristol VRT/SL3/6LXB	Eastern Coach Works	H43/31F	1977	Ex Hampshire Bus, 1992
129	RJT157R	Bristol VRT/SL3/6LXB	Eastern Coach Works	H43/31F	1977	Ex Hampshire Bus, 1991

174-185

	Leyland Leopard PSU3F/4R*	Willowbrook 003	C49F	1980-81	Ex Cumberland, 1991
					*179/80 are PSU3E/4R

174	OVL473	177	MSV533	180	4585SC	182	866NHT	184	LSK547
175	5889SC	178	PRM632X	181	4009SC	183	LSK545	185	LSK548
176	BSK744	179	BSK756						

186	147YFM	Leyland Leopard PSU3E/4R	Willowbrook 003	C49F	1982	Ex Hastings & District, 1991
187	ANU19T	Leyland Leopard PSU3E/4R	Plaxton Supreme IV Exp	C49F	1978	Ex East Midland, 1989
188	ANU20T	Leyland Leopard PSU3E/4R	Plaxton Supreme IV Exp	C49F	1978	Ex East Midland, 1989
189	ANU21T	Leyland Leopard PSU3E/4R	Plaxton Supreme IV Exp	C49F	1978	Ex East Midland, 1989
196	XMS247R	Leyland Leopard PSU3C/3R	Alexander AY	DP49F	1977	Ex Northern Scottish, 1991
197	OSJ630R	Leyland Leopard PSU3C/3R	Alexander AY	DP49F	1977	Ex Northern Scottish, 1991
198	OSJ642R	Leyland Leopard PSU3C/3R	Alexander AY	B53F	1977	Ex Northern Scottish, 1991

251-275

	Mercedes-Benz 709D	Alexander AM	B25F	1990

251	G251TSL	253	G253TSL	255	G255TSL	257	G257TSL	275	G275TSL
252	G252TSL	254	G254TSL	256	G256TSL				

308-312

	Mercedes-Benz 709D	Alexander AM	DP25F	1990

308	G197PAO	309	G198PAO	310	G199PAO	311	G200PAO	312	G201PAO

407	KRS586V	Volvo B58-61		Plaxton Supreme IV	C52FT	1980	Ex Highwayman, Errol, 1989
414	MSL35X	Volvo B58-61		Duple Dominant III	C57F	1981	Ex Cumberland, 1981

513-518

	Dennis Dart 9.8SDL3017	Alexander Dash	B41F	1992

513	J513FPS	515	J515FPS	516	J516FPS	517	J517FPS	518	J518FPS
514	J514FPS								

602-618

	AEC Routemaster 5RM	Park Royal	H36/28R	1960-65	Ex London Buses, 1985-87

602	EDS50A	607	LDS210A	609	XSL596A	614	LDS201A	616	ALD968B
606	LDS402A	608	LDS67A	611	LDS190A	615	EDS561B	618	CUV121C

620	NMY633E	AEC Routemaster R2RH2	Park Royal	H32/24F	1967	Ex LRT Engineering, 1987
621	NMY634E	AEC Routemaster R2RH2	Park Royal	H32/24F	1967	Ex London Buses, 1987

Previous Registrations:

145CLT	JSR43X	BSK756	KVV237V	LDS402A	145CLT
147YFM	VKN833X	EDS50A	WLT560	LSK545	UVV152W
4009SC	UVV150W	EDS561B	858DYE	LSK547	UVV153W
4585SC	KVV240V	KRS586V	866NHT, LUA250V	LSK548	UVV154W
5889SC	PRM629X	LDS67A	274CLT	MSL35X	5889SC, PVO22X
866NHT	UVV151W	LDS190A	449CLT	MSV533	PRM631X
9492SC	TSO19X	LDS201A	607DYE	OVL473	PRM628X
BSK744	PRM630X	LDS210A	245CLT	XSL596A	289CLT
BSK756	KVV237V	LDS402A	145CLT		

STRATHCLYDE'S BUSES

Strathclyde Buses Ltd, 197 Victoria Road, Glasgow, G42 7AD

This company was formed in 1986 to acquire the Strathclyde PTE bus fleet. Despite competition from former SBG companies and others, it remains the major provider of bus services in the city, and has established itself in new locations such as Cumbernauld, Dumbarton and significantly East Kilbride which until recently was almost the sole preserve of Central Scottish.

There have been no major additions to the fleet since the arrival of a large order for Volvo Citybuses in 1989-90, though of interest are three Leyland Olympians received in 1991 to cover for Citybuses returned for warranty work. A number of secondhand Metroriders have been obtained.

It is anticipated that the company will be sold to its management and employees during 1992.

Depots are at Knightswood, Larkfield, Parkhead and Possilpark.

The liveries are orange (Strathclyde red) and black (buses); orange, white and black (coaches).

Sole survivor of the initial trio of the front-engined Ailsas is AV3. It is seen at the St Enoch Square terminal in Glasgow. One of the features of the B55 is the traditional driver access through his own door.
Murdoch Currie

One of the final batch of Leyland Atlanteans crosses the bridge over the River Kelvin on Greater Western Road. Max Fowler

There are three Marshall-bodied double deckers in the Strathclyde fleet, two Volvo-Ailsas and the prototype Volvo Citybus. A118 is a Volvo-Ailsa seen in Paisley on a route that partly covers an erstwhile Graham's of Paisley service. Murdoch Currie

One of the final batch of Volvo-Ailsa B55s shows the forward radiator and, behind the driver's window, the water filler cap of these vehicles. Seating some 79 passengers, A124 is seen as it prepares to depart the Royal Burgh of Rutherglen for Glasgow. Graeme Yuill

Roe, whose factory is now the home of Optare, bodied ten Leyland Olympians for Glasgow in 1981. The Roe design differs from the more common Eastern Coach Works version in the windscreen area. LO4, a highbridge version, is seen at Govan bus station and interchange. Max Fowler

The greenhouse effect! Leyland Olympian LO20 stands in front of the St Enoch Centre in Glasgow. This is one of six Olympians fitted with Alexander RH-type bodywork. Max Fowler

MBC25, photographed in Johnstone, has since lost its coach seats to a newer Metrobus. However, when seen in April 1991 it carried a version of the latest coach livery. Graeme Yuill

Volvo Citybus AH31 is seen in Clydebank on a route which in part parallels Kelvin Central's Routemaster-operated services 5 and 6. David Little

The only Ailsa to have been constructed as a single decker is Strathclyde AS1, seen in wintry conditions while on a visit to Knightswood depot. Fitted with a version of the Marshall Camair body, it seats fifty.
Murdoch Currie

The Volvo B10M Citybus single deckers have been fitted with coach seats for tours and charters, though they appear on ordinary service when not so required. The bodywork for the six is split between Plaxton and Caetano and most have white relief to the livery. Representing the Plaxton Derwent style is AS4, seen heading for Easterhouse, while the Caetano Stagecoach design is seen on AS6 on a route normally operated by minibuses.
Stewart Brown

The two MCW Metroliners, C13 and C14, await a private party in Glasgow city centre. These vehicles are fitted with wheelchair lifts in their forward doorway. Max Fowler

The MCW MetroRider was available in two lengths and two widths. The narrow, shorter model, MF150, has a normal seating capacity of 25. These are the most common type in the Strathclyde fleet and M40, the first of the 1987 intake, is seen in Clydebank. David Little

STRATHCLYDE'S BUSES Fleet List

A1-40
Volvo-Ailsa B55-10 MkIII — Alexander RV — H44/35F — 1981

A1	TGG377W	A11	CSU219X	A19	CSU227X	A27	CSU235X	A34	CSU242X
A2	TGG378W	A12	CSU220X	A20	CSU228X	A28	CSU236X	A35	CSU243X
A4	TGG380W	A13	CSU221X	A21	CSU229X	A29	CSU237X	A36	CSU244X
A5	TGG381W	A14	CSU222X	A22	CSU230X	A30	CSU238X	A37	CSU245X
A7	TGG383W	A15	CSU223X	A23	CSU231X	A31	CSU239X	A38	CSU246X
A8	TGG384W	A16	CSU224X	A24	CSU232X	A32	CSU240X	A39	CSU247X
A9	TGG385W	A17	CSU225X	A25	CSU233X	A33	CSU241X	A40	CSU248X
A10	TGG386W	A18	CSU226X	A26	CSU234X				

A41-116
Volvo-Ailsa B55-10 MkIII — Alexander RV — H44/35F — 1982-83

A41	KGG101Y	A57	KGG117Y	A72	KGG132Y	A87	OGG183Y	A102	A565SGA
A42	KGG102Y	A58	KGG118Y	A73	KGG133Y	A88	OGG184Y	A103	A566SGA
A43	KGG103Y	A59	KGG119Y	A74	KGG134Y	A89	OGG185Y	A104	A567SGA
A44	KGG104Y	A60	KGG141Y	A75	KGG135Y	A90	OGG186Y	A105	A568SGA
A45	KGG105Y	A61	KGG125Y	A76	KGG136Y	A91	OGG187Y	A106	A732PSU
A46	KGG106Y	A62	KGG122Y	A77	KGG137Y	A92	OGG188Y	A107	A733PSU
A47	KGG107Y	A63	KGG123Y	A78	KGG138Y	A93	OGG189Y	A108	A734PSU
A48	KGG108Y	A64	KGG124Y	A79	KGG139Y	A94	OGG190Y	A109	A735PSU
A49	KGG109Y	A65	KGG121Y	A80	KGG140Y	A95	OGG191Y	A110	A736PSU
A50	KGG110Y	A66	KGG126Y	A81	KGG120Y	A96	OGG192Y	A111	A737PSU
A51	KGG111Y	A67	KGG127Y	A82	OGG178Y	A97	A560SGA	A112	A738PSU
A52	KGG112Y	A68	KGG128Y	A83	OGG179Y	A98	A561SGA	A113	A739PSU
A53	KGG113Y	A69	KGG129Y	A84	OGG180Y	A99	A562SGA	A114	A741PSU
A54	KGG114Y	A70	KGG130Y	A85	OGG181Y	A100	A563SGA	A115	A742PSU
A55	KGG115Y	A71	KGG131Y	A86	OGG182Y	A101	A564SGA	A116	A743PSU
A56	KGG116Y								

A117	A483UYS	Volvo-Ailsa B55-10 MkIII	Marshall	H44/35F	1984
A118	A484UYS	Volvo-Ailsa B55-10 MkIII	Marshall	H44/35F	1984

A119-133
Volvo-Ailsa B55-10 MkIII — Alexander RV — H44/35F — 1984

A119	B999YUS	A122	B23YYS	A125	B26YYS	A128	B29YYS	A131	B32YYS
A120	B21YYS	A123	B24YYS	A126	B27YYS	A129	B30YYS	A132	B33YYS
A121	B22YYS	A124	B25YYS	A127	B28YYS	A130	B31YYS	A133	B34YYS

AH1	ESU378X	Volvo Citybus B10M-50	Marshall	H47/39F	1982

AH2-6
Volvo Citybus B10M-50 — Alexander RV — H47/27FL — 1984

AH2	A600TNS	AH3	A601TNS	AH4	A603TNS	AH5	A602TNS	AH6	A604TNS

AH7-56
Volvo Citybus B10M-50 — Alexander RV — H47/37F — 1989

AH7	F89JYS	AH17	F99JYS	AH27	G412OGD	AH37	G285OGE	AH47	G295OGE
AH8	F90JYS	AH18	F790LSU	AH28	G413OGD	AH38	G286OGE	AH48	G296OGE
AH9	F91JYS	AH19	F791LSU	AH29	G414OGD	AH39	G287OGE	AH49	G297OGE
AH10	F92JYS	AH20	F792LSU	AH30	G415OGD	AH40	G288OGE	AH50	G298OGE
AH11	F93JYS	AH21	F793LSU	AH31	G416OGD	AH41	G289OGE	AH51	G299OGE
AH12	F94JYS	AH22	F794LSU	AH32	G280OGE	AH42	G290OGE	AH52	G300OGE
AH13	F95JYS	AH23	F795LSU	AH33	G281OGE	AH43	G291OGE	AH53	G301OGE
AH14	F96JYS	AH24	G409OGD	AH34	G282OGE	AH44	G292OGE	AH54	G302OGE
AH15	F97JYS	AH25	G410OGD	AH35	G283OGE	AH45	G293OGE	AH55	G303OGE
AH16	F98JYS	AH26	G411OGD	AH36	G284OGE	AH46	G294OGE	AH56	G304OGE

AH57-101
Volvo Citybus B10M-50 — Alexander RV — H47/37F — 1990

AH57	G685PNS	AH66	G694PNS	AH75	G703PNS	AH84	G528RDS	AH93	G537RDS
AH58	G686PNS	AH67	G695PNS	AH76	G704PNS	AH85	G529RDS	AH94	G538RDS
AH59	G687PNS	AH68	G696PNS	AH77	G521RDS	AH86	G530RDS	AH95	G539RDS
AH60	G688PNS	AH69	G697PNS	AH78	G522RDS	AH87	G531RDS	AH96	G540RDS
AH61	G689PNS	AH70	G698PNS	AH79	G523RDS	AH88	G532RDS	AH97	G541RDS
AH62	G690PNS	AH71	G699PNS	AH80	G524RDS	AH89	G533RDS	AH98	G542RDS
AH63	G691PNS	AH72	G700PNS	AH81	G525RDS	AH90	G534RDS	AH99	G543RDS
AH64	G692PNS	AH73	G701PNS	AH82	G526RDS	AH91	G535RDS	AH100	G544RDS
AH65	G693PNS	AH74	G702PNS	AH83	G527RDS	AH92	G536RDS	AH101	G545RDS

AS1	NHS782Y	Volvo-Ailsa B55	Marshall Camair	B50F	1983	
AS2	MGE185P	Ailsa B55-10	Alexander AV/SPTE	B38F	1972	
AS3	F384FYS	Volvo B10M-56	Plaxton Derwent	DP46F	1988	
AS4	F385FYS	Volvo B10M-56	Plaxton Derwent	DP46F	1988	
AS5	E31BTO	Volvo B10M-56	Plaxton Derwent	DP46F	1988	Ex Graham, Paisley, 1990
AS6	C982KHS	Volvo B10M-61	Caetano Stagecoach	DP53F	1986	Ex Graham, Paisley, 1990
AS7	C983KHS	Volvo B10M-61	Caetano Stagecoach	DP53F	1986	Ex Graham, Paisley, 1990
AS8	C188RVV	Volvo B10M-61	Caetano Stagecoach	DP55F	1986	Ex Graham, Paisley, 1990

AV3-18

Ailsa B55-10 — Alexander AV — H44/35F — 1975

AV3	GGG302N	AV6	MGE181P	AV11	MGE186P	AV14	MGE189P	AV17	MGE192P
AV4	MGE179P	AV7	MGE182P	AV12	MGE187P	AV15	MGE190P	AV18	MGE193P
AV5	MGE180P	AV8	MGE183P	AV13	MGE188P	AV16	MGE191P		

C5	BNS234S	Leyland Leopard PSU3E/4R	Duple Dominant II Express	C45FL	1978
C9	JGE29T	Leyland Leopard PSU3E/4R	Duple Dominant II Express	C45FL	1979
C12	OGD660V	Leyland Leopard PSU3E/4R	Duple Dominant II Express	C51F	1980
C13	A740RNS	MCW Metroliner CR126/3	MCW	C49FL	1983
C14	A741RNS	MCW Metroliner CR126/4	MCW	C49FL	1983
C15	B730CHS	Volvo B10M-56	Plaxton Paramount 3200 Ex	C53F	1985
C16	B200DGG	Leyland Tiger TRCLXC/2RH	Alexander TE	C49F	1985
LA664	HGD870L	Leyland Atlantean AN68/1R	Alexander AL	H45/29F	1973

LA757-952

Leyland Atlantean AN68/1R — Alexander AL — H45/29F — 1974-75

LA757	NGB125M	LA765	OYS162M	LA777	OYS174M	LA787	OYS184M	LA951	KSU827P
LA760	NGB128M	LA775	OYS172M	LA781	OYS178M	LA791	OYS188M	LA952	KSU828P

LA1030-1150

Leyland Atlantean AN68A/1R — Alexander AL — H45/31F — 1976-77

LA1030	MDS693P	LA1104	TGE823R	LA1118	TGE837R	LA1129	TGG744R	LA1139	TGG754R
LA1031	MDS694P	LA1106	TGE825R	LA1120	TGE839R	LA1130	TGG745R	LA1140	TGG755R
LA1034	MDS697P	LA1108	TGE827R	LA1121	TGG736R	LA1131	TGG746R	LA1141	TGG756R
LA1043	MDS706P	LA1109	TGE828R	LA1122	TGG737R	LA1132	TGG747R	LA1142	TGG757R
LA1049	MDS712P	LA1110	TGE829R	LA1123	TGG738R	LA1133	TGG748R	LA1143	TGG758R
LA1052	RUS303R	LA1111	TGE830R	LA1124	TGG739R	LA1134	TGG749R	LA1144	TGG759R
LA1097	RUS348R	LA1112	TGE831R	LA1125	TGG740R	LA1135	TGG750R	LA1147	TGG762R
LA1099	RUS350R	LA1113	TGE832R	LA1126	TGG741R	LA1136	TGG751R	LA1148	TGG763R
LA1100	RUS351R	LA1114	TGE833R	LA1127	TGG742R	LA1137	TGG752R	LA1150	TGG765R
LA1101	TGE820R	LA1116	TGE835R	LA1128	TGG743R	LA1138	TGG753R		

LA1151-1250

Leyland Atlantean AN68A/1R — Alexander AL — H45/33F — 1977-78

LA1151	UGG370R	LA1172	UGG391R	LA1192	WUS570S	LA1212	XUS583S	LA1232	XUS603S
LA1152	UGG371R	LA1173	UGG392R	LA1194	WUS572S	LA1214	XUS585S	LA1233	XUS604S
LA1153	UGG372R	LA1174	UGG393R	LA1195	WUS573S	LA1215	XUS586S	LA1234	XUS605S
LA1154	UGG373R	LA1175	UGG394R	LA1196	WUS574S	LA1216	XUS587S	LA1235	XUS606S
LA1155	UGG374R	LA1176	UGG395R	LA1197	WUS575S	LA1217	XUS588S	LA1236	XUS607S
LA1156	UGG375R	LA1177	UGG396R	LA1199	WUS577S	LA1218	XUS589S	LA1237	XUS608S
LA1157	UGG376R	LA1178	UGG397R	LA1200	WUS578S	LA1219	XUS590S	LA1239	XUS610S
LA1158	UGG377R	LA1179	UGG398R	LA1201	XUS572S	LA1221	XUS592S	LA1240	XUS611S
LA1159	UGG378R	LA1180	UGG399R	LA1202	XUS573S	LA1222	XUS593S	LA1241	XUS612S
LA1160	UGG379R	LA1181	UGG400R	LA1203	XUS574S	LA1223	XUS594S	LA1242	XUS613S
LA1161	UGG380R	LA1182	UGG401R	LA1204	XUS575S	LA1224	XUS595S	LA1243	XUS614S
LA1162	UGG381R	LA1183	UGG402R	LA1205	XUS576S	LA1225	XUS596S	LA1244	XUS615S
LA1163	UGG382R	LA1184	UGG403R	LA1206	XUS577S	LA1226	XUS597S	LA1245	XUS616S
LA1164	UGG383R	LA1185	UGG404R	LA1207	XUS578S	LA1227	XUS598S	LA1246	XUS617S
LA1166	UGG385R	LA1186	WUS579S	LA1208	XUS579S	LA1228	XUS599S	LA1247	XUS618S
LA1167	UGG386R	LA1189	WUS567S	LA1209	XUS580S	LA1229	XUS600S	LA1248	XUS619S
LA1168	UGG387R	LA1190	WUS568S	LA1210	XUS581S	LA1230	XUS601S	LA1249	XUS620S
LA1169	UGG388R	LA1191	WUS569S	LA1211	XUS582S	LA1231	XUS602S	LA1250	XUS621S
LA1170	UGG389R								

LA1251-1350

Leyland Atlantean AN68A/1R Alexander AL H45/33F 1979-80

LA1251 FSU68T	LA1271 FSU88T	LA1291 FSU108T	LA1311 LSU368V	LA1331 LSU388V
LA1252 FSU69T	LA1272 FSU89T	LA1292 FSU109T	LA1312 LSU369V	LA1332 LSU389V
LA1253 FSU70T	LA1273 FSU90T	LA1293 FSU110T	LA1313 LSU370V	LA1333 LSU390V
LA1254 FSU71T	LA1274 FSU91T	LA1294 FSU111T	LA1314 LSU371V	LA1334 LSU391V
LA1255 FSU72T	LA1275 FSU92T	LA1295 FSU112T	LA1315 LSU372V	LA1335 LSU392V
LA1256 FSU73T	LA1276 FSU93T	LA1296 FSU113T	LA1316 LSU373V	LA1336 LSU393V
LA1257 FSU74T	LA1277 FSU94T	LA1297 FSU114T	LA1317 LSU374V	LA1337 LSU394V
LA1258 FSU75T	LA1278 FSU95T	LA1298 FSU115T	LA1318 LSU375V	LA1338 LSU395V
LA1259 FSU76T	LA1279 FSU96T	LA1299 FSU116T	LA1319 LSU376V	LA1339 LSU396V
LA1260 FSU77T	LA1280 FSU97T	LA1300 FSU117T	LA1320 LSU377V	LA1340 LSU397V
LA1261 FSU78T	LA1281 FSU98T	LA1301 FSU118T	LA1321 LSU378V	LA1341 LSU398V
LA1262 FSU79T	LA1282 FSU99T	LA1302 FSU119T	LA1322 LSU379V	LA1342 LSU399V
LA1263 FSU80T	LA1283 FSU100T	LA1303 FSU120T	LA1323 LSU380V	LA1343 LSU400V
LA1264 FSU81T	LA1284 FSU101T	LA1304 FSU121T	LA1324 LSU381V	LA1344 LSU401V
LA1265 FSU82T	LA1285 FSU102T	LA1305 FSU122T	LA1325 LSU382V	LA1345 LSU402V
LA1266 FSU83T	LA1286 FSU103T	LA1306 FSU123T	LA1326 LSU383V	LA1346 LSU403V
LA1267 FSU84T	LA1287 FSU104T	LA1307 FSU124T	LA1327 LSU384V	LA1347 LSU404V
LA1268 FSU85T	LA1288 FSU105T	LA1308 FSU125T	LA1328 LSU385V	LA1348 LSU405V
LA1269 FSU86T	LA1289 FSU106T	LA1309 FSU126T	LA1329 LSU386V	LA1349 LSU406V
LA1270 FSU87T	LA1290 FSU107T	LA1310 FSU127T	LA1330 LSU387V	LA1350 LSU407V

LA1351-1449

Leyland Atlantean AN68A/1R Alexander AL H45/33F 1980-81

LA1351 RDS565W	LA1371 RDS550W	LA1391 RDS580W	LA1411 RDS600W	LA1430 SUS598W
LA1352 RDS566W	LA1372 RDS551W	LA1392 RDS581W	LA1412 RDS601W	LA1432 SUS600W
LA1353 RDS567W	LA1373 RDS552W	LA1393 RDS582W	LA1413 RDS602W	LA1433 SUS601W
LA1354 RDS568W	LA1374 RDS553W	LA1394 RDS583W	LA1414 RDS603W	LA1434 SUS602W
LA1355 RDS569W	LA1375 RDS554W	LA1395 RDS584W	LA1415 RDS604W	LA1435 SUS603W
LA1356 RDS570W	LA1376 RDS555W	LA1396 RDS585W	LA1416 RDS605W	LA1436 SUS604W
LA1357 RDS571W	LA1377 RDS556W	LA1397 RDS586W	LA1417 RDS606W	LA1437 SUS605W
LA1358 RDS572W	LA1378 RDS557W	LA1398 RDS587W	LA1418 RDS607W	LA1438 SUS606W
LA1359 RDS573W	LA1379 RDS558W	LA1399 RDS588W	LA1419 RDS608W	LA1439 SUS607W
LA1360 RDS574W	LA1380 RDS559W	LA1400 RDS589W	LA1420 RDS609W	LA1440 UGB193W
LA1361 RDS540W	LA1381 RDS560W	LA1402 RDS591W	LA1421 RDS610W	LA1441 CUS296X
LA1362 RDS541W	LA1382 RDS561W	LA1403 RDS592W	LA1422 RDS611W	LA1442 CUS297X
LA1363 RDS542W	LA1383 RDS562W	LA1404 RDS593W	LA1423 RDS612W	LA1443 UGB196W
LA1364 RDS543W	LA1384 RDS563W	LA1405 RDS594W	LA1424 RDS613W	LA1444 CUS298X
LA1365 RDS544W	LA1385 RDS564W	LA1406 RDS595W	LA1425 RDS614W	LA1445 CUS299X
LA1366 RDS545W	LA1386 RDS575W	LA1407 RDS596W	LA1426 RDS615W	LA1446 CUS300X
LA1367 RDS546W	LA1387 RDS576W	LA1408 RDS597W	LA1427 RDS616W	LA1447 CUS301X
LA1368 RDS547W	LA1388 RDS577W	LA1409 RDS598W	LA1428 RDS617W	LA1448 CUS302X
LA1369 RDS548W	LA1389 RDS578W	LA1410 RDS599W	LA1429 RDS618W	LA1449 UGB202W
LA1370 RDS549W	LA1390 RDS579W			

LO1	VGB364W	Leyland Olympian B45/TL11/1R	Alexander RH	H46/30F	1980

LO2-11

Leyland Olympian ONLTL11/1R Roe H46/31F 1981

LO2	CGG825X	LO4	CGG827X	LO6	CGG829X	LO8	CGG831X	LO10	CGG833X
LO3	CGG826X	LO5	CGG828X	LO7	CGG830X	LO9	CGG832X	LO11	CGG834X

LO12-16

Leyland Olympian ONTL11/1R Eastern Coach Works H46/31F 1982

LO12	CGG835X	LO13	CGG836X	LO14	CGG837X	LO15	CGG838X	LO16	CGG839X

LO17-21

Leyland Olympian ONTL11/1R Alexander RH H47/29F 1982

LO17	ESU4X	LO18	ESU5X	LO19	ESU6X	LO20	ESU7X	LO21	ESU8X

LO22-46

Leyland Olympian ONTL11/1R Eastern Coach Works H47/31F 1983

LO22	KGG142Y	LO27	KGG147Y	LO32	KGG152Y	LO37	KGG157Y	LO42	A371TGB
LO23	KGG143Y	LO28	KGG148Y	LO33	KGG153Y	LO38	KGG158Y	LO43	A372TGB
LO24	KGG144Y	LO29	KGG149Y	LO34	KGG154Y	LO39	KGG159Y	LO44	A373TGB
LO25	KGG145Y	LO30	KGG150Y	LO35	KGG155Y	LO40	KGG160Y	LO45	A374TGB
LO26	KGG146Y	LO31	KGG151Y	LO36	KGG156Y	LO41	KGG161Y	LO46	A375TGB

LO47	J136FYS	Leyland Olympian ON2R50G13Z4 Leyland	H47/31F	1991
LO48	J137FYS	Leyland Olympian ON2R50G13Z4 Leyland	H47/31F	1991
LO49	J138FYS	Leyland Olympian ON2R50G13Z4 Leyland	H47/31F	1991

M39	E55LBK	MCW MetroRider MF150/70	MCW	B25F	1988	Ex Southampton, 1990

M40-71

	MCW MetroRider MF150/55*	MCW	B23F	1987	*M40/1 are MF151/8

M40	E995WNS	**M47**	E932XYS	**M54**	E939XYS	**M60**	E945XYS	**M66**	E951XYS
M41	E996WNS	**M48**	E933XYS	**M55**	E940XYS	**M61**	E946XYS	**M67**	E952XYS
M42	E927XYS	**M49**	E934XYS	**M56**	E941XYS	**M62**	E947XYS	**M68**	E953XYS
M43	E928XYS	**M50**	E935XYS	**M57**	E942XYS	**M63**	E948XYS	**M69**	E954XYS
M44	E929XYS	**M51**	E936XYS	**M58**	E943XYS	**M64**	E949XYS	**M70**	E955XYS
M45	E930XYS	**M52**	E937XYS	**M59**	E944XYS	**M65**	E950XYS	**M71**	E956XYS
M46	E931XYS	**M53**	E938XYS						

M72-81

	MCW MetroRider MF150/56	MCW	B22F*	1988	*M75/6/9/81 are B13FL

M72	E307YDS	**M74**	E309YDS	**M76**	E311YDS	**M78**	E313YDS	**M80**	E315YDS
M73	E308YDS	**M75**	E310YDS	**M77**	E312YDS	**M79**	E314YDS	**M81**	E316YDS

M82-113

	MCW MetroRider MF154/12	MCW	B33F	1988	

M82	E179BNS	**M89**	E186BNS	**M96**	E193BNS	**M102**	E199BNS	**M108**	E205BNS
M83	E180BNS	**M90**	E187BNS	**M97**	E194BNS	**M103**	E200BNS	**M109**	E206BNS
M84	E181BNS	**M91**	E188BNS	**M98**	E195BNS	**M104**	E201BNS	**M110**	E207BNS
M85	E182BNS	**M92**	E189BNS	**M99**	E196BNS	**M105**	E202BNS	**M111**	E208BNS
M86	E183BNS	**M93**	E190BNS	**M100**	E197BNS	**M106**	E203BNS	**M112**	E209BNS
M87	E184BNS	**M94**	E191BNS	**M101**	E198BNS	**M107**	E204BNS	**M113**	E210BNS
M88	E185BNS	**M95**	E192BNS						

M114	F238EDS	MCW MetroRider MF154/1	MCW	C28F	1989	
M115	H844UUA	Optare MetroRider MR09	Optare	B29F	1991	Ex Optare demonstrator, 1991

M116-120

	MCW MetroRider MF158	MCW	B31F*	1988	Ex Colchester, 1991
					*M116 is DP29F

M116	F111NPU	**M117**	F112NPU	**M118**	F113NPU	**M119**	F114NPU	**M120**	F115NPU

M121	H398SYG	Optare MetroRider MR09	Optare	B29F	1990	Ex Optare demonstrator, 1991
M123	F672YOK	MCW MetroRider MF150/113	MCW	B23F	1988	Ex West Midlands Travel, 1991
M124	F673YOK	MCW MetroRider MF150/113	MCW	B23F	1988	Ex West Midlands Travel, 1991

MB1-5

	MCW Metrobus DR101/5	MCW	H46/31F	1979

MB1	GGA750T	**MB2**	GGA751T	**MB3**	GGA752T	**MB4**	GGA753T	**MB5**	GGA754T

MB6-20

	MCW Metrobus DR102/26	Alexander RH	H45/33F	1982

MB6	EUS101X	**MB9**	EUS104X	**MB12**	EUS107X	**MB15**	EUS110X	**MB18**	EUS113X
MB7	EUS102X	**MB10**	EUS105X	**MB13**	EUS108X	**MB16**	EUS111X	**MB19**	EUS114X
MB8	EUS103X	**MB11**	EUS106X	**MB14**	EUS109X	**MB17**	EUS112X	**MB20**	EUS115X

MB21-30

	MCW Metrobus DR102/31	MCW	H46/31F	1983

MB21	KGG162Y	**MB23**	KGG164Y	**MB25**	KGG166Y	**MB27**	KGG168Y	**MB29**	KGG170Y
MB22	KGG163Y	**MB24**	KGG165Y	**MB26**	KGG167Y	**MB28**	KGG169Y	**MB30**	KGG171Y

MB31-43

	MCW Metrobus DR102/36	MCW	H46/31F*	1983	*MB35 is H46/23FL

MB31	MUS309Y	**MB34**	MUS312Y	**MB37**	A731RNS	**MB40**	A734RNS	**MB42**	A736RNS
MB32	MUS310Y	**MB35**	MUS313Y	**MB38**	A732RNS	**MB41**	A735RNS	**MB43**	A737RNS
MB33	MUS311Y	**MB36**	A730RNS	**MB39**	A733RNS					

MB44	A738RNS	MCW Metrobus DR132/4	MCW	H46/31F	1983
MB45	A739RNS	MCW Metrobus DR132/4	MCW	H46/31F	1983

MB46-70

	MCW Metrobus DR102/72	MCW	H46/31F*	1989	*MBCs are DPH43/29F

MB46	G384OGD	**MB51**	G389OGD	**MB56**	G394OGD	**MB61**	G399OGD	**MBC66**	G404OGD
MB47	G385OGD	**MB52**	G390OGD	**MB57**	G395OGD	**MBC62**	G400OGD	**MB67**	G405OGD
MB48	G386OGD	**MB53**	G391OGD	**MB58**	G396OGD	**MBC63**	G401OGD	**MB68**	G406OGD
MB49	G387OGD	**MB54**	G392OGD	**MB59**	G397OGD	**MBC64**	G402OGD	**MB69**	G407OGD
MB50	G388OGD	**MB55**	G393OGD	**MB60**	G398OGD	**MBC65**	G403OGD	**MB70**	G408OGD

Special Liveries:
Overall advertisements: A129, AH2, 53, 64, 87/8, 93/9, LA1426, MB58.

STRATHTAY

Strathtay Scottish Omnibuses Ltd, Seagate Bus Station, Dundee, DD1 2HR

Strathtay was formed in 1985 from the Tayside depots of Midland and Northern. It was to be the only SBG company to be sold to a non-Scottish buyer, being now owned by The Yorkshire Traction Company Ltd. However, the new owner has retained the existing management and the vehicles carry the same livery. So apart from the arrival of a few vehicles from Yorkshire and Lincolnshire, there is little evidence of a new order. The Yorkshire connection has brought the Bristol VRT to the fleet for the first time.

Largely as a result of the loss of tenders, services west of Perth have been abandoned in favour of local arch-rival Stagecoach, and as a result the depot at Crieff has closed.

Routemaster operation by Strathtay in Perth ceased late in 1991, but the type is still to be found in Dundee.

Depots are at Arbroath, Blairgowrie, Dundee, Forfar, Montrose and Perth. The livery is french blue, orange and white.

The remaining Strathtay Routemasters now operate in and around Dundee and most are in the livery displayed on SR20. Once RM917 with London Buses, it is seen heading out of the city for Kingoodie.
Stewart Brown

Evidence of the new ownership was the arrival of seven Bristol VRTs from the parent company, Yorkshire Traction. Painted into Strathtay livery at Barnsley they are fitted with the Leyland 510 engine used in the Leyland National. Mike Fowler

Strathtay acquired
five Daimler
Fleetlines from
Greater Manchester
in 1987. Fitted with
Northern Counties
bodywork, they add
another design of
bodywork. SD21 is
seen in Dundee on
cross-city service 76.
C.M. Anderson

Ten Leyland
Olympians were
transferred to
Strathtay from
Northern Scottish on
formation. Four were
bodied by Alexander,
of which one, SO4, is
seen in Montrose.
The remaining six
were bodied by
Eastern Coach Works
and SO10 is seen
setting out from
Montrose for
Ferryden.
Stewart Brown

The four Leyland Tigers with Alexander P-type bodies are to be found on Perth city services. SBT4 is seen in Perth working service 6 to Moncreiff.
Murdoch Currie

SL40 is typical of the Scottish Bus Group's purchases for stage work. Fitted with Alexander's AYS-type body this Leyland Leopard is seen in Dundee.
Mick Fowler

Once Northern NPE64, Leyland Leopard SL23 undergoes a driver changeover at Arbroath depot on the limited stop service 40X. Strathtay have taken the opportunity to purchase many cherished index marks, one of the unusual ones being VOH640.
Murdoch Currie

Leyland Tiger ST8 is seen in a wet Dundee bus station. Fitted with the early version of the Duple Laser it supports both the Tiger's head and Leyland badges.
Mike Fowler

Originally a Northern vehicle, Tiger ST11 is fitted with an Alexander TE-type body. It is seen in Dundee having worked service 40X from Arbroath.
Stewart Brown

A number of minibuses have been acquired for school contracts including SS5, a Mercedes-Benz with Pilcher Greene conversion.
Murdoch Currie

Strathtay   **115**

The Dormobile Renaults were acquired to compete with Stagecoach on Perth city services. However, they are now deployed throughout the company's area. SS13 is seen while outward bound from Perth in Bridge of Earn. Max Fowler

SS23 is a Mercedes-Benz L508D with a Whittaker conversion. It is based at Arbroath where it was photographed in July 1991. Stewart Brown

STRATHTAY Fleet List

SB1-7

		Bristol VRT/SL3/501		Eastern Coach Works	H43/31F*	1976-77	Ex Yorkshire Traction, 1991 *SB1/2/6 are H43/34F

SB1	KKY834P	SB3	OWE853R	SB5	OWE857R	SB6	KKY833P	SB7	OWE858R
SB2	KKY835P	SB4	OWE854R						

SBT1	A112ESA	Leyland Tiger TRBTL11/2R	Alexander P	B52F	1983	Ex Northern Scottish, 1987
SBT2	A113ESA	Leyland Tiger TRBTL11/2R	Alexander P	B52F	1983	Ex Northern Scottish, 1987
SBT3	A114ESA	Leyland Tiger TRBTL11/2R	Alexander P	B52F	1983	Ex Northern Scottish, 1987
SBT4	A115ESA	Leyland Tiger TRBTL11/2R	Alexander P	B52F	1983	Ex Northern Scottish, 1987
SD11	CWG914L	Daimler Fleetline CRG6LXB	Alexander AD	H44/31F	1973	Ex Northern Scottish, 1985
SD12	ULS673T	Leyland Fleetline FE30AGR	Eastern Coach Works	H43/32F	1979	Ex Midland Scottish, 1985
SD13	YSR152T	Leyland Fleetline FE30AGR	Eastern Coach Works	H43/32F	1978	Ex Northern Scottish, 1985
SD14	ASA25T	Leyland Fleetline FE30AGR	Eastern Coach Works	H43/32F	1978	Ex Northern Scottish, 1985
SD15	LMS156W	Leyland Fleetline FE30AGR	Alexander AD	H44/31F	1980	Ex Midland Scottish, 1985
SD16	LMS168W	Leyland Fleetline FE30AGR	Alexander AD	H44/31F	1980	Ex Midland Scottish, 1985

SD17-22

Daimler Fleetline CRG6LXB — Northern Counties — H43/32F — 1976 — Ex Greater Manchester, 1987

SD17	LJA476P	SD18	LJA477P	SD19	LJA478P	SD21	LJA481P	SD22	LJA483P

SL19	ORU738	Leyland Leopard PSU3E/4R	Duple Dominant Express	C49F	1977	Ex Northern Scottish, 1985
SL20	365DXU	Leyland Leopard PSU3E/4R	Duple Dominant Express	C49F	1977	Ex Northern Scottish, 1985
SL21	670CLT	Leyland Leopard PSU3D/4R	Alexander AT	C49F	1978	Ex Midland Scottish, 1985
SL22	XHR877	Leyland Leopard PSU3D/4R	Alexander AT	C49F	1978	Ex Midland Scottish, 1985
SL23	VOH640	Leyland Leopard PSU3E/4R	Alexander AT	C49F	1979	Ex Northern Scottish, 1985
SL24	XNR453	Leyland Leopard PSU3E/4R	Alexander AT	C49F	1979	Ex Northern Scottish, 1985
SL26	YSV318	Leyland Leopard PSU3E/4R	Alexander AT	C49F	1979	Ex Northern Scottish, 1985
SL27	691DYE	Leyland Leopard PSU3E/4R	Duple Dominant I Express	C49F	1979	Ex Northern Scottish, 1985
SL28	YJU694	Leyland Leopard PSU3E/4R	Duple Dominant I Express	C49F	1979	Ex Northern Scottish, 1985
SL29	VLT217	Leyland Leopard PSU3E/4R	Duple Dominant II Express	C49F	1979	Ex Midland Scottish, 1985
SL30	VLT221	Leyland Leopard PSU3E/4R	Duple Dominant II Express	C49F	1979	Ex Midland Scottish, 1985
SL31	ULS330T	Leyland Leopard PSU3E/4R	Alexander AYS	B53F	1979	Ex Midland Scottish, 1985
SL32	143CLT	Leyland Leopard PSU3F/4R	Duple Dominant II Express	C49F	1980	Ex Midland Scottish, 1985
SL34	866PYC	Leyland Leopard PSU3F/4R	Alexander AT	C49F	1980	Ex Northern Scottish, 1985

SL35-43

Leyland Leopard PSU3E/4R* — Alexander AYS — B53F — 1980-82 — Ex Northern Scottish, 1985
*SL39-43 are PSU3G/4R

SL35	GSO85V	SL37	GSO87V	SL39	XSS39Y	SL41	XSS41Y	SL43	XSS43Y
SL36	GSO86V	SL38	GSO88V	SL40	XSS40Y	SL42	XSS42Y		

SL44	LMS385W	Leyland Leopard PSU3F/4R	Alexander AYS	DP49F	1980	Ex Midland Scottish, 1985
SL45	TMS409X	Leyland Leopard PSU3G/4R	Alexander AYS	B53F	1982	Ex Midland Scottish, 1985
SL46	XMS424Y	Leyland Leopard PSU3G/4R	Alexander AYS	B53F	1982	Ex Midland Scottish, 1985

SL54-61

Leyland Leopard PSU3D/4R — Alexander AYS — B53F — 1977 — Ex Fife Scottish, 1987

SL54	YSF74S	SL56	YSF79S	SL59	YSF82S	SL60	YSF87S	SL61	YSF88S
SL55	YSF75S	SL57	YSF80S						

SL63	ULS323T	Leyland Leopard PSU3E/4R	Alexander AYS	B53F	1979	Ex Kelvin Scottish, 1987
SL65	ULS321T	Leyland Leopard PSU3E/4R	Alexander AYS	DP49F	1979	Ex Kelvin Scottish, 1987
SL66	ULS335T	Leyland Leopard PSU3E/4R	Alexander Midland	B53F	1979	Ex Kelvin Scottish, 1987
SL68	WLT316	Leyland Leopard PSU3E/4R	Duple Dominant II Express	C49F	1979	Ex Kelvin Scottish, 1988

SM1-11

MCW Metrobus DR102 — Alexander RL — H45/33F — 1982-86 — SM1-8 ex Midland Scottish, 1985

SM1	ULS627X	SM4	ULS632X	SM6	BLS424Y	SM8	B97PKS	SM10	D310DSR
SM2	ULS628X	SM5	ULS633X	SM7	BLS433Y	SM9	D309DSR	SM11	D311DSR
SM3	ULS631X								

SM12-16

MCW Metrobus DR102/60 — Alexander RL — H47/33F — 1987

SM12	E412GES	SM13	E413GES	SM14	E414GES	SM15	E415GES	SM16	E416GES

SO1	SSA8X	Leyland Olympian ONLXB/1R	Alexander RL	H45/32F	1981	Ex Northern Scottish, 1985
SO2	SSA9X	Leyland Olympian ONLXB/1R	Alexander RL	H45/32F	1981	Ex Northern Scottish, 1985
SO3	SSA10X	Leyland Olympian ONLXB/1R	Alexander RL	H45/32F	1981	Ex Northern Scottish, 1985
SO4	SSA11X	Leyland Olympian ONLXB/1R	Alexander RL	H45/32F	1981	Ex Northern Scottish, 1985

SO5-10

Leyland Olympian ONLXB/1R — Eastern Coach Works — H45/32F — 1982 — Ex Northern Scottish, 1985

SO5	TSO18X	SO7	TSO25X	SO8	TSO26X	SO9	TSO27X	SO10	TSO28X
SO6	TSO22X								

SO11-19

Leyland Olympian ONLXB/1RV — Alexander RL — H47/32F — 1986-87

SO11	C111BTS	SO16	C116BTS	SO17	D817EES	SO18	D818EES	SO19	D819EES

SO20-25

Leyland Olympian ONLXB/1R — Alexander RL — DPH41/32F — 1983 — Ex Fife Scottish, 1988

SO20	PSU371	SO22	PSU373	SO23	PSU374	SO24	PSU376	SO25	PSU375
SO21	PSU372								

SR1-25

SR1-25		AEC Routemaster 5RM		Park Royal		H36/28R	1959-64 Ex London Buses, 1986-88		

SR1u	WTS225A	SR5u	WTS404A	SR14	YSL76B	SR20	WTS102A	SR23	AST415A
SR2u	WTS245A	SR6w	YSL32B	SR17	WTS109A	SR21	XSL220A	SR24	WTS186A
SR3u	WTS329A	SR12	WTS101A	SR19	WTS128A	SR22	AST416A	SR25	WTS333A
SR4u	YTS973A								

SS4	A342ASF	Mercedes-Benz L608D	Mercedes-Benz	DP16F	1983	Ex Scottish CI for Spastics, 1988
SS5	GYS77X	Mercedes-Benz L508D	Pilcher-Greene	DP12F	1982	Ex Jewish Assn for Handicapped, 1989

SS6-18

SS6-18		Renault S56		Dormobile Routemaker	B25F	1989

SS6	G889FJW	SS9	G892FJW	SS12	G895FJW	SS15	G898FJW	SS17	G900FJW
SS7	G890FJW	SS10	G893FJW	SS13	G896FJW	SS16	G899FJW	SS18	G901FJW
SS8	G891FJW	SS11	G894FJW	SS14	G897FJW				

SS19	D307MHS	Dodge S56	Alexander AM	B21F	1986	Ex Kelvin Central, 1990
SS20	D308MHS	Dodge S56	Alexander AM	B21F	1986	Ex Kelvin Central, 1990
SS21	D309MHS	Dodge S56	Alexander AM	B21F	1986	Ex Kelvin Central, 1990
SS22	SSS539X	Mercedes-Benz L508D	Reeve Burgess	C19F	1981	Ex Mair, Dyce, 1990
SS23	EUS798X	Mercedes-Benz L508D	Whittaker	C19F	1982	Ex Barnes, Bedlington, 1990
SS24	A755UGE	Mercedes-Benz 207D	Devon Conversions	C12F	1984	Ex McFall, Glasgow, 1990
SS25	D566VBV	Freight Rover Sherpa 374	Dormobile	B16F	1986	Ex RoadCar, 1991
SS26	D568VBV	Freight Rover Sherpa 374	Dormobile	B16F	1986	Ex RoadCar, 1991
SS27	D570VBV	Freight Rover Sherpa 374	Dormobile	B16F	1986	Ex RoadCar, 1991
SS28	E104UNE	Mercedes-Benz 609D	PMT	C19F	1988	Ex Shearings, 1991
ST3	WLT743	Leyland Tiger TRCTL11/3R	East Lancashire (1992)	DP55F	1982	Ex Northern Scottish, 1985
ST4	WLT921	Leyland Tiger TRCTL11/3R	Duple 340 (1987)	C48FT	1982	Ex Northern Scottish, 1985
ST6	VLT183	Leyland Tiger TRBTL11/2R	Duple Dominant II Express	C45F	1983	Ex Midland Scottish, 1985
ST7	VLT298	Leyland Tiger TRBTL11/2R	Alexander TE	C46F	1983	Ex Midland Scottish, 1985
ST8	FSU309	Leyland Tiger TRCTL11/3RH	Duple Laser	C46FT	1984	Ex Midland Scottish, 1985
ST9	VLT93	Leyland Tiger TRCTL11/3RH	Duple Laser	C46FT	1984	Ex Midland Scottish, 1985
ST10	VLT45	Leyland Tiger TRCTL11/3RH	Duple Laser 2	C46FT	1985	Ex Midland Scottish, 1985
ST11	WLT917	Leyland Tiger TRCTL11/2RP	Alexander TE	C47F	1985	Ex Northern Scottish, 1985
ST12	WLT427	Leyland Tiger TRCTL11/2RP	Alexander TE	C47F	1985	Ex Northern Scottish, 1985
ST17	821DYE	Leyland Tiger TRCTL11/3R	East Lancashire (1992)	DP55F	1981	Ex Kelvin Scottish, 1985
ST18	415VYA	Leyland Tiger TRCTL11/3RH	Alexander TC	C55F	1987	

ST19-23

ST19-23		Leyland Tiger TRCLXC/2RH		Alexander TE	C49F	1985 Ex Kelvin Central, 1989

ST19	HSK765	ST20	HSK766	ST21	HSK791	ST22	HSK792	ST23	WLT784

ST24	WLT610	Leyland Tiger TRCLXC/2RH	Duple 320	C49FT	1986	Ex Kelvin Central, 1990
ST25	WLT943	Leyland Tiger TRCTL11/3RZ	Duple 340	C49FT	1987	Ex Kelvin Central, 1990
ST26	WLT759	Leyland Tiger TRCTL11/3RZ	Duple 340	C49FT	1987	Ex Kelvin Central, 1990

Previous Registrations:

143CLT	GLS948V	PSU375	A990FLS	WTS102A	WLT917
365DXU	RRS54R	PSU376	A989FLS	WTS109A	VLT93
415VYA	D718FES	VLT45	B133PMS	WTS128A	VLT221
670CLT	GLS266S	VLT93	A127EGG	WTS186A	143CLT
691DYE	CRS72T	VLT183	BLS110Y	WTS245A	VLT298
821DYE	BSG546W, 17CLT, XDS685W	VLT217	ULS648T	WTS329A	WLT759
866PYC	JSA105V	VLT221	ULS649T	WTS333A	WLT316
AST415A	VLT45	VLT298	BMS512Y	WTS225A	WLT943
AST416A	VLT191	VOH640	CRS64T	WTS404A	WLT702
FSU309	A126ESG, VLT42, A651XGG	WLT316	ULS650T	XHR877	GLS272S
ORU738	RRS45R	WLT427	B334LSO	XNR453	CRS65T
HSK765	C258FGG	WLT610	C114JCS	XSL220A	VLT26
HSK766	C259FGG	WLT743	VSS4X	YJU694	CRS75T
HSK791	C260FGG	WLT759	D316SGB	YSL32B	821DYE
HSK792	C261FGG	WLT784	C262FGG	YSL76B	ALD911B
PSU371	A985FLS	WLT917	B333LSO	YSR152T	ASA21T
PSU372	A986FLS	WLT921	VSS5X	YSV318	CRS67T
PSU373	A987FLS	WLT943	D315SGB	YTS973A	17CLT
PSU374	A988FLS	WTS101A	VLT183		

Special Liveries:
Scottish Citylink: ST4,9,10,25/6.

TAYSIDE

Tayside Public Transport Co Ltd, 44-48 East Dock Street, Dundee, DD1 3JS

The company was established in 1986 to continue the bus operations of Tayside Regional Council, itself the successor to Dundee's Corporation trams, buses and (two) trolleybuses.

In what is understood to be a unique situation, every employee subscribed £500 to Taybus Holdings Ltd which in June 1991 bought Tayside Public Transport from the Regional Council

The company continues as the main provider of city transport in Dundee. The coach fleet was substantially augmented in 1990 when the neighbouring business of Greyhound Luxury Coaches was acquired. Coaches now operate under a Tayside Greyhound banner.

There have been a few changes to the bus fleet which because of the operator's preference for Volvo products has the unusual distinction of having no rear-engined vehicles.

The depot is at East Dock Street and the liveries are cream, mid blue and dark blue for buses with white and mid blue for coaches.

Since 1977 the standard Tayside bus has been the Ailsa construction of the Volvo based chassis and latterly the Volvo product. For most of the time the bodywork has been by Alexander. An example of the early version is 264, seen in Reform Street, Dundee.
Stewart Brown

Following an accident, 272 was converted to open-top configuration and renumbered 300. It is seen working the Tesco contract service.
Stewart Brown

Mark III Volvo-Ailsa 46 was painted in a representation of the Dundee Corporation green livery in recognition of the city's octo-centenary in 1991. Mike Fowler

Once a devotee of dual doors, Tayside is gradually rebuilding vehicles to single door configuration. Northern Counties-bodied Volvo-Ailsa 56 was still to be so treated when photographed in Albert Square, Dundee in June 1991. Murdoch Currie

The first order for Volvo Citybus included two fitted out with coach bodies by East Lancashire. No. 89 is seen on local service 4 passing through the city. Stewart Brown

The newest buses in the fleet are fifteen Volvo Citybuses fitted with Alexander R-type bodies featuring flat glass screens on both upper and lower decks. J. Burnett

'Dennis the Menace' collided with a pillar of the Tay Bridge, so now there are only three Wee Buses left. Photographed in Dundee centre is 'Beryl the Peril'. M.M. Fowler

TAYSIDE Fleet List

1-35

Ailsa B55-10 MkII | Alexander AV | H44/31D* | 1980 | * 1,2 are H44/34F

1	CSL601V	8	CSL608V	15	CSL615V	22	DSP922V	29	DSP929V
2	CSL602V	9	CSL609V	16	CSL616V	23	DSP923V	30	DSP930V
3	CSL603V	10	CSL610V	17	CSL617V	24	DSP924V	31	DSP931V
4	CSL604V	11	CSL611V	18	CSL618V	25	DSP925V	32	DSP932V
5	CSL605V	12	CSL612V	19	CSL619V	26	DSP926V	33	DSP933V
6	CSL606V	13	CSL613V	20	CSL620V	27	DSP927V	34	DSP934V
7	CSL607V	14	CSL614V	21	DSP921V	28	DSP928V	35	DSP935V

36-50

Volvo-Ailsa B55-10 MkIII | Alexander RV | H48/36F | 1981

36	HSR36X	39	HSR39X	42	HSR42X	45	HSR45X	48	HSR48X
37	HSR37X	40	HSR40X	43	HSR43X	46	HSR46X	49	HSR49X
38	HSR38X	41	HSR41X	44	HSR44X	47	HSR47X	50	HSR50X

51-60

Volvo-Ailsa B55-10 MkIII | Northern Counties | H48/36F | 1983

51	OSN851Y	53	OSN853Y	55	OSN855Y	57	OSN857Y	59	OSN859Y
52	OSN852Y	54	OSN854Y	56	OSN856Y	58	OSN858Y	60	OSN860Y

61-85

Volvo-Ailsa B55-10 MkIII | East Lancashire | H48/36F* | 1983 | *68-71/4/6/7/80-2 are H51/33D

61	OSN861Y	66	OSN866Y	71	OSN871Y	76	A76SSP	81	A81SSP
62	OSN862Y	67	OSN867Y	72	OSN872Y	77	A77SSP	82	A82SSP
63	OSN863Y	68	OSN868Y	73	OSN873Y	78	A78SSP	83	A83SSP
64	OSN864Y	69	OSN869Y	74	OSN874Y	79	A79SSP	84	A84SSP
65	OSN865Y	70	OSN870Y	75	OSN875Y	80	A80SSP	85	A85SSP

86-90

Volvo Citybus B10M-50 | East Lancashire | H51/38F* | 1984 | *89/90 are CH45/33F

86	A286TSN	87	A287TSN	88	A288TSN	89	PYJ136	90	OTS271

91-105

Volvo Citybus B10M-50 | Alexander RV | H47/37F | 1989

91	G91PES	94	G94PES	97	G97PES	100	G100PES	103	G103PES
92	G92PES	95	G95PES	98	G98PES	101	G101PES	104	G104PES
93	G93PES	96	G96PES	99	G99PES	102	G102PES	105	G105PES

140u	NSP340R	Ailsa B55-10	Alexander AV	H44/31D	1976
141u	NSP341R	Ailsa B55-10	Alexander AV	H44/31D	1976
184	ETS964	Daimler CVG6	Metro Cammell	H37/28R	1955

201	D701EES	Dodge S56	Alexander AM	B23F	1987	
202	D702EES	Dodge S56	Alexander AM	B23F	1987	
204	D704EES	Dodge S56	Alexander AM	DP23F	1987	
223	NSV622	Volvo B58-56	Plaxton Supreme IV Exp	C53F	1982	Ex Greyhound, Dundee, 1990
224	VSR591	Volvo B58-56	Plaxton Supreme IV Exp	C49FT	1980	Ex Greyhound, Dundee, 1990
225	NSV621	Volvo B58-56	Plaxton Supreme IV Exp	C49FT	1980	Ex Greyhound, Dundee, 1990
226	PSR781	Volvo B58-56	Plaxton Supreme IV Exp	C49FT	1980	Ex Greyhound, Dundee, 1990
227	220BSR	Volvo B10M-56	Plaxton Paramount 3200 Ex	C49F	1983	Ex Greyhound, Dundee, 1990
228	2741AP	Leyland Leopard PSU3G/4R	Plaxton Supreme V Exp	C53F	1982	
229	2133PL	Leyland Leopard PSU3G/4R	Plaxton Supreme V Exp	C53F	1982	
230	5414PH	Leyland Leopard PSU3G/4R	Plaxton Supreme V Exp	C53F	1982	
231	7017PF	Leyland Leopard PSU3G/4R	Plaxton Supreme V Exp	C53F	1982	
232	DXC330	Leyland Tiger TRCTL11/1R	Reeve Burgess Riviera	C35F	1984	
233	EUE489	Leyland Tiger TRCTL11/1R	Reeve Burgess Riviera	C35F	1984	
234	LVG263	Leyland Tiger TRCTL11/1R	Reeve Burgess Riviera	C35F	1984	
235	LXJ462	Leyland Tiger TRCTL11/1R	Reeve Burgess Riviera	C35F	1984	

236-270

		Ailsa B55-10 MkII	Alexander AV	H44/31D	1977-79

236u	SSN236S	243u	SSN243S	251u	SSN251S	258u	WTS258T	265u	WTS265T
237u	SSN237S	244u	SSN244S	252	SSN252S	259u	WTS259T	266	WTS266T
238u	SSN238S	246u	SSN246S	253	SSN253S	260	WTS260T	267	WTS267T
239u	SSN239S	247	SSN247S	254	SSN254S	261	WTS261T	268u	WTS268T
240u	SSN240S	248u	SSN248S	255	SSN255S	262	WTS262T	269	WTS269T
241u	SSN241S	249	SSN249S	256	WTS256T	263	WTS263T	270	WTS270T
242u	SSN242S	250	SSN250S	257	WTS257T	264	WTS264T		

273	WTS273T	Ailsa B55-10 MkII	Alexander AV	H44/31D	1979	
274	WTS274T	Ailsa B55-10 MkII	Alexander AV	H44/31D	1979	
275	WTS275T	Ailsa B55-10 MkII	Alexander AV	H44/31D	1979	
276	WTS276T	Ailsa B55-10 MkII	Alexander AV	H44/31D	1979	
300	WTS272T	Ailsa B55-10 MkII	Alexander AV	O44/31D	1979	
TC1	LIW9278	Volvo B10M-61	Ikarus Blue Danube	C49F	1988	Ex Greyhound, Dundee, 1990
TC2	LIW9279	Volvo B10M-61	Ikarus Blue Danube	C49F	1988	Ex Greyhound, Dundee, 1990
TC3	CTS917	Volvo B10M-61	Irizar Pyrennean	C49FT	1984	Ex Greyhound, Dundee, 1990
TC4	AJX158	Volvo B10M-61	Irizar Pyrennean	C49FT	1984	Ex Greyhound, Dundee, 1990
TC5	LXI2961	Volvo B10M-61	Irizar Pyrennean	C49FT	1985	Ex Greyhound, Dundee, 1990
TC6	LXI2630	Volvo B10M-61	Irizar Pyrennean	C49FT	1985	Ex Greyhound, Dundee, 1990
TC7	6689DP	Volvo B10M-61	Irizar Pyrennean	C49FT	1986	Ex Tramontana, Carfin, 1986
TC8	666TPJ	Volvo B10M-61	Irizar Pyrennean	C49FT	1987	
TC9	PSU339	Dennis Javelin 12SDA1911	Duple 320	C53FT	1988	
TC10	PSU340	Dennis Javelin 12SDA1911	Duple 320	C53FT	1988	
TC11	USU661	Dennis Javelin 12SDA1911	Duple 320	C53FT	1989	
TC12	USU662	Dennis Javelin 12SDA1911	Duple 320	C53FT	1989	
TC13	UHK585	Leyland Tiger TRCTL11/3RH	Plaxton Paramount 3500	C51F	1984	
TC14	XLD627	Leyland Tiger TRCTL11/3RH	Plaxton Paramount 3500	C51F	1984	
TC15	ETS117	Volvo B10M-56	Plaxton Supreme V Exp	C53F	1982	Ex Greyhound, Dundee, 1990
TC16	NSV616	Volvo B10M-56	Plaxton Paramount 3200 Ex	C45FT	1983	Ex Greyhound, Dundee, 1990

Previous Registrations:

220BSR	OES342Y	EUE489	B833VSR	OTS271	A290TSN
2133PL	KES303X	LIW9278	E736KSP	PSR781	DSR478V
2741AP	KES302X	LIW9279	E737KSP	PSU339	E307KES
5414PH	KES304X	LVG263	B834VSR	PSU340	E308KES
666TPJ	D312ETS	LXI2961	B917CSU	PYJ136	A289TSN
6689DP	D491NSU	LXI2630	B918CSU	UHK585	A709SSR
7017PF	KES305X	LXJ462	B835VSR	USU661	F313NSP
AJX158	A947VGG	NSV616	OES343Y	USU662	F314NSP
CTS917	A946VGG	NSV621	DSR477V	VSR591	DSR476V
DXC330	B832VSR	NSV622	KSP698X	XLD627	A710SSR
ETS117	LSP502X				

Special Liveries:
Dundee Corporation: 184
Overall Advertisements: 48, 70, 95.

Named Vehicles:
89 *River Tay*, 90 *River Tummel*, 201 *Beryl the Peril*, 202 *Korky the Cat*, 204 *Desperate Dan*, 228 *Glen Clova*, 229 *Glen Lyon*, 230 *Glen Shee*, 231 *Glen Esk*, 232 *Strathearn*, 233 *Strathmore*, 234 *Strathtay*, 235 *Strathtummel*, 300 *Broughty Castle*, TC9 *Glen Almond*, TC10 *Glen Garry*, TC7 *Dundee, City of Discovery*, TC8 *Bonnie Dundee*, TC11 *Glen Eagles*, TC12 *Glen Devon*, TC13 *Loch Tay*, TC14 *Loch Rannoch*,

WESTERN

Western Scottish Omnibuses Ltd, Nursery Avenue, Kilmarnock, KA1 3JD

Western has for many years been the principal bus and coach operator in south-west Scotland. In 1985, in anticipation of deregulation, the depots, vehicles and services based in Glasgow, Renfrewshire, Largs and Rothesay were hived off to a new company, Clydeside Scottish Omnibuses Ltd. However, when it was announced that the Scottish Bus Group companies were to be sold individually, it was decided to re-merge Western and Clydeside, a move which was not popular with Clydeside staff. The Clydeside faction eventually agreed with Western management that if Western was sold to the management/employee team, then the Clydeside area would be sold on to an employee-owned company, Clydeside 2000, which had backing from Luton & District.

Partly because of the foregoing, Western was the last of the SBG companies to be sold, being sold to the management and employees in October 1991. The depots, vehicles and services based in Glasgow, Renfrewshire and Largs were immediately sold to Clydeside 2000. Thus Western is restored to the position which existed from 1985 to 1989 when it served Ayrshire, Dumfries and Galloway, and Carlisle, but on this occasion retains Rothesay on the Isle of Bute.

There is a fair amount of competition from a variety of other operators throughout the area, though that in Dumfries lessened with the collapse of the Dickson business in 1991.

As with most other former SBG companies, there is a lack of newer vehicles in the fleet. The red and cream livery is now virtually extinct, most vehicles being in the black, white, grey and red livery, a stylish version of which has been developed for coaches.

Depots are at Ayr, Cumnock, Dumfries, Girvan, Kilmarnock, Rothesay and Stranraer. Some vehicles are coded L for London Service pool, though Western no longer has the Citylink contract.

NR829 is one of a pair of Daimler Fleetlines fitted with Alexander bodywork that were acquired from Kelvin Scottish in 1987. Seen at Irvine Cross, it still displays the message that Western was 'The Best British Bus Company' in 1987.
S. McDonald

Photographed while still on hire and carrying GM Buses livery and a temporary fleet number/is one of eight Atlanteans that have now been taken into the fleet. Max Fowler

The Volvo Citybuses are usually to be found on the trunk route from Ayr through Kilmarnock to Glasgow. V898, re-numbered|from V998 since the photograph was taken, has the uncommon Alexander RVC body. It is seen leaving Buchanan bus station, Glasgow on a Citylink journey to Ayr. Murdoch Currie

A typical Leopard bus in what was, until recently, Western's standard livery is L677 photographed while on a Kilmarnock town service. Alistair Douglas

Western was the only Scottish Bus Group company not to take delivery of new Leyland Nationals, but has since received several transferred from other companies. Several came from Kelvin Central though EGB89T, now renumbered L770, is the only surviving Mk1. It has been fitted with a DAF engine by Western.
Max Fowler

Some livery experiments are in progress utilising more grey and less black. The fleetname, as shown on Leyland Leopard L629, now features red flashes above and below the lettering.
Murdoch Currie

Extensively refurbished prior to entering service with Western is L777, one of the former Kelvin National 2s which have survived much longer than did many of the original type. While the majority of National 2s remain within former SBG companies many are now to be found elsewhere.
Stewart Brown

Western Scottish has traditionally retained vehicles south of the border at Carlisle though operations into Carlisle have now ceased. The area once used as Western's depot is now the bus station, while vehicles were moved to the Ribble depot, now transferred to Cumberland. Seen in Carlisle towards the end of operation is S479, one of the Seddons allocated to Dumfries. Murdoch Currie

Dennis Dorchester N421 with Alexander TC coachwork is seen in what is now regarded as the dual purpose livery. It is departing from Brodick Pier on the Isle of Arran, having just disembarked from the ferry of the same name. David Little

Dennis Dorchester N140 is now in the current Western Scottish coach livery of black and white with centre panels in two shades of grey. The body is the Plaxton Paramount 3500, one of six of the type in Western's fleet, all of which carry second-hand index marks, four transferred from London Routemasters.
Murdoch Currie

Ayr's 'Buzzers' are Alexander bodied Dodge S56s and these are gradually receiving the latest Western livery, though some have a black roof. Seen on service 1 in Ayr town centre is D225.
Max Fowler

Western hold the contract for Strathclyde PTE's Dial-a-Bus services in Ayrshire for which five Talbot Freeways are allocated. Sporting both Western and Strathclyde Transport names is T278, seen in Ayr in July 1991.
Murdoch Currie

WESTERN Fleet List

H105	VLT81	Duple 425 SDAK1503	Duple	C51FT	1986	
H106	VLT206	Duple 425 SDAK1503	Duple	C51FT	1986	
H107	VLT54	Duple 425 SDAK1503	Duple	C51FT	1985	
H108	J8WSB	Duple 425 SDAK1503	Duple	C49FT	1992	
N111	H661UWR	Dennis Javelin 11SDL1905	Duple 320	C53F	1991	Ex Wallace Arnold, 1992
N113	J13WSB	Dennis Javelin 11SDL1905	Plaxton Paramount 3200 III	C53F	1992	
N114	J14WSB	Dennis Javelin 11SDL1905	Plaxton Paramount 3200 III	C53F	1992	
N115	J15WSB	Dennis Javelin 11SDL1905	Plaxton Premiére	C53F	1992	

N140-145

Dennis Dorchester SDA810 — Plaxton Paramount 3500 — C55F — 1985 — *N143/4 are C51F

N140	VLT226	N142	VLT272	N143	YSV730	N144	YSV735
N141	WLT441						

N145 VLT245

V146-151

Volvo B10M-61 — Duple Goldliner IV — C46FT — 1982-83 Seating varies

V146	ESU435	V148	WLT538	V149	WLT774	V150	WLT809
V147	GSU950						

V151 WLT915

L172	13CLT	Leyland Tiger TRCTL11/3RZ	Duple 340	C48FT	1987	Ex Kelvin Central, 1990
L173	WLT546	Leyland Tiger TRCTL11/3RZ	Duple 340	C48FT	1987	Ex Kelvin Central, 1990
V185	WLT447	Volvo B10MT-53	Plaxton Paramount 4000RS	CH55/9FT	1985	Ex Highland Scottish, 1986

V191-197

Volvo B10M-61 — Plaxton Paramount 3500 — C44FT* — 1985 — *Seating varies

V191	VCS391	V194	VLT37	V195	WLT978	V196	WLT465

V197 WLT697

V198	WLT720	Volvo B10M-61	Berkhof Esprite	C53F	1985

Z201-218

Mercedes-Benz L608D — Alexander AM — B21F — 1986 — Ex Kelvin Scottish, 1987

Z201	C101KDS	Z207	D107NUS	Z210	D110NUS	Z213	D113NUS
Z204	C104KDS	Z208	D108NUS	Z211	D111NUS	Z214	D114NUS
Z205	C105KDS	Z209	D109NUS	Z212	D112NUS	Z215	D115NUS
Z206	C106KDS						

Z216 D116NUS, Z217 D117NUS, Z218 D118NUS

D222-260

Dodge S56 — Alexander AM — B25F* — 1987 — *D258 is DP25F

D222	D222NCS	D230	D230NCS	D238	D238NCS	D246	D246NCS
D223	D223NCS	D231	D231NCS	D239	D239NCS	D247	D247NCS
D224	D224NCS	D232	D232NCS	D240	D240NCS	D248	D248NCS
D225	D225NCS	D233	D233NCS	D241	D241NCS	D249	D249NCS
D226	D226NCS	D234	D234NCS	D242	D242NCS	D250	D250NCS
D227	D227NCS	D235	D235NCS	D243	D243NCS	D251	D251NCS
D228	D228NCS	D236	D236NCS	D244	D244NCS	D252	D252NCS
D229	D229NCS	D237	D237NCS	D245	D245NCS	D253	D253NCS

D254 D254NCS, D255 D255NCS, D256 D256NCS, D257 D257NCS, D258 D258NCS, D259 D259NCS, D260 D260NCS

Z262-271

Mercedes-Benz L608D — Alexander AM — B21F* — 1986 — Ex Kelvin Scottish, 1987 / *Z271 is DP21F

Z262	D122NUS	Z264	D124NUS	Z268	D128NUS	Z270	D130NUS
Z263	D123NUS	Z266	D136NUS	Z269	D129NUS		

Z271 D121NUS

T273	D94EKV	Talbot Freeway	Talbot	DP12FL	1987	Ex Carriageways, Wolfstean, 1992

T274-278

Talbot Freeway — Talbot — DP12FL — 1989-90

T274	F334JHS	T275	F335JHS	T276	F336JHS	T277	G825VGA

T278 G831VGA

D281-289

Dodge S56 — Alexander AM — B25F* — 1987 — Ex Clydeside Scottish, 1989 / *D281 is DP25F

D281	D301SDS	D283	D303SDS	D285	D305SDS	D287	D307SDS
D282	D302SDS	D284	D304SDS	D286	D306SDS		

D289 D309SDS

S400	803DYE	Seddon Pennine 7	Alexander AT	C24FL	1976	
R402	HDS566H	Daimler Fleetline CRG6LXB	Alexander AD	O44/31F	1970	Ex Clydeside Scottish, 1989

N403-410

Dennis Dorchester SDA801 — Plaxton Paramount 3200 Ex C49F — 1983 — N404/5/7-10 ex Clydeside, 1989

N403	703DYE	**N405**	WLT727	**N407**	WLT830	**N409**	WLT444	**N410** WLT874
N404	VLT104	**N406**	WLT794	**N408**	WLT652			

N416-421

Dennis Dorchester SDA811 — Alexander TC — C55F — 1987

N416	D216NCS	**N418**	D218NCS	**N419**	D219NCS	**N420**	D220NCS	**N421** D221NCS
N417	D217NCS							

V423	WLT439	Volvo B10M-61	Duple Dominant IV	C46FT	1981	
V424	WLT416	Volvo B10M-61	Duple Dominant IV	C55F	1981	Ex Clydeside Scottish, 1989
V426	WLT526	Volvo B10M-61	Duple Dominant IV	C55F	1982	Ex Clydeside Scottish, 1989
V427	FSU737	Volvo B10M-61	Duple Dominant IV	C46FT	1982	
V428	FSU739	Volvo B10M-61	Duple Dominant IV	C46FT	1982	
V429	VLT219	Volvo B10M-61	Duple Dominant IV	C46FT	1981	Ex Clydeside Scottish, 1989
V430	VLT154	Volvo B10M-61	Duple Dominant IV	C55F	1981	Ex Clydeside Scottish, 1989
V431	WLT415	Volvo B10M-61	Duple Dominant IV	C46FT	1981	
V432	VLT73	Volvo B10M-61	Duple Dominant IV	C51F	1981	Ex Clydeside Scottish, 1989

S434-482

Seddon Pennine 7 — Alexander AT — C49F* — 1979-80 *S438/9 are C45F, S470 is DP53F
S436/7/9/40/57-72/9 are ex Clydeside Scottish, 1988-89

S434	DSD934V	**S443**	DSD943V	**S452**	DSD952V	**S463**	DSD963V	**S476** DSD976V
S435	DSD935V	**S444**	DSD944V	**S453**	DSD953V	**S464**	DSD964V	**S477** DSD977V
S436	DSD936V	**S445**	DSD945V	**S454**	DSD954V	**S470**	DSD970V	**S478** DSD978V
S437	DSD937V	**S447**	DSD947V	**S455**	DSD955V	**S472**	DSD972V	**S479** DSD979V
S438	WLT501	**S448**	DSD948V	**S456**	DSD956V	**S473**	DSD973V	**S480** DSD980V
S439	WGA908V	**S449**	DSD949V	**S457**	DSD957V	**S474**	DSD974V	**S481** DSD981V
S440	DSD940V	**S450**	DSD950V	**S460**	DSD960V	**S475**	DSD975V	**S482** DSD982V
S442	DSD942V	**S451**	DSD951V	**S462**	DSD962V			

L499	PGA829V	Leyland Leopard PSU3F/4R	Alexander AT	C49F	1980	Ex Kelvin Scottish, 1988

S518-546

Seddon Pennine 7 — Alexander AY — B53F* — 1978-80 *S526 is DP49F

S518	YSD818T	**S523**	YSD823T	**S529**	ASD829T	**S535**	ASD835T	**S543** ASD843T
S519	YSD819T	**S525**	ASD825T	**S531**	ASD831T	**S536**	ASD836T	**S544** ASD844T
S520	YSD820T	**S526**	ASD826T	**S532**	ASD832T	**S537**	ASD837T	**S545** DSD983V
S521	YSD821T	**S527**	ASD827T	**S533**	ASD833T	**S542**	ASD842T	**S546** DSD984V
S522	YSD822T	**S528**	ASD828T	**S534**	ASD834T			

S551-564

Seddon Pennine 7 — Alexander AY — DP49F — 1979

S551	BSD851T	**S553**	BSD853T	**S558**	BSD858T	**S560**	BSD860T	**S563** BSD863T
S552	BSD852T	**S556**	BSD856T	**S559**	BSD859T	**S562**	BSD862T	**S564** BSD864T

L600	YSD350L	Leyland Leopard PSU3/3R	Alexander AY	B41F	1973	Ex Northern Scottish, 1987
L602	KSJ940P	Leyland Leopard PSU3B/4R	Alexander AYS	B53F	1976	
L629	GMS285S	Leyland Leopard PSU3E/4R	Alexander AYS	B53F	1978	Ex Kelvin Scottish, 1987
L630	GMS292S	Leyland Leopard PSU3D/4R	Alexander AYS	B53F	1978	Ex Kelvin Scottish, 1987

L631-687

Leyland Leopard PSU3D/4R — Alexander AY — B53F — 1977-78

L631	TSJ31S	**L667**	TSJ67S	**L671**	TSJ71S	**L679**	TSJ79S	**L685** TSJ85S
L632	TSJ32S	**L668**	TSJ68S	**L676**	TSJ76S	**L680**	TSJ80S	**L686** TSJ86S
L633	TSJ33S	**L669**	TSJ69S	**L677**	TSJ77S	**L683**	TSJ83S	**L687** TSJ87S
L664	TSJ64S	**L670**	TSJ70S	**L678**	TSJ78S			

L692-769

Leyland Leopard PSU3E/4R — Alexander AY — B53F* — 1978-80 *L737 is DP49F
L695-717/33 are ex Clydeside Scottish, 1989

L692	YCS92T	**L731**	BSJ931T	**L745**	GCS45V	**L751**	GCS51V	**L761** GCS61V
L695	BSJ895T	**L733**	GCS33V	**L746**	GCS46V	**L753**	GCS53V	**L762** GCS62V
L696	BSJ896T	**L737**	GCS37V	**L747**	GCS47V	**L757**	GCS57V	**L765** GCS65V
L717	BSJ917T	**L738**	GCS38V	**L748**	GCS48V	**L758**	GCS58V	**L769** GCS69V
L730	BSJ930T	**L741**	GCS41V	**L749**	GCS49V	**L760**	GCS60V	

L770	EGB89T	Leyland National 11351A/1R		B52F	1978	Ex Kelvin Central, 1989

L771-791

| | | | | | | | | | | Leyland National 2 NL116L11/1R | | B48F | 1980-81 | Ex Kelvin Scottish, 1988 |

L771	WAS771V	**L776**	MDS866V	**L780**	YFS308W	**L784**	RFS584V	**L788**	WAS768V
L773	RFS583V	**L777**	MDS859V	**L781**	MSO18W	**L785**	NLS985W	**L789**	NLS989W
L774	YFS304W	**L778**	MDS858V	**L782**	RFS582V	**L786**	SNS826W	**L790**	YFS310W
L775	MDS865V	**L779**	RFS579V	**L783**	NLS983W	**L787**	MSO17W	**L791**	YFS309W

A800	UNA853S	Leyland Atlantean AN68A/1R	Park Royal	H43/32F	1978	Ex GM Buses, 1991
A801	UNA863S	Leyland Atlantean AN68A/1R	Park Royal	H43/32F	1978	Ex GM Buses, 1991
A802	WVM884S	Leyland Atlantean AN68A/1R	Park Royal	H43/32F	1978	Ex GM Buses, 1991
A803	WVM877S	Leyland Atlantean AN68A/1R	Park Royal	H43/32F	1978	Ex GM Buses, 1991
A804	ANA211T	Leyland Atlantean AN68A/1R	Northern Counties	H43/32F	1978	Ex GM Buses, 1991
A805	BNC936T	Leyland Atlantean AN68A/1R	Park Royal	H43/32F	1979	Ex GM Buses, 1991
A806	RJA702R	Leyland Atlantean AN68A/1R	Northern Counties	H43/32F	1977	Ex GM Buses, 1991
A807	UNA772S	Leyland Atlantean AN68A/1R	Park Royal	H43/32F	1978	Ex GM Buses, 1991
R828	LMS160W	Leyland Fleetline FE30AGR	Alexander AD	H44/31F	1980	Ex Kelvin Central, 1989
R829	SMS122P	Daimler Fleetline CRG6LXB	Alexander AD	H44/31F	1976	Ex Kelvin Scottish, 1987
R830	SMS127P	Daimler Fleetline CRG6LXB	Alexander AD	H44/31F	1976	Ex Kelvin Scottish, 1987

R832-838

| | | | | | | | | | | Leyland Fleetline FE30AGR | | Eastern Coach Works | H43/32F | 1978 | Ex Northern Scottish, 1987 |

R832	ASA22T	**R834**	ASA24T	**R836**	ASA26T	**R837**	ASA27T	**R838**	ASA28T
R833	ASA33T								

R839	ULS669T	Leyland Fleetline FE30AGR	Eastern Coach Works	H43/32F	1978	Ex Kelvin Central, 1987
R840	ULS660T	Leyland Fleetline FE30AGR	Eastern Coach Works	H43/32F	1978	Ex Kelvin Central, 1987
R841	ULS658T	Leyland Fleetline FE30AGR	Eastern Coach Works	H43/32F	1978	Ex Kelvin Central, 1987
R842	OSG59V	Leyland Fleetline FE30AGR	Eastern Coach Works	H43/32F	1978	Ex Kelvin Central, 1987

R844-889

| | | | | | | | | | | Leyland Fleetline FE30AGR | | Northern Counties | H44/31F | 1978-79 | R859-76/80/5/7 ex Clydeside, 1988-89 |

R844	TSJ34S	**R853**	XSJ653T	**R861**	XSJ661T	**R870**	BCS870T	**R880**	ECS880V
R846	XSJ646T	**R854**	XSJ654T	**R862**	XSJ662T	**R871**	BCS871T	**R882**	ECS882V
R847	XSJ647T	**R855u**	XSJ655T	**R865**	XSJ665T	**R873**	BCS873T	**R883**	ECS883V
R848	XSJ648T	**R856u**	XSJ656T	**R866**	XSJ666T	**R876**	ECS876V	**R885**	ECS885V
R849	XSJ649T	**R857**	XSJ657T	**R867**	XSJ667T	**R877**	ECS877V	**R887**	ECS887V
R850	XSJ650T	**R858**	XSJ658T	**R868**	XSJ668T	**R878**	ECS878V	**R888**	BCS865T
R851	XSJ651T	**R859**	XSJ659T	**R869**	XSJ669T	**R879**	ECS879V	**R889**	BCS869T
R852	XSJ652T	**R860**	XSJ660T						

V894	E864RCS	Volvo Citybus B10M-50	Alexander RV	DPH41/25F	1987	
V895	E865RCS	Volvo Citybus B10M-50	Alexander RV	DPH45/35F	1987	
V896	E866RCS	Volvo Citybus B10M-50	Alexander RV	DPH45/35F	1987	
V897	E867RCS	Volvo Citybus B10M-50	Alexander RV	DPH45/29F	1987	
V898	B175FFS	Volvo Citybus B10M-50	Alexander RVC	CH42/28F	1984	Ex Fife Scottish, 1987
V899	B60EGG	Volvo Citybus B10M-50	Alexander RVC	CH42/28F	1984	Ex Fife Scottish, 1987
1059	UCS659	Albion Lowlander LR7	Alexander	H40/31F	1963	
1074	YYS174	Bedford C521	Duple	C21FM	1960	Ex David MacBrayne, 1970
1082	RCS382	Leyland PD3/3	Alexander	L35/32RD	1961	

Previous Registrations:

13CLT	D317SGB	VLT219	NCS119W	WLT546	D318SGB
803DYE	MSJ370P	VLT226	B200CGA	WLT652	TSD158Y
703DYE	TSD153Y	VLT245	B199CGA	WLT697	B197CGA
ESU435	GGE130X	VLT272	B202CGA	WLT720	B198CGA
FSU737	GGE127X	WGA908V	DSD939V, WLT652	WLT727	TSD155Y
FSU739	GGE128X	B60EGG	WLT144, B176FFS	WLT774	TSD149Y
GSU950	GGE131X	WLT415	NCS121W	WLT794	TSD156Y
HDS566H	SMS402H, 703DYE	WLT416	NCS114W	WLT809	TSD150Y
VCS391	B191CGA	WLT439	NCS123W	WLT830	TSD157Y
VLT37	B194CGA	WLT441	B201CGA	WLT874	TSD152Y
VLT54	C207HSD	WLT444	TSD159Y	WLT915	TSD151Y
VLT73	NCS118W	WLT447	B925BGA	WLT978	B195CGA
VLT81	C205HSD	WLT465	B196CGA	YSV730	B203CGA
VLT104	TSD154Y	WLT501	DSD938V	YSV735	B204CGA
VLT154	NCS115W	WLT526	GGE126X		
VLT206	C206HSD	WLT538	TSD148Y		

Special Liveries:

Service X16 promotional livery:	N143/4.	Scottish Citylink: N142, V146-51, L172/3, V194-8, N416-20, V423/7-9/31
Scottish General:	L602	Overall Advertisements: D228/9/53, R402, S434, S552, L671, R873

ALLANDER/ LOCH LOMOND COACHES

Allander Coaches Ltd, Unit 19, Cloberfield Industrial Estate, Milngavie, G62 7LN

Allander has for many years been in the contract, private hire and extended tour business. It was also involved for a time in a joint venture with Newton of Dingwall operating express services from Central Scotland to Inverness and the north. The coach fleet has a livery of orange and black and is based at Milngavie. In 1988, the business of Loch Lomond Coaches was acquired. Loch Lomond had attempted to set up a network of local services around Dumbarton and the Vale of Leven following deregulation, but had run into difficulties. Loch Lomond was continued by Allander as a separate entity and the services developed.

During 1991, an accommodation was reached with the main competitor, Kelvin Central, to co-ordinate services and timetables. Later in 1991, the Loch Lomond depot in Alexandria was abandoned and vehicles moved to Kelvin Central's Old Kilpatrick depot, though major maintenance is carried out at Milngavie. Loch Lomond vehicles are red and cream.

ALLANDER Fleet List

GDZ795	Leyland Leopard PSU3C/4R	Willowbrook Warrior (1989)	B55F	1975	Ex Thorne, Bubwith, 1988
OSJ615R	Leyland Leopard PSU3C/3R	Alexander AYS	B53F	1976	Ex Western Scottish, 1988
OSJ616R	Leyland Leopard PSU3C/3R	Alexander AYS	B53F	1976	Ex Western Scottish, 1988
OSJ618R	Leyland Leopard PSU3C/3R	Alexander AYS	B53F	1976	Ex Western Scottish, 1988
OSJ619R	Leyland Leopard PSU3C/3R	Alexander AYS	B53F	1976	Ex Western Scottish, 1988
PRA11R	Leyland Leopard PSU3C/4R	Alexander AT	B53F	1976	Ex Happy Days, Woodseaves, 1990
PRA12R	Leyland Leopard PSU3C/4R	Alexander AT	B53F	1976	Ex Happy Days, Woodseaves, 1990
PRA14R	Leyland Leopard PSU3C/4R	Alexander AT	B53F	1976	Ex Happy Days, Woodseaves, 1990
UOI772	Leyland Leopard PSU3C/4R	Willowbrook Warrior (1990)	B53F	1977	Ex Parish, Hawarden, 1988
Q652WWJ	Leyland Leopard PSU5C/4R	Alexander ATS	B51F	1979	Ex Gobig, Mirfield, 1989
758WNN	Volvo B58-56	Plaxton P'mount 3200(1991)	C53F	1979	Ex Marbill, Beith, 1991
3786AT	Volvo B58-61	Plaxton P'mount 3200(1987)	C57F	1980	Ex Beaudside, Bootle, 1987
2154K	Volvo B10M-61	Van Hool Alizée	C53F	1983	
4143AT	Volvo B10M-46	Van Hool Alizée	C38FT	1987	
2367AT	Volvo B10M-46	Van Hool Alizée	C38FT	1988	
7921AT	Volvo B10M-61	Van Hool Alizée	C50FT	1988	
E359VUM	Leyland Tiger TRBTL11/2RP	Plaxton Derwent	B54F	1988	Ex Plaxton demonstrator, 1988
F962MGA	Volvo B10M-61	Ikarus Blue Danube	C49FT	1989	
F442YSJ	Volvo B10M-61	Ikarus Blue Danube	C49FT	1989	
F453FKY	Volvo B10M-61	Ikarus Blue Danube	C49FT	1989	
G411PGG	Mercedes-Benz 811D	Reeve Burgess Beaver	B33F	1989	
G902MNS	Mercedes-Benz 811D	Reeve Burgess Beaver	B33F	1989	Ex Whitelaw, Stonehouse, 1991
9446AT	Volvo B10M-60	Van Hool Alizée	C48FT	1990	
J232HVK	Toyota HDB30R	Caetano Optimo	C18F	1991	

Previous Registrations:

2154K	NYS54Y, 9446AT, PGE926Y	9446AT	2154K, H103XNS
2367AT	E194YGG	F962MGA	F451FKY, 9446AT
3786AT	JRY569V	F442YSJ	F452FKY, 2154AT
4143AT	E477WUS	GDZ795	LPT903P
758WNN	GRF447V	UOI772	VCA995R, 2154K, WGD792R
7921AT	F147EYS		

Named vehicles:
758WNN *Highland Prince*, F962MGA *Highland Princess*, F442YSJ *Highland Diplomat*, F453FKY *Highland Ambassador*.

ARRAN COACHES

Arran Transport and Trading Co. Ltd, The Pier, Brodick, Isle of Arran

The island of Arran is located in the Firth of Clyde and is reached by ferry from Ardrossan. The Arran Transport and Trading Company was established in 1967 to take over the operations of A.C.Lennox of Whiting Bay and Lennox Motors (Brodick) Ltd. While in the 1950s there had been 20-bus operators on the island, by 1973 Arran Coaches had a monopoly.

For many years, Arran operators were limited to vehicles not exceeding 7ft 6ins wide, but the current fleet includes larger vehicles including a 12 metre coach. There are garages at Brodick and Whiting Bay, and the livery is red and white.

An Arran Coaches Bedford at Brodick Pier on the service to Brodick Castle with the ferry from Ardrossan in the background.
Murdoch Currie

ARRAN COACHES Fleet List

HCS350N	Bedford YRQ	Plaxton Derwent	DP45F	1975	
PSD845R	Bedford YLQ	Plaxton Supreme Express	C45F	1977	
CCS459T	Bedford YMT	Duple Dominant Express	C53F	1979	
MCS138W	Bedford YMT	Duple Dominant II Express	C53F	1981	
MCS139W	Bedford YLQ	Duple Dominant II	C45F	1981	
A934WYS	Leyland Tiger TRCTL11/3R	Marshall	B54F	1984	Ex MOD, 1991
B764DEG	Ford Transit 150	Dormobile	B16F	1985	
D167TRA	Bedford YMT	Duple Dominant	B55F	1986	Ex British Coal, 1991
D917GRU	Bedford YMT	Plaxton Derwent	B53F	1987	Ex Tillingbourne, 1991
D918GRU	Bedford YMT	Plaxton Derwent	B53F	1987	Ex Tillingbourne, 1991
D799USB	Bedford YMT	Duple Dominant	B55F	1987	
E638YUS	Mercedes-Benz 609D	Reeve Burgess	C19F	1988	
G262EHD	DAF SB2305DHTD585	Plaxton Paramount 3200 III	C57F	1989	
G574FSD	Mercedes-Benz 709D	Reeve Burgess Beaver	B25F	1990	

Previous Registrations:
A934WYS   20KB51

BAIRD / COWAL

Alexander Baird Ltd, West End Garage, Dunoon, Argyll
Cowal Motor Services Ltd, 1/3 Auchamore Road, Dunoon, Argyll

Dunoon, the principal town of the Cowal area, was once a bustling holiday resort. More recently it has hosted the US Navy, but the Polaris base is in process of closing down. For many years, bus services in the area were provided by Dunoon Motor Services Ltd, while the principal coach tour operators were Gold Line and Baird's Royal Blue.

Dunoon Motor Services ceased suddenly in 1964. A new company, Cowal Motor Services, under the same management as Baird, stepped in to the breach and has been the main provider of bus services since. In 1968, Gold Line ceased trading leaving Baird with a virtual monopoly. Inevitably in the current climate, the bulk of the work is contracted by Strathclyde PTE. The two companies share premises in Dunoon and vehicles are exchanged between fleets from time to time. Most are in a red, cream and black livery.

BAIRD Fleet List

Note - B indicates Alexander Baird and C the Cowal Motor Services subsidiary.

B	CHA444K	Leyland Leopard PSU3A/4R	Willowbrook	DP49F	1971	Ex Midland Red South, 1985
C	TSN513M	Bedford SB5	Duple Vega 31	C41F	1974	Ex Tantivy, St Helier, 1990
C	SCS366M	Leyland Leopard PSU3/3R	Alexander AY	DP49F	1974	Ex Western Scottish, 1985
B	SCS367M	Leyland Leopard PSU3/3R	Alexander AY	DP49F	1974	Ex Western Scottish, 1985
B	GCS792N	Leyland Leopard PSU3/3R	Alexander AY	DP49F	1974	Ex Western Scottish, 1985
C	JSB445P	Bedford SB5	Duple Dominant	C41F	1975	Ex Craig, Campbeltown, 1985
C	KSJ950P	Seddon Pennine 7	Alexander AY	B53F	1976	Ex Western Scottish, 1987
C	NSJ2R	Seddon Pennine 7	Alexander AY	B53F	1976	Ex Western Scottish, 1987
C	RSD980R	Seddon Pennine 7	Alexander AY	DP49F	1977	Ex Western Scottish, 1988
C	RSD981R	Seddon Pennine 7	Alexander AY	DP49F	1977	Ex SBG Engineering, 1988
C	RSD990R	Seddon Pennine 7	Alexander AY	DP49F	1977	Ex Western Scottish, 1988
C	RCS706R	Seddon Pennine 7	Alexander AT	C49F	1977	Ex Arthur, Coatbridge, 1989
C	CFS820S	Seddon Pennine 7	Alexander AY	B53F	1978	Ex Lowland Scottish, 1989
B	YYJ298T	Leyland Leopard PSU5C/4R	Plaxton Supreme IV	C53F	1978	Ex Rennie, Dunfermline, 1990
B	YYJ300T	Leyland Leopard PSU5C/4R	Plaxton Supreme IV	C53F	1978	Ex Rennie, Dunfermline, 1990
B	JTM116V	Volvo B58-61	Plaxton Supreme IV	C57F	1979	Ex Limebourne, London SW1, 1985
B	FVA147W	Volvo B10M-61	Plaxton Viewmaster IV	C47FT	1981	Ex Webber, Blisland, 1989

Previous Registrations:
TSN513M   J15799

CLYDE COAST

Clyde Coast Services Ltd, 55 Montgomerie Street, Ardrossan

Clyde Coast Services was formed as a co-operative in 1928 by defectors from A1, and had only one route, that from Saltcoats to Largs. The co-operative arrangement ceased some years ago, and the company now works from a single base in Ardrossan. The company operates high specification coaches on contract and private hire work.

A number of Leyland Nationals has been obtained in recent years for use on bus services. In 1991, an express service from West Kilbride to Glasgow was introduced. Later that year, the local service in Largs operated by Martin was taken over. A new express service from Fairlie and Largs to Glasgow is now operating, and there are also new services from Saltcoats to Dalry and Beith. The livery of blue and white has been modified on service buses to blue and light blue. Six new Van Hool coaches have been delivered in a new coach livery of dark blue metallic with a light blue band.

A former Yorkshire Traction Leyland National, N4 is seen at work with Clyde Coast Services. Only the Leyland Nationals now carry fleet numbers. Murdoch Currie

CLYDE COAST Fleet List

N1-N6				Leyland National 11351A/1R					B49F	1977-78	Ex Yorkshire Traction, 1989-90
N1	PPM894R	**N3**	WWA122S	**N4**	SWE441S			**N5**	SWE443S	**N6**	XAK454T
N2	XAK451T										

N7	TVF617R	Leyland National 11351A/1R		B49F	1977	Ex Marbill, Beith, 1991
N8	NHA255M	Leyland National 1151/1R/2501		B51F	1973	Ex Midland Red West, 1990
N9	NHA256M	Leyland National 1151/1R/2501		B51F	1973	Ex Midland Red West, 1990
N10	MHD336L	Leyland National 1151/1R/0501		B50F	1972	Ex Sheffield & District, 1990

PYD984V	Volvo B58-56	Duple Dominant II Express	C53F	1980	Ex Marbill, Beith, 1991
WGB554W	Volvo B58-56	Duple Dominant II Express	C53F	1980	Ex Crawford, Neilston, 1991
341AYF	Leyland Olympian ONTL11/2R	Eastern Coach Works	DPH45/28F	1983	Ex Alder Valley, 1991
B577LPE	Leyland Olympian ONTL11/2RSp	Eastern Coach Works	DPH45/28F	1985	Ex Alder Valley, 1991
B429PJF	Ford Transit 150	Robin Hood	B16F	1985	Ex Martin, Largs, 1991
C567TUT	Ford Transit 150	Dormobile	B16F	1986	Ex Martin, Largs, 1991
E938SSD	Volvo B10M-61	Van Hool Alizée	C50FT	1988	
F986HGE	Volvo B10M-60	Plaxton Paramount 3500	C53F	1989	Ex Park, Hamilton, 1990

	Volvo B10M-60		Van Hool Alizée	C52FT	1991	
J867JNS		J869JNS		J870JNS	J871JNS	J989JNS
J868JNS						

Previous Registrations:

341AYF	YPJ503Y		WGB554W	RHS855W, 935BRU

EDINBURGH TRANSPORT / SILVER COACH LINES

Silver Coach Lines Ltd, 81 Salamander Street, Edinburgh, EH6 7JZ

This company has been operating high specification coaches catering mainly for the overseas tourist trade for a number of years. Originally known as Silver Fox Coaches, the company was for a time owned by Alexander, the Falkirk coachbuilder. Following disposal by Alexander, the name was changed to Silver Coach Lines, the quality of the coaches upgraded and a new silver, black, orange and blue livery introduced. There was a brief involvement in an Edinburgh-Glasgow express service jointly with Green's of Kirkintilloch. Given the upmarket nature of the operation, it came as a surprise that the company should be interested in tendering for local service work, but that is what has happened. A separate 'Edinburgh Transport' unit has been set up using mainly Leyland Nationals, but also Scotland's only Optare Deltas. The Edinburgh Transport livery is orange and blue.

SILVER COACH LINES Fleet List

	B529LSG	Fiat 35.8	Robin Hood	C9F	1985	
	B726MBC	Volvo B10M-61	Caetano Algarve	C53F	1985	Ex Park, Hamilton, 1987
	D270FSG	Toyota HB31R	Caetano Optimo	C14F	1987	
	F792NNL	Toyota HB31R	Caetano Optimo	C19F	1989	
	F793NNL	Toyota HB31R	Caetano Optimo	C19F	1989	
	F794NNL	Toyota HB31R	Caetano Optimo	C19F	1989	
	F795NNL	Toyota HB31R	Caetano Optimo	C19F	1989	
	PSU610	Kässbohrer Setra S210HD	Kässbohrer Tornado	C28FT	1989	
	PSU611	Kässbohrer Setra S210HD	Kässbohrer Tornado	C28FT	1989	
	PSU612	Kässbohrer Setra S210HD	Kässbohrer Tornado	C35F	1989	
	PSU613	Kässbohrer Setra S210HD	Kässbohrer Tornado	C35F	1989	
		Kässbohrer Setra S215HD	Kässbohrer Tornado	C49FT	1989	
	PSU614	PSU615	PSU616	PSU617	PSU618	
	PSU619	Kässbohrer Setra S215HR	Kässbohrer Rational	C53F	1989	
	PSU620	Kässbohrer Setra S215HR	Kässbohrer Rational	C53F	1989	
	PSU621	Kässbohrer Setra S215HR	Kässbohrer Rational	C53F	1989	
	PSU698	Kässbohrer Setra S215HD	Kässbohrer Tornado	C49FT	1990	
	SGR566R	Leyland National 11351A/1R		B49F	1977	Ex Go-Ahead Northern, 1990
ET101	SGR553R	Leyland National 11351A/1R		B49F	1976	Ex Green, Kirkintilloch, 1990
ET102	NEN962R	Leyland National 11351A/1R		B49F	1976	Ex Green, Kirkintilloch, 1990
ET103	RBU183R	Leyland National 11351A/1R		B49F	1976	Ex Green, Kirkintilloch, 1990
ET104	NEV682M	Leyland National 1151/1R/0402		B49F	1973	Ex Paterson, Bannockburn, 1991
ET105	NEN959R	Leyland National 11351A/1R		B49F	1976	Ex Green, Kirkintilloch, 1990
ET106	SGR553R	Leyland National 11351A/1R		B49F	1976	Ex Go-Ahead Northern, 1990
ET107	VPT603R	Leyland National 11351A/1R		B49F	1977	Ex Go-Ahead Northern, 1990
ET201	F379UCP	Mercedes-Benz 609D	Reeve Burgess Beaver	B24F	1988	Ex Yorkshire Rider, 1990
ET301	G785PWL	DAF SB220LC550	Optare Delta	B47F	1989	Ex DAF demonstrator, 1990
ET302	F792DWT	DAF SB220LC550	Optare Delta	B47F	1989	Ex Optare demonstrator, 1990

Special Liveries:
Edinburgh Transport: ET101-302.

The blue and orange Edinburgh Transport livery, particularly on the Optare Deltas, creates a distinctive impression in Princes Street when compared with the traditional Lothian and SMT liveries. Mike Fowler

Leyland National WPT716R pulls out of the bus station into St Andrew Square, Edinburgh. Mike Fowler

GAELICBUS

Alexander MacConnacher & Son, Brecklet Garage, Ballachulish, PA39 4JG

The history of this operator can be traced back to 1919 when Alexander MacConnacher offered for hire a model T Ford car which he had assembled himself. In 1921 he obtained the first charabanc in the area and thereafter developed a tours business together with hotel interests. In the 1970s, the fleetname Gaelic Coaches was adopted.

Since 1986, local services have been operated principally around Fort William, but stretching also to Oban and Inverness, all in competition with Highland Scottish. The Gaelicbus fleetname was introduced at this time. Vehicles are based at Ballachulish, and are in a livery of dark and light green.

The Leyland Nationals in the Gaelicbus fleet are from GM Buses, but came via OK at Bishop Auckland.

A Plaxton-bodied Ford loads in Oban on the Fort William service which follows the coast through Connel and Ballachulish, the home of this operator.
Murdoch Currie

Parked at Corpach is one of several Duple-bodied AEC Reliances still active in the Gaelicbus fleet.
Murdoch Currie

GAELICBUS Fleet List

HNB21N	Leyland National 10351/1R		B41F	1975	Ex OK, Bishop Auckland, 1989	
HNB23N	Leyland National 10351/1R		B41F	1975	Ex OK, Bishop Auckland, 1989	
HNE636N	Leyland National 10351/1R		B41F	1975	Ex OK, Bishop Auckland, 1989	
HJA129N	Leyland National 10351/1R		B41F	1975	Ex OK, Bishop Auckland, 1989	
NOC597R	Leyland Fleetline FE30AGR	Park Royal	H43/33F	1976	Ex West Midlands Travel, 1989	
NOC724R	Leyland Fleetline FE30AGR	East Lancashire	H43/33F	1977	Ex West Midlands Travel, 1989	
SWW158R	Ford R1114	Plaxton Supreme III	C53F	1977	Ex Ganal, Shotts, 1988	
RRP860R	Bristol VRT/SL3/6LXB	Eastern Coach Works	H43/31F	1977	Ex United Counties, 1991	
	AEC Reliance 6U3ZR	Duple Dominant	B53F	1977-79	Ex Hutchison, Overtown, 1986-88	
UGB13R	ESU424T	JGE346T		JGE347T		JGE348T
ESU423T	ESU425T					
DJA558T	Ford R1114	Plaxton Supreme IV	C53F	1979	Ex Stirk, Staindrop, 1985	
JGE516T	Ford R1114	Plaxton Supreme IV	C53F	1979	Ex Yule, Pitlochry, 1987	
549KYA	Van Hool T815H	Van Hool Alicron	C50FT	1984	Ex Berrington & Steele, 1988	

Previous Registrations:
549KYA   A780VLG

GOLDEN EAGLE

John B.G. Irvine, Muirhall Garage, Salsburgh, ML7 4LS

This old established firm is run by a branch of a Lanarkshire family steeped in the transport business. The service from Airdrie to Salsburgh and Shotts continues to be the main activity of the operator, though there has of late been some augmentation and variation to deal with the effects of deregulation. A fleet of modern coaches is maintained for private hire work. Fleet livery is red and cream and all vehicles are garaged at Salsburgh.

GOLDEN EAGLE Fleet List

AUS417S	AEC Reliance 6U3ZR	Marshall	B51F	1978	
AUS418S	AEC Reliance 6U3ZR	Marshall	B51F	1978	
HGA747T	AEC Reliance 6U3ZR	Duple Dominant	B51F	1979	
UNS973W	Leyland Leopard PSU3E/4R	Duple Dominant	B55F	1981	
HSC166X	Leyland Cub CU435	Duple Dominant	B31F	1981	Ex Lothian, 1991
866KTV	Volvo B10M-61	Van Hool Alizée	C53F	1985	
D864PGB	Volvo B10M-61	Van Hool Alizée	C53F	1986	
E129BSU	Volvo B10M-61	Van Hool Alizée	C53FT	1988	
F706WCS	Volvo B10M-56	Duple 300	B53F	1988	
F235ESU	Volvo B10M-60	Van Hool Alizée	C53FT	1989	
G432UHS	Volvo B10M-55	Plaxton Derwent	B55F	1990	
H991YUS	Mercedes-Benz 709D	Reeve Burgess Beaver	B25F	1990	
J716USF	Mercedes-Benz 709D	Alexander AM	DP25F	1991	
J39HSU	Volvo B10M-60	Van Hool Alizée	C53F	1992	

Previous Registrations:
866KTV   B761KRB

A Marshall-bodied AEC Reliance uplifts a private party at Hamilton Interchange. Murdoch Currie

HENDERSON TRAVEL

Henderson Travel, Unit 2, Whistleberry Industrial Estate, Hamilton

This operator came to prominence with deregulation having successfully obtained Strathclyde PTE contracts for minibus services. Several tendered services are now operated, some requiring the use of full size vehicles. Most of the services are in Lanarkshire, but some are within the Glasgow city boundary.

HENDERSON TRAVEL Fleet List

HCS789N	Leyland Leopard PSU3/3R	Alexander AYS	B53F	1975	Ex Northern Scottish, 1990
HCS790N	Leyland Leopard PSU3/3R	Alexander AYS	B53F	1975	Ex Northern Scottish, 1990
HCS796N	Leyland Leopard PSU3/3R	Alexander AYS	B53F	1975	Ex Northern Scottish, 1990
HCS818N	Leyland Leopard PSU3/3R	Alexander AYS	B53F	1975	Ex Northern Scottish, 1990
Q201SDS	Leyland Leopard PSU3E/4R	Willowbrook Warrior (1991)	B55F	19??	Ex ??
LIW3462	Leyland Leopard PSU3?/4R	Willowbrook Warrior (1991)	B55F	19??	Ex ??
A451BSC	Mercedes-Benz L307D	Devon Conversions	B12C	1983	
B947ASU	Volvo B10M-56	Van Hool	B51F	1984	Ex Hutchison, Overtown, 1991
B879GSG	Mercedes-Benz L608D	Devon Conversions	C23F	1984	
B665BTU	Mercedes-Benz L608D	Coachcraft	C21F	1985	Ex Collison, Stonehouse, 1986
B250KSX	Mercedes-Benz L608D	Devon Conversions	C21F	1985	Ex Western, Newbridge, 1986
C350RSF	Mercedes-Benz L608D	Devon Conversions	C23F	1985	
E508KSC	Mercedes-Benz 609D	Alexander AM	C22F	1987	
E996VYS	Mercedes-Benz 609D	Reeve Burgess Beaver	C19F	1987	
E268XGB	Mercedes-Benz 609D	Reeve Burgess Beaver	C19F	1987	
E157XHS	Volvo B10M-56	Plaxton Derwent	B54F	1988	Ex Hutchison, Overtown, 1991
E635LSF	Mercedes-Benz 609D	Alexander AM	C25F	1988	
E504YSU	Mercedes-Benz 709D	Alexander AM	B25F	1988	Ex Caldwell, Greenock, 1989
E508YSU	Mercedes-Benz 709D	Alexander AM	B25F	1988	Ex Caldwell, Greenock, 1989
E766MSC	Mercedes-Benz 709D	Alexander AM	C25F	1988	Ex Wilson, Port Glasgow, 1989
F346TSC	Mercedes-Benz 811D	Alexander AM	C33F	1988	
F362TSC	Mercedes-Benz 609D	Alexander AM	C25F	1988	
F593YSC	Mercedes-Benz 609D	Alexander AM	C25F	1989	
G109CSF	Mercedes-Benz 609D	Alexander AM	C25F	1989	
G399FSF	Mercedes-Benz 811D	PMT	C33F	1990	
G198GNY	Mercedes-Benz 811D	Optare StarRider	B33F	1991	Ex Shamrock, Pontypridd, 1991
H897JCS	Mercedes-Benz 811D	Reeve Burgess Beaver	C33F	1991	
J440UFS	Mercedes-Benz 709D	Alexander AM	C25F	1991	

HUTCHISON

Hutchison's Coaches (Overtown) Ltd, 5 Castlehill Road, Overtown, Wishaw, ML2 0QS

This is another of the original Lanarkshire bus operators with a history extending since before the Great War. Until the 1960s, there were routes from Wishaw to Larkhall and to Overtown as well as contract work carrying miners. In the sixties, a network of routes linking Wishaw and Motherwell was established despite the fierce opposition of Scottish Bus Group subsidiary, Central SMT.

Since deregulation, express services to Glasgow have been added. There is still a significant element of crew operation. A modern luxury coach fleet is available for hire. The fleet livery is blue and cream, but some coaches are silver with red trim. The depot is in Overtown.

Until recently this was Scotland's only Dennis Dart. Despite the Carlyle badges, it was one of the few bodied at Blackpool by Duple.
Alistair Douglas

F708WCS, a Duple 300-bodied Volvo B10M is seen in Wishaw bound for Motherwell. There are now thirteen of this model in the Hutchison fleet.
Murdoch Currie

For several years the 12-metre Volvo B10M was chosen by Hutchison for the stage vehicle requirement. Eight of the type, all fitted with Duple Dominant bus bodies, were added to the fleet in 1986. When fitted to the Volvo B10M this body has a step in the window level as exemplified by **D391PYS**. Murdoch Currie

HUTCHISON Fleet List

C811JGB	Bedford YMP	Lex	B37F	1985	

	Volvo B10M-61	Duple Dominant	B55F	1986	
D497NYS	D499NYS	D391PYS	D376RHS		D377RHS
D498NYS	D390PYS	D375RHS			

KSK929	Volvo B10M-61	Van Hool Alizée	C50DLT	1987	
KSK930	Volvo B10M-61	Van Hool Alizée	C50DLT	1987	
KSK931	Volvo B10M-61	Duple 340	C55F	1988	
KSK932	Volvo B10M-61	Duple 340	C55F	1988	
KSK933	Volvo B10M-61	Duple 340	C55F	1988	
KSK934	Volvo B10M-61	Duple 340	C55F	1988	
E65TCS	Volvo B10M-61	Van Hool Alizée	C55F	1988	Ex A1, Ardrossan, 1990
E156XHS	Volvo B10M-56	Plaxton Derwent	B54F	1988	
E809XHS	Ford Transit VE6	Deansgate	C12C	1988	

	Volvo B10M-56	Duple 300	B53F	1988-89	F771-4JYS are type B10M-55
E158XHS	E871BGG	F707WCS	F771JYS		F773JYS
E159XHS	F338VSD	F708WCS	F772JYS		F774JYS
E870BGG	F339VSD	F709WCS			

F775JYS	Volvo B10M-60	Duple 320	C59F	1989	
F776JYS	Volvo B10M-60	Duple 320	C59F	1989	
G456MGG	Dennis Dart 9SDL3002	Duple	B35F	1990	
G457MGG	Volvo B10M-60	Jonckheere Deauville	C51FT	1990	
G370CCV	Volvo B10M-60	Van Hool Alizée	C49FT	1990	Ex Ford, Gunnislake, 1991
G931TUS	Volvo B10M-60	Plaxton Paramount 3500 III	C53F	1990	
H558YYS	Ford Transit VE6	Scott	C14C	1991	
H721YYS	Volvo B10M-60	Van Hool Alizée	C49FT	1991	
H722YYS	Volvo B10M-60	Van Hool Alizée	C49FT	1991	
J17BUS	Volvo B10M-60	Duple 300	B53F	1992	
J18BUS	Volvo B10M-60	Duple 300	B53F	1992	
J19BUS	Volvo B10M-60	Van Hool Alizée	C53FT	1992	
J20BUS	Volvo B10M-60	Van Hool Alizée	C53FT	1992	

Previous Registrations:

KSK929	D365RHS		KSK932	E153XHS
KSK930	D366RHS		KSK933	E154XHS
KSK931	E152XHS		KSK934	E155XHS

McGILL'S

McGill's Bus Service Ltd, Muriel Street, Barrhead, Renfrewshire, G78 1QE

The McGill family operated buses in Ayrshire for a time, but the present company has its origins in the acquisition in 1933 of O'Hara's Barrhead to Paisley service. Expansion in the 1950s brought a second Barrhead-Paisley route, a local service in Paisley, and an extension through Paisley to Renfrew Ferry. More recently a Barrhead-Glasgow service has been introduced, as well as tendered duties between Barrhead and Neilston.

Once a mainly double deck fleet, the standard vehicle is now the Leyland National, with the added interest of a former demonstration Lynx. The garage is in Barrhead and the buses are painted red and grey.

There are a number of former demonstration Leyland Lynxes in Scotland. H733HWK was the first example of the Lynx 2 to be fitted with a stepped floor, rather than the ramp floor option. It had been painted all-over red when photographed in Paisley. Murdoch Currie

The McGill's fleet has been a keen operator of the Leyland National for many years, with many versions, including the articulated examples based on DAB chassis, built at Roe's with National parts. Now one of the oldest examples in the fleet, XYS596S is seen at Paisley Cross. M. Currie

KRS536V is one of two secondhand Leyland National 2s to join the fleet, the other example coming from Edmunds of Rassau. The vehicle is unusual in that it has retained its service number display — 3G is the duty number. Stewart Brown

McGILL'S Fleet List

	Leyland National 11351A/1R		B52F	1977-79	
TDS611R	XYS595S	DYS636T		DYS637T	LGA977V
TDS612R	XYS596S				
GGE171T	Leyland National 10351A/1R		B41F	1979	Ex Strathclyde PTE, 1986
AAK112T	Leyland National 10351B/1R		B44F	1979	Ex Somerbus, Paulton, 1989
KRS536V	Leyland National 2 NL106L11/1R		B44F	1980	Ex Northern Scottish, 1991
	Leyland National 2 NL116AL11/1R		B52F	1981	KKG ex Edmunds, Rassau, 1986
UGE388W	UGE389W	KKG109W		BHS206X	BHS207X
B724AGD	Leyland National 2 NL116TL11/1R		B52F	1984	
B725AGD	Leyland National 2 NL116HLXCT/1R		B52F	1985	
C263FGG	Leyland National 2 NL116HLXCT/1R		B52F	1986	
C264FGG	Leyland National 2 NL116HLXCT/1R		B52F	1986	
H733HWK	Leyland Lynx LX2R11C15Z4S Leyland Lynx 2		B51F	1990	Ex VL Bus demonstrator, 1991

Previous Registrations:
KRS536V   GSO2V.

MOFFAT & WILLIAMSON

Moffat & Williamson Ltd, Main Road, Gauldry, Fife, DD6 8RQ

This firm was born in 1978 of a merger between two old-established operators, Moffat of Cardenden, and Williamson of Gauldry. For some years, a proportion of the fleet carried Williamson's blue and cream livery and the remainder were in Moffat's cream and brown. Today, all of the fleet is in Moffat's colours. Both operators were involved in contract work and hiring, and this was continued by the new company. The full effects of deregulation were slower to develop in Fife than elsewhere and it was not until 1988 that Moffat & Williamson launched its competitive challenge to Fife Scottish, the region's principal operator.

Commercial services were introduced on the Glenrothes-Kirkcaldy corridor and then in Glenrothes itself and North-east Fife together with a range of tendered services on behalf of Fife Regional Council. The company has probably the largest fleet of Bristol VRTs in Scotland, but other types are represented in the fleet including ex Kelvin Scottish Leopards. The depots are at Gauldry and in Glenrothes.

Bristol VRT YBW600R once plied the streets of Oxford, but now departs Dundee for the Tay Bridge and a different university town.
Alistair Douglas

The latest double-deck arrivals are former Portsmouth Leyland Atlanteans displaced in that town by minibuses. Originally dual-doored, they are being converted to single door by their new owners.
Murdoch Currie

MTV762P is a former Nottingham Leyland Leopard with Duple Dominant E bodywork. The 'Economy' version of the Dominant was produced alongside the coach and bus versions using the coach shell but fitted with bus seating.
Murdoch Currie

Six former Kelvin Scottish Leopards are very similar to the Fife vehicles with which they compete in the Kirkcaldy area. GMS299S, previously with Midland Scottish and Kelvin Scottish, is seen at Glenrothes bus station.
Murdoch Currie

MOFFAT & WILLIAMSON Fleet List

PRG125J	Daimler Fleetline CRG6LXB	Alexander L	H48/37F	1971	Ex Grampian, 1982
PRG129J	Daimler Fleetline CRG6LXB	Alexander L	H48/37F	1971	Ex Grampian, 1982
LAL320K	Leyland Leopard PSU3B/4R	Plaxton Elite II Express	C53F	1972	Ex Barton, 1978
VNB169L	Leyland Atlantean AN68/1R	Park Royal	H43/32F	1972	Ex Skill, Nottingham, 1988
GOG630N	Bristol VRT/SL3/6LXB	MCW	H43/34F	1974	Ex Brixham Coaches, 1988
GOG642N	Bristol VRT/SL3/6LXB	MCW	H43/34F	1974	Ex Brixham Coaches, 1988
GUA380N	Bristol VRT/SL2/6G	Eastern Coach Works	H43/31F	1974	Ex Devon General, 1987
GUD751N	Bristol VRT/SL2/6G	Eastern Coach Works	H43/34F	1974	Ex Devon General, 1987
JWL993N	Bristol VRT/SL2/6G	Eastern Coach Works	H43/34F	1975	Ex Devon General, 1987
JWL994N	Bristol VRT/SL2/6G	Eastern Coach Works	H43/34F	1975	Ex Devon General, 1987
JWL996N	Bristol VRT/SL2/6G	Eastern Coach Works	H43/34F	1975	Ex Thames Transit, 1989
JWL997N	Bristol VRT/SL2/6G	Eastern Coach Works	H43/34F	1975	Ex Thames Transit, 1989
JRB744N	Leyland Leopard PSU3C/4R	Duple Dominant E	DP53F	1975	Ex Nottingham, 1989
LAL749P	Leyland Leopard PSU3C/4R	Duple Dominant E	DP53F	1975	Ex Nottingham, 1989
PJO445P	Bristol VRT/SL3/6LX	Eastern Coach Works	H43/34F	1975	Ex Thames Transit, 1989
PJO448P	Bristol VRT/SL3/6LX	Eastern Coach Works	H43/34F	1975	Ex Thames Transit, 1989

Reg	Chassis	Body	Layout	Year	Notes
MNU186P	Daimler Fleetline CRG6LX	Northern Counties	H47/30D	1976	Ex Nottingham, 1988
MNU189P	Daimler Fleetline CRG6LX	Northern Counties	H47/30D	1976	Ex Nottingham, 1988
MNU193P	Daimler Fleetline CRG6LX	Northern Counties	H47/30D	1976	Ex Nottingham, 1988
MTV756P	Leyland Leopard PSU3C/4R	Duple Dominant E	DP53F	1976	Ex Nottingham, 1989
MTV762P	Leyland Leopard PSU3C/4R	Duple Dominant E	DP53F	1976	Ex Nottingham, 1989
OUP679P	Bristol VRT/SL3/6LX	Eastern Coach Works	H43/31F	1976	Ex Devon General, 1987
MOD572P	Bristol VRT/SL3/6LXB	Eastern Coach Works	H43/32F	1976	Ex Devon General, 1987
LPB123P	Leyland Leopard PSU5A/4R	Duple Dominant	C57F	1976	Ex Watson, Southampton, 1982
121ASV	Leyland Leopard PSU3C/4R	Plaxton Supreme III	C53F	1976	Ex King, Dunblane, 1986
RWT544R	Bristol VRT/SL3/6LX	Eastern Coach Works	H43/31F	1976	Ex York City & District, 1989
RWT545R	Bristol VRT/SL3/6LX	Eastern Coach Works	H43/31F	1976	Ex York City & District, 1989
RWT546R	Bristol VRT/SL3/6LX	Eastern Coach Works	H43/31F	1976	Ex York City & District, 1989
SWW299R	Bristol VRT/SL3/6LX	Eastern Coach Works	H43/31F	1976	Ex York City & District, 1989
YBW600R	Bristol VRT/SL3/6LX	Eastern Coach Works	H43/31F	1976	Ex Thames Transit, 1989
YBW606R	Bristol VRT/SL3/6LX	Eastern Coach Works	H43/31F	1976	Ex Thames Transit, 1989
UGG390R	Leyland Atlantean AN68A/1R	Alexander AL	H45/33F	1977	Ex Skill, Nottingham, 1988
FSU374	Leyland Leopard PSU3E/4R	Plaxton Supreme III	C53F	1977	Ex Blue Emblem, London SE13, 1985
TPJ67S	Bristol LHS6L	Eastern Coach Works	B35F	1977	Ex Eastbourne, 1991

	Leyland Leopard PSU3E/4R	Alexander AYS	B53F	1978	Ex Kelvin Scottish, 1988
GMS276S	GMS277S	GMS280S	GMS294S		GMS299S

Reg	Chassis	Body	Layout	Year	Notes
VDV123S	Bristol VRT/SL3/6LXB	Eastern Coach Works	H43/31F	1978	Ex Devon General, 1989
122ASV	Leyland Leopard PSU5B/4R	Duple Dominant	C57F	1978	Ex Armstrong, Bletchley, 1985
CMJ448T	Leyland Leopard PSU3E/4R	Plaxton Supreme IV Exp	C53F	1978	Ex Frames Rickards, Brentford, 1984
YTS791T	Leyland Leopard PSU3E/4R	Plaxton Supreme IV	C53F	1979	Ex Cosgrove, Dundee, 1985
FSU375	Leyland Leopard PSU5C/4R	Plaxton Supreme IV	C57F	1979	Ex Shamrock & Rambler, 1984
BGY588T	Leyland Leopard PSU5C/4R	Plaxton Supreme IV	C50F	1979	Ex NT London, 1984
JGE514T	Ford R1114	Plaxton Supreme IV Exp	C53F	1979	

	Leyland Atlantean AN68A/1R	Alexander AL	H45/32F*	1979	Ex Thames Transit, 1991
					*335/6/41 are H45/34F, 344 is H45/28D
YBK335V	YBK337V	YBK339V	YBK341V		YBK343V
YBK336V	YBK338V	YBK340V	YBK342V		YBK344V

Reg	Chassis	Body	Layout	Year	Notes
DES263V	Ford T152	Plaxton Supreme IV	C35F	1980	
LVS440V	Leyland Leopard PSU3E/4R	Plaxton Supreme IV	C53F	1980	Ex Burdett, Mosbrough, 1987
LFJ848W	Bristol LHS6L	Eastern Coach Works	B35F	1980	Ex Thames Transit, 1991
LFJ850W	Bristol LHS6L	Eastern Coach Works	B35F	1980	Ex Thames Transit, 1991
CGA189X	Mercedes-Benz L307D	Reeve Burgess	C12F	1981	
FSU371	Leyland Tiger TRCTL11/3R	Plaxton Supreme IV	C53F	1982	Ex Bicknell, Godalming, 1984
FSU372	Leyland Tiger TRCTL11/2R	Plaxton Supreme VI	C53F	1982	Ex Whyte, Newmarchar, 1987
FSU394	Leyland Tiger TRCTL11/3R	Plaxton Paramount 3500	C48FT	1983	Ex Ebdon, Sidcup, 1984
A79RGE	Fiat 35.8	Reeve Burgess	C12F	1983	
BSK789	Volvo B10M-61	Plaxton Paramount 3500 II	C49FT	1985	Ex Dodsworth, Boroughbridge, 1990
BSK790	Leyland Tiger TRCTL11/3RZ	Plaxton Paramount 3500 III	C53F	1985	Ex Shearings, 1989
YBK159	Volvo B10M-61	Van Hool Alizée	C51F	1985	Ex Cotter, Glasgow, 1987
FSU393	Leyland Tiger TRCTL11/3RZ	Van Hool Alizée	C53F	1987	Ex Travellers, Hounslow, 1990
FSU395	Leyland Tiger TRCTL11/3RZ	Van Hool Alizée	C53F	1987	Ex Travellers, Hounslow, 1990
E368YGB	Mercedes-Benz 609D	Scott	C25F	1987	Ex Stirling, Kilsyth, 1988
E596JSP	Mercedes-Benz 609D	Reeve Burgess Beaver	C23F	1988	
E431YHL	Mercedes-Benz 709D	Reeve Burgess Beaver	B25F	1988	
G146GOL	Iveco Daily 49.10	Carlyle Dailybus	B25F	1989	Ex Carlyle, 1991
G149GOL	Iveco Daily 49.10	Carlyle Dailybus	B25F	1989	Ex Carlyle, 1991
G743DSG	Iveco Daily 49.10	Carlyle Dailybus	B24F	1989	
G744DSG	Iveco Daily 49.10	Carlyle Dailybus	B24F	1989	
G731FSC	Iveco Daily 49.10	Carlyle Dailybus	B25F	1990	
G315TKO	Iveco Daily 49.10	Dormobile Routemaker	B25F	1990	Ex Dormobile demonstrator, 1990
G318UES	Mercedes-Benz 811D	Reeve Burgess Beaver	C25F	1990	
J437MDB	DAF Sherpa 400	Dormobile	B18F	1992	
J438MDB	DAF Sherpa 400	Dormobile	B18F	1992	

Previous Registrations:

121ASV	TLS735P	FSU374	VMJ959S
122ASV	YBM533S	FSU375	EDF261T
BSK780	B509UNB	FSU393	D233HMT
BSK789	B706WUA	FSU394	FNM859Y
FSU371	RPC58X	FSU395	D231HMT
FSU372	MAX335X		

JOHN MORROW

John Morrow, 813 South Street, Glasgow

John Morrow, an established coach hirer in Clydebank, began in 1988 to develop a network of local services in competition with Kelvin Scottish, later Kelvin Central, and Strathclyde Buses. Most of the services are based on Clydebank, but the operating area extends eastward into Glasgow and west to Dumbarton and the Vale of Leven. Morrow operates two contracted services in Glasgow city centre, the inter-station service and the service to the Exhibition and Conference Centre, using vehicles in special liveries. A feature of several of the routes is the use of service numbers once used by Central SMT. The fleet base is now in South Street, Glasgow and the fleet livery is cream with brown and buff stripes.

BYW392V is a short version of the Leyland National from the London Buses fleet. It is seen in the current livery application while on the service from Clydebank to Dumbarton. Morrow uses old Central SMT service numbers, a nice historical touch.
Murdoch Currie

One of two contract services in Glasgow city centre is the inter-station service 98. YYE286T is painted in Strathclyde livery on the sides with yellow front and rear.
Graeme Yuill

Following a brief career with Green's of Kirkintilloch, former GM Buses single deck Fleetline TWH697T is now in the Morrow fleet. The conversion from double-deck was made following an accident with a bridge. Murdoch Currie

JOHN MORROW Fleet List

1	NFM854M	Leyland National 1151/1R/0405		DP48F	1974	Ex Crosville Wales, 1988
2	HPF304N	Leyland National 10351/1R		B41F	1975	Ex Green, Kirkintilloch, 1990
3	BYW392V	Leyland National 10351A/2R		B36D	1979	Ex London Buses, 1990
4	UPB295S	Leyland National 10351A/1R		B41F	1977	Ex London Country NW, 1990
5	UFG50S	Leyland National 11351A/2R		B49D	1977	Ex D Stewart, Dalmuir, 1990
6	ORP459M	Leyland National 1151/1R		B52F	1973	Ex United Counties, 1988
7	SPC288R	Leyland National 10351A/1R		B41F	1977	Ex London Country NW, 1990
8	HCA967N	Leyland National 11351/1R		DP48F	1974	Ex Crosville Wales, 1989
9	TVF618R	Leyland National 11351A/1R		B49F	1977	Ex Green, Kirkintilloch, 1992
10	YYE279T	Leyland National 10351/2R		B36D	1978	Ex London Buses, 1990
11	PJJ350S	Leyland National 10351A/1R		B41F	1977	Ex East Kent, 1989
12	BYW375V	Leyland National 10351A/2R		B36D	1979	Ex London Buses, 1990
14	TVF615R	Leyland National 11351A/1R		B52F	1977	Ex Marbill, Beith, 1991
15	PJJ347S	Leyland National 10351A/1R		B41F	1977	Ex East Kent, 1989
16	OVV517R	Leyland National 11351A/1R		B49F	1976	Ex United Counties, 1989
17	SGR556R	Leyland National 11351A/1R		B49F	1977	Ex Go-Ahead Northern, 1991
18	PVF358R	Leyland National 11351A/1R		B52F	1976	Ex Marbill, Beith, 1991
19	HPF320N	Leyland National 10351/1R		B41F	1975	Ex London Country NW, 1990
20	KNV506P	Leyland National 11351A/1R		B49F	1975	Ex MacTavish, Hardgate, 1990
22	YYE286T	Leyland National 10351A/2R		B36D	1979	Ex London Buses, 1990
23	TWH697T	Leyland Fleetline FE30AGR	NCME/GMB	B28F	1978	Ex Green, Kirkintilloch, 1991
	HHA147L	Leyland National 1151/1R/2401		B52F	1973	Ex Armstrong, Bletchley, 1990
	UWY301L	Leyland National 1151/1R/0401		B52F	1973	Ex West Yorkshire, 1990
	NFM828M	Leyland National 1151/1R/0405		DP48F	1973	Ex Green, Kirkintilloch, 1990
	NGB10P	Volvo B58-61	Plaxton Supreme III	C57F	1976	Ex Campbell, Clydebank, 1991
	ANA108Y	Leyland Tiger TRCTL11/3R	Plaxton Paramount 3500	C48FT	1983	Ex London & Country, 1990

Special Liveries:
SECC special service: 19
Strathclyde Transport: 22

ROYAL MAIL POST BUS

The Postbus Controller, Royal Mail Inverness, 14 Queensgate, Inverness, IV1 1AA

ROYAL MAIL POST BUS - Scottish Regions Fleet List

6760002 D572YSA	Ford Sierra Estate		4-seat	1987	

6770001-13 Land Rover Land Rover 4-seat 1987

6770001 D283YRS	**6770005** D678FAS	**6770008** D681FAS	**6770011** D684FAS	**6770013** D685FAS
6770002 D282YRS	**6770006** D679FAS	**6770009** D682FAS		

7750002 F911EUS	Freight Rover Sherpa 285	Post Office	B14C	1988
7770023 E113FAS	Land Rover	Land Rover	4-seat	1988
8760002 F121NST	Ford Sierra Estate		4-seat	1988
8760003 F122NST	Ford Sierra Estate		4-seat	1988
9100103 H397YAS	Land Rover 90	Land Rover	4-seat	1990
9100116 G470UHS	Land Rover 90	Land Rover	4-seat	1990
9730218 G120JSC	Freight Rover Sherpa 285	Post Office	B14C	1990
9730240 H359YGG	Freight Rover Sherpa 285	Post Office	B14C	1990

9760002 G340UES	Freight Rover Sherpa 285	Post Office	B11C	1990
0100072 J436GDS	Land Rover 90	Land Rover	4-seat	1991

0750095-115 DAF Sherpa 285 Post Office B11C 1990-91 0750114 is 16-seat

0750095 G394VST	**0750101** H848XSL	**0750107** J546FSU	**0750110** J549FSU	**0750113** J282EST
0750096 G395VST	**0750103** J543FSU	**0750108** J547FSU	**0750111** J550FSU	**0750114** J305EST
0750098 H828XSL	**0750104** J544FSU	**0750109** J548FSU	**0750112** J306AAA	**0750115** J450GDS
0750099 H931VSL	**0750105** J545FSU			

0760001-18 Ford Sierra Estate 4-seat 1991

0760001 H399YAS	**0760005** H394YAS	**0760009** H403YAS	**0760013** H409YAS	**0760016** H384YAS
0760002 H401YAS	**0760006** H402YAS	**0760010** H404YAS	**0760014** H410YAS	**0760017** H408YAS
0760003 H392YAS	**0760007** H395YAS	**0760011** H406YAS	**0760015** H407YAS	**0760018** H852XSL
0760004 H393YAS	**0760008** H383YAS	**0760012** H396YAS		

0760019-33 Peugeot 405 Estate 4-seat 1991

0760019 H871CSU	**0760024** H644CST	**0760027** H645CST	**0760029** H649CST	**0760032** J307EST
0760021 H642CST	**0760025** H643CST	**0760028** H646CST	**0760031** H869CSU	**0760033** H422CNS
0760022 H870CSU	**0760026** H872CSU			

1750007-71 DAF Sherpa 285 Post Office B11C 1991-92

1750007 J962VSG	**1750020** J626FAS	**1750028** J841VSF	**1750037** J640FAS	**1750066** J475FRS
1750014 J330EST	**1750021** J639FAS	**1750030** J832VSF	**1750059** J473FSR	**1750067** J602ESL
1750015 J622FAS	**1750022** J627FAS	**1750032** J834VSF	**1750062** J472FSR	**1750068** J477FRS
1750016 J621FAS	**1750024** J638FAS	**1750033** J831VSF	**1750063** J590ESL	**1750069** J470FRS
1750017 J623FAS	**1750025** J166VSF	**1750034** J833VSF	**1750064** J474FSR	**1750070** J476FRS
1750018 J624FAS	**1750026** J203VSF	**1750035** J382HYS	**1750065** J601ESL	**1750071** J471FRS
1750019 J625FAS	**1750027** J221VSF	**1750036** J383HYS		

1760002-25 Peugeot 405 Estate 4-seat 1992

1760002 J641FAS	**1760008** J974VSG	**1760013** J643FAS	**1760016** J973VSG	**1760022** J408HYS
1760003 J961VSG	**1760009** J970VSG	**1760014** J642FAS	**1760020** J381HYS	**1760023** J471ASO
1760004 J969VSG	**1760010** J971VSG	**1760015** J963VSG	**1760021** J756ASO	**1760025** H912FDU
1760005 J975VSG	**1760011** J972VSG			

1770100-105 Land Rover 90 Land Rover 4-seat 1992

1770100 J478FSR	**1770102** J480FSR	**1770103** J481FSR	**1770104** J482FSR	**1770105** J483FSR
1770101 J479FSR				

SKYE-WAYS

Clan Garage (Kyle) Ltd, Ferry Pier, Kyle of Lochalsh, IV40 8AF

Clan Garage has been operating buses for many years, though initially only in a small way. In the 1970s, the fleet grew with vehicles operating around Kyle and on the Isle of Skye. An express service linking Skye with Glasgow was operated using the old-established 'Skye-Ways' name. Later these services were operated jointly with Scottish Citylink for a time, but more recently there has been a split with Citylink and Clan has been developing an independent Skye-Ways network in competition with Citylink. There has for some time now been at least one double decker in the fleet, usually required for school contracts, but interestingly during recent summers it has been used on ordinary service on Skye. The fleet livery is blue and the main depot is at Kyle.

Double decker buses are relatively rare on the Isle of Skye, though recently Clan Coaches have been using Bristol VRT ANV775J on a regular service from Portree to the ferry terminal at Kyleakin. Murdoch Currie

SKYE-WAYS Fleet List

VHV109G	AEC Reliance 6U3ZR	Plaxton Panorama Elite	C45C	1969	Ex Glenton, London SE15, 1976
BAN115H	AEC Reliance 6U3ZR	Plaxton Panorama Elite	C34C	1970	Ex Glenton, London SE15, 1977
ANV775J	Bristol VRT/SL6G	Eastern Coach Works	H39/31F	1971	Ex United Counties, 1989
TME134M	AEC Reliance 6U3ZR	Plaxton Elite III	C38C	1974	Ex Glenton, London SE15, 1981
LSO82P	Ford A0609	Alexander AS	B27F	1976	Ex Munro, Ardelve, 1990
TNS597W	Ford R1114	Duple Dominant II	C53F	1981	Ex Ganal, Shotts, 1990
OFA990	Volvo B10M-61	Van Hool Alizée	C46FT	1981	Ex Patterson, Kilbirnie, 1989
NFB892	Volvo B10M-61	Van Hool Alizée	C50FT	1983	Ex Park, Hamilton, 1985
A47OVF	Leyland Tiger TRCTL11/3RH	Plaxton Paramount 3500	C50F	1984	Ex Ambassador Travel, 1991
A49OVF	Leyland Tiger TRCTL11/3RH	Plaxton Paramount 3500	C50F	1984	Ex Ambassador Travel, 1991
NFL881	Volvo B10M-61	Van Hool Alizée	C49FT	1985	Ex Cotter, Glasgow, 1987
NCC745	Volvo B10M-61	Van Hool Alizée	C49FT	1985	Ex Cotter, Glasgow, 1988
12EWO	Volvo B10M-61	Van Hool Alizée	C50FT	1987	
E208JST	Renault Master T35D	Coachwork Conversions	C12F	1988	

	Volvo B10M-60	Van Hool Alizée	C52FT	1989-90	
F782UJS	G454TST	G761WAS	G811WST		H258AAS

G93PGB	Volvo B10M-60	Van Hool Alizée	C46FT	1989	Ex Bruce, Airdrie, 1991
J699DJS	Toyota HDB30R	Caetano Optimo II	C21F	1991	
J780DJS	Toyota HDB30R	Caetano Optimo II	C21F	1991	

Previous Registrations:

12EWO	D800EST, D846FST	A49OVF	A902KAH, PIJ3379
A47OVF	A901KAH, PIJ8513	NFB892	MSU581Y

STOKES

William Stokes & Sons Ltd, 22 Carstairs Road, Carstairs, ML11 8QD

Stokes is another of the long established Lanarkshire companies, operating a mix of local services (commercial and tendered), contract and private hire work. Stokes vehicles will as always be found in and around Lanark, but they also operate to Hamilton and to Peebles in Borders Region. The fleet of red and cream vehicles is maintained at Carstairs.

F480FGE is a Plaxton-bodied Leyland Tiger, one of four with the Derwent style body in the Stokes fleet. It is seen at Hamilton bound for Lanark, a town no longer served by the local former Scottish Bus Group operator, Kelvin Central. Max Fowler

STOKES Fleet List

TGB529R	Leyland Leopard PSU3D/4R	Duple Dominant Express	C49F	1976	
WDS223S	Leyland Leopard PSU3E/4R	Duple Dominant II Express	C49F	1977	
EGA609T	Leyland Leopard PSU3E/4R	Duple Dominant II Express	C53F	1978	
HGE51T	Leyland Leopard PSU3E/4R	Plaxton Supreme IV Exp	C53F	1979	
UGA428W	Bristol LHS6L	Duple Dominant I Express	C33F	1981	
ESU815X	Bristol LHS6L	Plaxton Supreme V	C33F	1982	
WSU857	Leyland Tiger TRCTL11/2R	Plaxton Paramount 3200 Ex	C49F	1983	
MSU300Y	Leyland Tiger TRCTL11/2R	Duple Dominant II Express	C53F	1983	
WSU858	Leyland Tiger TRCTL11/2R	Duple Laser Express	C53F	1983	
B186YUS	Mercedes-Benz L307D	Reeve Burgess	B12F	1984	
WSU209	Leyland Tiger TRCTL11/3RH	Van Hool Alizée	C53F	1986	
WSU864	Van Hool T815	Van Hool Alicron	C53F	1987	Ex Clarke, London SE20, 1987
F479FGE	Leyland Tiger TRBTL11/2RP	Plaxton Derwent	B54F	1988	
F480FGE	Leyland Tiger TRBTL11/2RP	Plaxton Derwent	B54F	1988	
F343GUS	Leyland Tiger TRBTL11/2RP	Plaxton Derwent	B54F	1988	
F344GUS	Leyland Tiger TRBTL11/2RP	Plaxton Derwent	B54F	1988	
WSU859	Volvo B10M-60	Ikarus Blue Danube	C49FT	1989	
WSU860	Dennis Javelin 11SDL1905	Plaxton Paramount 3200 III	C32FT	1989	Ex Green, Kirkintilloch, 1990
H716LOL	Mercedes-Benz 811D	Carlyle	B33F	1990	
H717LOL	Mercedes-Benz 811D	Carlyle	B33F	1990	
H718LOL	Mercedes-Benz 811D	Carlyle	B33F	1990	
H719LOL	Mercedes-Benz 811D	Carlyle	B33F	1990	
WSU871	Van Hool T815	Van Hool Alicron	C53F	1991	

Previous Registrations:

WSU209	C180EME		WSU860	G850VAY
WSU857	MSU299Y		WSU864	D298HMT
WSU858	A846TDS		WSU871	H290TDT
WSU859	G586KKU			

WEST COAST MOTORS

Craig of Campbeltown Ltd, Benmhor, Campbeltown, PA28 6DN

For almost 50 years, the Kintyre peninsula was served by two principal operators, Craig Brothers and A & P McConnochie. Both connected at Tarbert with MacBrayne's service to Glasgow. In 1970, Craig took over McConnochie's business, and in the same year Western succeeded MacBrayne on the Glasgow service. In 1983, West Coast took over the Oban area services of MacColl, giving it a detached operation well to the north of its main area. In 1985 Midland Scottish replaced Western as the Bus Group operator in South Argyll. The Glasgow service was by then a Scottish Citylink route, and West Coast became a joint operator with Citylink.

The following year, the services of Stag Garage, Lochgilphead, were taken over. In 1987 Midland passed its depot and services at Ardrishaig to West Coast in exchange for the latter's Oban area services. Thus West Coast became the major operator in South Argyll. Subsequently, an operating base was re-established in Oban to cater for tendered work that had been gained. The main depots are at Campbeltown and Ardrishaig. The fleet livery is red, dark red and cream.

WEST COAST MOTORS Fleet List

	Reg	Chassis	Body	Code	Year	Notes
—	MSB929J	Bedford YRQ	Plaxton Derwent	B49F	1971	Ex MacDonald & Maclellan, 1986
—	VSB164M	Bedford YRT	Plaxton Derwent	B60F	1974	
—	KGG184N	Bedford YRQ	Plaxton Panorama Elite	C45F	1975	Ex Earnside, Glenfarg, 1976
—	JSB870P	Bedford YRT	Duple Dominant	B66F	1975	
—	RSB7S	Bedford YLQ	Plaxton Supreme III Exp	C45F	1977	
—	RSB8S	Bedford YLQ	Duple Dominant II	C45F	1977	
—	WSB186V	Bedford YMT	Duple Dominant	B63F	1979	
—	WSB187V	Bedford YMT	Duple Dominant	B63F	1979	
—	BVA789V	Leyland Leopard PSU3F/5R	Plaxton Supreme IV	C49F	1980	Ex Premier, 1991
—	CJE452V	Leyland Leopard PSU3F/5R	Plaxton Supreme IV	C49F	1980	Ex Premier, 1991
—	FSL615W	Bedford YLQ	Plaxton Supreme IV	C45F	1980	Ex Henderson, Coaltown, 1985
—	SLS630W	Ford Transit 150	Dormobile	B16F	1981	Ex McPherson, Penicuik, 1989
—	DSB118X	Leyland Leopard PSU3E/4R	Plaxton Supreme IV Exp	C53F	1982	
—	DSB119X	Leyland Leopard PSU3E/4R	Plaxton Supreme IV Exp	C53F	1982	
—	A101KSB	Ford Transit 150	Dormobile	B14F	1984	Ex MacFarlane, Oban, 1988
—	A657UGD	Volvo B10M-61	Plaxton Paramount 3500	C53F	1984	Ex Park, Hamilton, 1986
—	B948ASU	Volvo B10M-56	Van Hool	B51F	1984	Ex Hutchison, Overtown, 1989
—	B192XJD	Volvo B10M-56	Plaxton Paramount 3200	C49F	1985	Ex Telling Golden Miller, 1989
—	D181TSB	Volvo B10M-61	Plaxton Paramount 3200 III	C57F	1986	
—	D177NNS	Freight Rover Sherpa 350D	Scott	C16F	1984	Ex Scott demonstrator, 1987
—	E260XGB	Mercedes-Benz 609D	Scott	C23F	1987	Ex Whitelaw, Stonehouse, 1990
—	E858WSB	Volvo B10M-61	Duple 340	C55F	1988	
—	E360XSB	Volvo B10M-61	Plaxton Paramount 3500 III	C53F	1988	
—	F131YSB	Ford Transit VE6	Deansgate	B14F	1988	
—	F532ASB	Volvo B10M-61	Plaxton Paramount 3200 III	C53F	1989	
—	F727ASB	Volvo B10M-61	Plaxton Paramount 3200 III	C53F	1989	
—	G450DSB	Volvo B10M-60	Duple 340	C55F	1990	
—	G897MCX	DAF MB230LT615	Van Hool Alizée	C49F	1990	
—	G21CEH	Volvo B10M-60	Plaxton Paramount 3500 III	C53F	1990	Ex Paramount Leisure, 1991
—	G120CEH	Volvo B10M-60	Plaxton Paramount 3500 III	C53F	1990	Ex Paramount Leisure, 1990
—	G69RGG	Volvo B10M-60	Plaxton Paramount 3500 III	C53F	1990	Ex Park, Hamilton, 1991
—	H522FSB	Mercedes-Benz 709D	Reeve Burgess Beaver	B25F	1990	
—	H165EJU	Toyota HDB30R	Caetano Optimo II	C21F	1991	Ex Green, Kirkintilloch, 1992
—	J807HSB	MAN 11.190	Optare Vecta	B41F	1992	

Special Liveries:
Scottish Citylink: F532ASB.

F727ASB is typical of the high standard of vehicle used by West Coast Motors in its long distance service to the Kintyre peninsula. It is a Plaxton-bodied Volvo B10M. Max Fowler

The Freight Rover Sherpa is used as a minibus base by several body conversion companies. Scott have produced a high floor model based on the 350 series van. D177NNS is seen while working the local service from Ardrishaig to Lochgilphead. Alistair Douglas

WHITELAW'S

Whitelaw's Coaches, The Cross, Stonehouse, Lanarkshire, ML9 3LQ

Whitelaw's was one of a number of established coach operators who took advantage of Central Scottish's misfortunes during the strikes of 1989. Services in and around Hamilton were introduced to fill the gap and were well established by the time that Central was back in business. What is unusual about this operator is the number of new buses obtained to operate the services. Early in 1992, there appeared to have been some negotiation between Whitelaw's and Kelvin Central resulting in rationalisation of routes and the transfer of some vehicles to Kelvin Central. The fleet livery is silver or grey with red, white and blue stripes. The vehicles are kept at Stonehouse.

CNH170X in Hamilton Bus Station is a Leyland Leopard with Eastern Coach Works' B51 body which was produced to the order of the National Bus Company. It was new to United Counties.
Murdoch Currie

Whitelaw's have several Leyland Lynxes in the fleet, including some of the Lynx 2 variety. One of the latest is J42GGB, an example with Cummins engine, seen at Hamilton on service 254 to Stonehouse.
Murdoch Currie

On a local service in Hamilton is OLS539P, one of several former Scottish Bus Group Leyland Leopards in the Whitelaw fleet. This one came from Midland Bluebird. Murdoch Currie

WHITELAW'S Fleet List

HEF380N	Leyland Leopard PSU3C/4R	Plaxton Elite Express II	DP55F	1975	Ex Tame Valley, Birmingham, 1991
HCS794N	Leyland Leopard PSU3/3R	Alexander AYS	B53F	1975	Ex Northern Scottish, 1990
HCS798N	Leyland Leopard PSU3/3R	Alexander AYS	B53F	1975	Ex Northern Scottish, 1990
OLS539P	Leyland Leopard PSU3/3R	Alexander AYS	B53F	1975	Ex Midland Scottish, 1991
SSU397R	Leyland Leopard PSU3D/4R	Alexander AYS	B53F	1976	Ex Midland Scottish, 1991
SAD129R	Leyland Leopard PSU3E/4R	Willowbrook 003	C47F	1977	Ex Vanguard, Bedworth, 1991
XMS245R	Leyland Leopard PSU3C/3R	Alexander AY	B53F	1977	Ex Midland Scottish, 1991
XMS254R	Leyland Leopard PSU3C/3R	Alexander AY	B53F	1977	Ex Midland Scottish, 1991
HNE251V	Leyland Leopard PSU5C/4R	Duple Dominant II	C50F	1980	Ex Ribble, 1991
JND257V	Leyland Leopard PSU5C/4R	Duple Dominant II	C50F	1980	Ex Ribble, 1991
JND258V	Leyland Leopard PSU5C/4R	Duple Dominant II	C50F	1980	Ex Ribble, 1991
JND263V	Leyland Leopard PSU5C/4R	Duple Dominant II	C50F	1980	Ex Ribble, 1991
MRJ280W	Leyland Leopard PSU5D/4R	Plaxton Supreme IV	C53F	1981	Ex Ribble, 1991
CNH170X	Leyland Leopard PSU3G/4RT	Eastern Coach Works B51	C49F	1982	Ex Luton & District, 1991
D32MWN	Leyland Lynx LX112TL11ZR1	Leyland	B51F	1987	Ex Rees & Williams, Morriston, 1991
E743TCS	Volvo B10M-61	Van Hool Alizée	C49FT	1988	Ex Rowe, Muirkirk, 1990
F380MUT	Volvo B10M-61	Plaxton Paramount 3500 III	C53F	1988	Ex Patterson, Birmingham, 1989
191WHW	Volvo B10M-61	Plaxton Paramount 3500 III	C53F	1989	Ex Patterson, Birmingham, 1989
7994WW	Volvo B10M-60	Plaxton Paramount 3500 III	C53F	1989	
9396WW	Volvo B10M-60	Plaxton Paramount 3500 III	C53F	1989	
G899MNS	Volvo B10M-55	Plaxton Derwent	B55F	1989	
G900MNS	Volvo B10M-55	Plaxton Derwent	B55F	1989	
G472PGE	Leyland Lynx LX112L10ZR1R	Leyland	B51F	1989	
G473PGE	Leyland Lynx LX112L10ZR1R	Leyland	B51F	1989	
G169LET	Volvo B10M-60	Plaxton Paramount 3500 III	C53F	1989	
G170LET	Volvo B10M-60	Plaxton Paramount 3500 III	C53F	1989	
7062WW	Volvo B10M-60	Jonckheere Deauville	C51FT	1989	Ex Antler, Rugeley, 1990
5896WW	Volvo B10M-60	Jonckheere Deauville	C48FT	1989	Ex Antler, Rugeley, 1990
G178RBD	Volvo B10M-60	Jonckheere Deauville	C51FT	1990	Ex Stirk, Staindrop, 1990
H51NDU	Leyland Lynx LX2R11C15Z4S	Leyland Lynx 2	B51F	1991	Ex Volvo demonstrator, 1991
J41GGB	Leyland Lynx LX2R11C15Z4S	Leyland Lynx 2	B51F	1991	
J42GGB	Leyland Lynx LX2R11C15Z4S	Leyland Lynx 2	B51F	1991	
J43GGB	Leyland Lynx LX2R11C15Z4S	Leyland Lynx 2	B51F	1992	
J45GGB	Leyland Lynx LX2R11C15Z4S	Leyland Lynx 2	B51F	1992	
J46GGB	Volvo B10M-60	Plaxton Paramount 3500 III	C53F	1991	

Previous Registrations:

191WHW	F805COJ	7062WW	F101CBD
5896WW	F102CBD	7994WW	F191EKY

WILSON'S

Wilson's Coaches Ltd, Medwyn Garage, Carnwath

The Wilson family have been operating buses since the 1920s, initially in Galashiels, but mostly based at Carnwath. A local service in Carluke was operated and there was an occasional service between Forth and Edinburgh. The Lanark local service came with the business of McKnight in 1966. A number of other Lanarkshire firms were acquired in the seventies. The majority of the fleet was employed on contract and hire work prior to 1986. Since deregulation, various tendered and commercial services have been operated in the Hamilton, Motherwell and Wishaw areas.

In 1990, the Lanark-based Nationwide Coaches was bought from the Whiteford family, increasing the fleet significantly and bringing additional coach work as well as further tendered services.

The depots are at Carnwath and Larkhall. Wilson's coaches are red and grey or silver, though some service buses are red and yellow. The Nationwide livery of white with red and orange bands is applied to a proportion of the fleet.

Photographed at Lanark bus station is OTF359K a Bristol RESL with East Lancashire bodywork originally from the Accrington Corporation fleet. Murdoch Currie

Bristol LH OJD44R came to Wilson's with the Nationwide business and is seen in Wishaw on the service to Torbothie. Alistair Douglas

The Nationwide name and livery has continued to be used on some vehicles in the Wilson's fleet. Former London Country YPD131Y is one of three Leyland Tigers from that source and is seen at Hamilton on the Clyde Valley service to Lanark. Alistair Douglas

WILSON'S Fleet List

SEL245H	Leyland Atlantean PDR1A/1	Alexander J	H43/31F	1969	Ex Lancaster, 1990
OTF359K	Bristol RESL6L	East Lancashire	DP42F	1972	Ex Hyndburn, 1987
MLK558L	Daimler Fleetline CRL6	Park Royal	H44/24D	1973	Ex Hewlett & Sutton, 1986
MLK668L	Daimler Fleetline CRL6	Park Royal	H44/27F	1973	Ex Graham, Paisley, 1986
GOL416N	Leyland National 11351/1R		B49F	1974	Ex Stevenson, Uttoxeter, 1987
SJG340N	Leyland National 10351/1R		B41F	1974	Ex East Kent, 1989
JOX494P	Leyland National 11351/1R		B49F	1974	Ex Stevenson, Uttoxeter, 1987
NGE172P	AEC Reliance 2U3RA	Plaxton Supreme	C53F	1976	Ex Nationwide, Carnwath, 1990
MDF115P	Leyland Leopard PSU3C/4R	Duple Dominant	C47F	1976	Ex Nightingale, B'Salterton, 1986
MDS678P	Leyland Atlantean AN68A/1R	Alexander AL	H45/31F	1976	Ex Stewart, Dalmuir, 1991

MDS685P	Leyland Atlantean AN68A/1R	Alexander AL	H45/31F	1976	Ex Strathclyde PTE, 1984
RUS318R	Leyland Atlantean AN68A/1R	Alexander AL	H45/31F	1976	Ex Boyce, Campsie, 1991
OJD44R	Bristol LH6L	Eastern Coach Works	B39F	1976	Ex Nationwide, Carnwath, 1990
DLS260S	Leyland Leopard PSU3E/4R	Duple Dominant Express	C53F	1977	Ex Scoughall, Dunbar, 1991
YWT521S	Ford R1114	Plaxton Supreme	C53F	1978	Ex Nationwide, Carnwath, 1990
AUS654S	Ford R1114	Plaxton Supreme	C53F	1978	Ex Nationwide, Carnwath, 1990
XBF59S	Leyland Leopard PSU3E/4R	Duple Dominant Express	C53F	1978	Ex Pride-of-the-Road, Royston, 1991
CGE809S	Ford R1114	Plaxton Supreme	C53F	1978	Ex Nationwide, Carnwath, 1990
SWS770S	Bristol LH6L	Eastern Coach Works	B43F	1978	Ex Bristol, 1986
DWY665T	Leyland Leopard PSU3E/4R	Plaxton Supreme Express	C49F	1979	Ex York City & District, 1991
MSG914T	Volvo B58-56	Plaxton Supreme IV	C53F	1979	Ex Allan, Gorebridge, 1986
YHU679V	Volvo B58-61	Duple Dominant II	C50F	1979	Ex French, Coldingham, 1986
JLF296V	Fiat 55F10	Reeve Burgess	C18F	1979	Ex Nationwide, Carnwath, 1990
UFR900V	Mercedes-Benz L207D	Devon Conversions	B12F	1979	Ex Nationwide, Carnwath, 1990
NGD26V	Volvo B58-61	Duple Dominant II	C53F	1980	Ex Southern, Barrhead, 1985
NNS234V	Volvo B58-56	Duple Dominant II	C53F	1980	Ex Mace, Glasgow, 1984
EYH811V	Leyland Leopard PSU3E/4R	Duple Dominant Express	C49F	1980	Ex Andrews, Sheffield, 1991
LSA22W	Mercedes-Benz L508D	Mercedes-Benz	B17F	1980	Ex Nationwide, Carnwath, 1990
CFS166W	Ford Transit 150	Deansgate	B12F	1981	Ex Nationwide, Carnwath, 1990
YST310W	Leyland Leopard PSU3E/4R	Duple Dominant	C49FT	1981	Ex Nationwide, Carnwath, 1990
SLJ387X	Leyland Leopard PSU5C/4R	Plaxton Supreme	C53F	1981	Ex Docherty, Auchterarder, 1991
DBH453X	Leyland Leopard PSU5D/4R	Duple Dominant	C53F	1982	Ex Safeway, Rainham, 1991
YWX537X	Leyland Leopard PSU3E/4R	Duple Dominant	C53F	1982	Ex Warrington, 1991
YPD110Y	Leyland Tiger TRCTL11/2R	Duple Dominant II Express	DP53F	1983	Ex Dorset Travel Services, 1991
YPD131Y	Leyland Tiger TRCTL11/2R	Duple Dominant II Express	DP53F	1983	Ex London Country NE, 1991
YPD134Y	Leyland Tiger TRCTL11/2R	Duple Dominant II Express	DP53F	1983	Ex London Country NW, 1991
NDS837Y	Mercedes-Benz L608D	Reeve Burgess	C25F	1983	Ex Nationwide, Carnwath, 1990
A620LCP	Ford R1114	Duple	C48FT	1983	Ex Nationwide, Carnwath, 1990
174NJO	Leyland Tiger TRCTL11/3R	Van Hool Alizée	C49F	1983	Ex Nationwide, Carnwath, 1990
GIL3270	DAF MB200DKFL600	Van Hool Alizée	C55F	1984	
GIL3271	DAF MB200DKFL600	Van Hool Alizée	C55F	1984	
NIB6694	DAF MB200DKFL600	Van Hool Alizée	C48F	1984	Ex Nationwide, Carnwath, 1990
9712WX	DAF SB200DHS585	Jonckheere Jubilee P50	C51FT	1984	Ex Nationwide, Carnwath, 1990
851GWL	Volvo B10M-61	Jonckheere P50	C53F	1984	
STL743	Volvo B10M-61	Van Hool Alizée	C50FT	1984	Ex Cotter, Morecambe, 1986
NIB6527	Volvo B10M-61	Jonckheere Jubilee P599	CH47/12FT	1984	Ex Nationwide, Carnwath, 1990
SV2923	DAF MB200DKVL600	Van Hool Alizée	C49FT	1985	
YCR874	Volvo B10M-61	Van Hool Alizée	C53F	1986	
JSV362	Leyland Tiger TRCTL11/3R	Plaxton Supreme V	C50F	1986	Ex Armchair, Brentford, 1991
C656JOA	Freight Rover Sherpa 310D	Coachcraft	C16F	1986	Ex Nationwide, Carnwath, 1990
C283RSF	DAF MB200DKVL600	Plaxton Paramount 3500	C53F	1986	
C360KGG	Volvo B10M-61	Van Hool Alizée	C52FT	1986	
D476DSX	Van Hool T815	Van Hool Alicron	C55F	1987	
D477DSX	Van Hool T815	Van Hool Alicron	C55F	1987	
E212GNV	DAF SB2300DHS585	Jonckheere Jubilee P50	C51FT	1987	Ex Hallmark, Luton, 1991
E408MSX	Volvo B10M-61	Plaxton Paramount 3500	C53FT	1988	
E871MSX	Volvo B10M-61	Van Hool Alizée	C53FT	1988	
F710SFS	Volvo B10M-61	Van Hool Alizée	C51F	1988	Ex Nationwide, Carnwath, 1990
F711SFS	Volvo B10M-61	Van Hool Alizée	C51F	1988	Ex Nationwide, Carnwath, 1990
F476XMS	Volvo B10M-46	Van Hool Alizée	C38F	1988	
F953WSF	Volvo B10M-60	Van Hool Alizée	C53F	1989	
F640XSF	Volvo B10M-60	Van Hool Alizée	C53F	1989	
F812XSG	Volvo B10M-60	Van Hool Alizée	C51F	1989	
F199PNR	Toyota HB31R	Caetano Optimo	C18F	1989	Ex Nationwide, Carnwath, 1990
F207PNR	DAF SB3000DKV601	Caetano Algarve	C53F	1989	Ex Nationwide, Carnwath, 1990
F208PNR	DAF SB3000DKV601	Caetano Algarve	C53F	1989	Ex Nationwide, Carnwath, 1990
F199PNR	Toyota HB31R	Caetano Optimo	C18F	1989	Ex Nationwide, Carnwath, 1990
F155DKU	Leyland Swift LBM6T/2RA	Reeve Burgess	B39F	1989	Ex Green, Kirkintilloch, 1991
	Volvo B10M-60	Van Hool Alizée	C53F	1990	Ex Nationwide, Carnwath, 1990
G339HSC	G341HSC	G342HSC		G343HSC	G344HSC
G340HSC					

Previous Registrations:

851GWL	A590XRP	NIB6527	A119XNH
9712WX	A125XNH	NIB6694	A542HRY
GIL3270	A975ESF	SV2923	B262MSC
GIL3271	A976ESF	YCR874	C245RSF
JSV362	XPP295X		